Strengthening Anti-Racist
Educational Leaders

Bloomsbury Race, Ethnicity and Belonging in Education

Series Editors: Paul Miller, Jeffrey S. Brooks and Lauri Johnson

The Bloomsbury Race, Ethnicity and Belonging in Education series is focused on understanding issues surrounding race, ethnicity and notions of (un)belonging in all aspects, phases and contexts of education, from early years to higher education and in non-traditional and informal settings. International in scope and open to contributions from all over the world, the series presents theoretically robust and empirically rigorous studies of students' and staff experiences of "race" and "belonging" in educational settings, where these experiences include a broad range of elements such as: student life, student representation and participation, curriculum design and delivery, diversity of reading lists and assessment, discipline and career progression, Anti-Blackness, political resistance, and related subjects such as populism, colonialism and imperialism.

Books in the series are united by the belief that "belonging" (and "unbelonging") is an important issue for all peoples, and that it is not possible to understand contemporary educational institutions or experiences without understanding the extent to which issues to do with racial and ethnic (in)equality can impact organisational and individual senses of identity, work, community, values and funding. In this way, the series offers a broad perspective on "race," "ethnicity" and "belonging" that considers the intersections of these ideas and contexts from a multiplicity of lenses. It offers a unique resource for academics and researchers working in the fields of educational leadership, sociology of education, anthropology of education and organisational behaviour, amongst others.

Advisory Board: Denise Armstrong (Brock University, Canada); Kadir Beycioglu (Dokuz Eylül University, Turkey) Tony Bush (University of Nottingham, UK); Christine Callender (University College London, UK); Susan C. Faircloth (Colorado State University, USA); Mark Gooden (Columbia University, USA); Tyrone Howard (UCLA, USA); Gaetane Jean-Marie (Rowan University, USA); Reva Joshee (University of Toronto, Canada); Gloria Ladson-Billings (University of Wisconsin, USA); Sadhana Manik (University of Kwa-Zulu-Natal, South Africa Uvanney Maylor (University of Bedfordshire, UK); Yoon Pak (University of Illinois, USA); Fazal Rizvi (University of Melbourne, Australia); Allan Walker (Education University of Hong Kong, Hong Kong); Camille Wilson (University of Michigan, USA)

Strengthening Anti-Racist Educational Leaders

Advocating for Racial Equity in Turbulent Times

Edited by Anjalé D. Welton and Sarah Diem

BLOOMSBURY ACADEMIC
LONDON • NEW YORK • OXFORD • NEW DELHI • SYDNEY

BLOOMSBURY ACADEMIC
Bloomsbury Publishing Plc
50 Bedford Square, London, WC1B 3DP, UK
1385 Broadway, New York, NY 10018, USA
29 Earlsfort Terrace, Dublin 2, Ireland

BLOOMSBURY, BLOOMSBURY ACADEMIC and the Diana logo are trademarks
of Bloomsbury Publishing Plc

First published in Great Britain, 2022
This paperback edition published in 2023

Copyright © Anjalé D. Welton and Sarah Diem and Bloomsbury 2022

Anjalé D. Welton, Sarah Diem and Bloomsbury have asserted their right under the
Copyright, Designs and Patents Act, 1988, to be identified as Author of this work.

Cover design: Charlotte James
Cover image © Prostock-Studio/ iStock

All rights reserved. No part of this publication may be reproduced or
transmitted in any form or by any means, electronic or mechanical, including
photocopying, recording, or any information storage or retrieval system,
without prior permission in writing from the publishers.

Bloomsbury Publishing Plc does not have any control over, or responsibility for, any
third-party websites referred to or in this book. All internet addresses given in
this book were correct at the time of going to press. The author and publisher
regret any inconvenience caused if addresses have changed or sites have
ceased to exist, but can accept no responsibility for any such changes.

A catalogue record for this book is available from the British Library.

Library of Congress Cataloging-in-Publication Data

Names: Welton, Anjalé D., editor. | Diem, Sarah, editor.
Title: Strengthening anti-racist educational leaders: advocating for
racial equity in turbulent times / Edited by Anjalé D. Welton and Sarah Diem.
Description: London; New York: Bloomsbury Academic, 2022. |
Series: Bloomsbury race, ethnicity and belonging in education |
Includes bibliographical references and index.
Identifiers: LCCN 2021023390 (print) | LCCN 2021023391 (ebook) |
ISBN 9781350167810 (hardback) | ISBN 9781350167827 (ebook) |
ISBN 9781350167834 (epub)
Subjects: LCSH: Racism in education–United States. | Educational
equalization–United States. | Educational leadership–United States. |
Social justice and education–United States.
Classification: LCC LC212.2.S79 2022 (print) |
LCC LC212.2 (ebook) | DDC 370.89–dc23
LC record available at https://lccn.loc.gov/2021023390
LC ebook record available at https://lccn.loc.gov/2021023391

ISBN: HB: 978-1-3501-6781-0
PB: 978-1-3502-2513-8
ePDF: 978-1-3501-6782-7
eBook: 978-1-3501-6783-4

Series: Bloomsbury Race, Ethnicity and Belonging in Education

Typeset by Integra Software Services Pvt. Ltd.

To find out more about our authors and books visit www.bloomsbury.com
and sign up for our newsletters.

Contents

List of Illustrations	vii
List of Contributors	viii
Series Editors' Foreword	xvi

Introduction: Strengthening Anti-racist Educational Leaders
Anjalé D. Welton and Sarah Diem   1

Part 1   The Sociopolitical Context of Anti-racist Educational Leadership

1. Anti-racist Leadership in Precarious Sociopolitical Contexts
   Anjalé D. Welton, Greg Johnson, and Sarah Diem   17
2. Anti-racism as Core Competency for Educational Leaders
   Matthew A. Rodriguez and Amanda E. Lewis   31
3. The Politics of the School–Prison Nexus: Racial Capitalism and Possibilities for Transformation in Schools and Beyond *Erica O. Turner, Abigail J. Beneke, María Velázquez and Rob Timberlake*   41

Part 2   Anti-racist Educational Leadership Preparation and Practice

4. Considerations for District-level Anti-racist Leadership Preparation
   Mary B. Herrmann and Jessica A. Herrmann   55
5. From the Inside Out: A Letter to Anti-racist Leaders
   Marcus Campbell and Michael Kucera   69
6. The Color of Coloniality: White Administrators' Expectations of Black Males in School Discipline *Daniel D. Liou and Adam Zang*   81
7. Understanding the Racialized Organization: African-centered Leadership and Their Unique Form of Culturally Responsive Leadership *Bodunrin O. Banwo and Muhammad Khalifa*   93

Part 3   Community Engagement, Activism, and Anti-racist Educational Leadership

8. Aligning Frameworks and Identifying Capacities for Anti-racist Advocacy Educational Leadership *Michelle D. Young and Angel Miles Nash*   109

9 Anti-racist Activist Leadership *Jason Salisbury and Meagan Richard* 121
10 Toward More Equitable Communities: Leadership Lessons for Systemic Social Change *Rhoda Freelon and Jeanette Taylor* 133
11 (Re)Imagining "Successful" University–District–Community Partnerships *Decoteau J. Irby, Bradley W. Carpenter, and Erica Young* 145

Part 4 Recognizing and Accounting for the Work of Anti-racist Leadership

12 The Invisible Labor of PK-20 BIPOC Leaders *Zelideh R. Martinez Hoy, Dennis J. Perkins Jr., and David Hoa Khoa Nguyen* 159
13 On the Backs of Black Women: Examining How the Supporting Administrative Role Is Entrenched in Racism *Asia Fuller Hamilton and Mykah Jackson* 169
14 Anti-racism for White People: From Inactivism to Activism *Jeffrey S. Brooks* 181
15 Sameness and Conformity in Predominately White School Districts *Sharon I. Radd* 193
16 Developing Anti-racist Leaders through Equity-expansive Technical Assistance *Kathleen A. King Thorius and Tiffany S. Kyser* 207

Notes 219
References 220
Index 253

Illustrations

Figures

1.1	Overall AP/honors enrollment by race and ethnicity, Oak Park and River Forest High School	24
7.1	Responsive school leadership defined by the imagined cultural ideal	98
7.2	Responsive school leadership defined by the imagined cultural ideal	102
8.1	Critical capacities of advocacy leaders	111
15.1	The self-replicating cycle of the Homogenous Whole	195

Table

15.1	Percentage of students who attend schools with racial peers by race in 2017	194

Contributors

Bodunrin O. Banwo is Assistant Professor in the Department of Leadership in Education at the University of Massachusetts, USA. His research focuses on the liberatory effects of communitarian programming in schools and on student development. Before receiving his PhD, Banwo served as a food access manager for the City of Baltimore and the Philadelphia-based nonprofit The Food Trust, a public school teacher, and a Peace Corps volunteer in Paraguay, South America.

Abigail J. Beneke is a PhD candidate in the Department of Educational Policy Studies at the University of Wisconsin-Madison, USA. Using a diverse range of conceptual tools from the anthropology and sociology of education policy, critical race theories, and philosophy of education, Beneke's research links federal, state, and local educational policymaking to school-level practice to examine the racial and economic politics of education reform, the politics and practice of school discipline and school discipline reform, and the role of schools and communities in challenging or reproducing inequality in public education.

Jeffrey S. Brooks is Professor of Educational Leadership and Associate Dean of Education in the School of Education at RMIT University in Melbourne, Australia. His research focuses on educational leadership, and he specifically explores the way leaders influence (and are influenced by) socio-cultural dynamics such as racism, globalization, social justice, and activism in schools and communities. Brooks is a two-time J. William Fulbright Senior Scholar alumnus, author of over 100 scholarly publications, and he has been a leader and team member in projects that have garnered over 8 million dollars in extramural funding.

Marcus Campbell is Assistant Superintendent and Principal at Evanston Township High School in the USA. Campbell is responsible for providing leadership in the development of district strategy and organizational change, including effective instructional practices, impactful diversity and equity initiatives, and responsive programs and services. He oversees the implementation of all district equity transformation programs, training, and initiatives to help improve the overall school culture for all students and to eliminate barriers to the equitable education of students from underrepresented backgrounds. His goal is to ensure that all students are educated and supported in a safe, equitable, culturally relevant, and student-centered learning environment.

Bradley W. Carpenter is Associate Professor in the Department of Educational Leadership at the Baylor University School of Education, USA. As a former school principal, Carpenter has a passion for working with public school districts and administrators, and helps aspiring principals and superintendents realize their identity as transformational leaders of school communities. His research focuses on leader wellbeing and self-care, development of equity-minded school leaders, and how discourses and policymaking shape educational policy. His latest publication, "Confronting COVID: Crisis Leadership, Turbulence, and Self-Care," is in *Frontiers in Education* (2021).

Sarah Diem is Professor in the Department of Educational Leadership and Policy Analysis at the University of Missouri, USA. She is also a Faculty Affiliate in the Harry S. Truman School of Government and Public Affairs and the Qualitative Inquiry Program in the College of Education and Human Development at the University of Missouri, USA. She researches the social, political, and geographic contexts of education, focusing primarily on how the politics and implementation of educational policies affect outcomes related to racial equity and opportunity within public schools. She is also interested in the ways in which future school leaders are being prepared to address racism in their school communities.

Rhoda Freelon is Assistant Professor in the Department of Educational Leadership and Policy Studies at University of Houston, USA. Her research interests examine the role of families, youth, and communities in advancing educational equity and racial justice in schools.

Asia Fuller Hamilton is Principal at Garden Hills Math, Engineering, and Leadership Academy in Champaign, Illinois, USA. Her research interests include Black girlhood/womanhood and equity leadership.

Jessica Herrmann serves as a Director of Student Services and former bilingual school psychologist in the suburbs of Chicago, Illinois, USA. Her areas of professional interest include equity and anti-racist leadership, social-emotional learning, systems of support, and school-based mental health services.

Mary B. Herrmann is Associate Professor in the Education Policy, Organization and Leadership Department at the University of Illinois at Urbana-Champaign, USA. Her teaching and research interests include leadership development, equity, and organizational learning. She has authored two books, *Decide to Lead, Building Capacity and Leveraging Change through Decision-Making* (2017) and *Learn to Lead, Lead to Learn: Leadership as a Work in Progress* (2020). She is a book reviewer and frequent contributor to *School Administrator* (AASA) and previously served in numerous leadership positions, including school superintendent.

Zelideh R. Martinez Hoy is Program Director and Faculty Member at the Bard Prison Initiative's Women's College Partnership in Indianapolis, Indiana, USA. Her research interests include access to public health and education, the emotional labor of professionals of Color and organizational change to account for historically marginalizing spaces. She has a PhD in Health Behavior and an MSEd in Higher Education and Student Affairs from Indiana University at Bloomington, USA.

Decoteau J. Irby is Associate Professor in the Department of Educational Policy Studies at the University of Illinois at Chicago, USA. His academic research explores how equity-focused school leadership improves Black children and youth's educational experiences. He has published numerous peer-reviewed journal articles about school organizations, educational leadership, and racism and is the author of *Stuck Improving: Racial Equity and School Leadership*.

Mykah Jackson is Principal of Yankee Ridge Elementary School in Urbana School District in Illinois, USA. She previously served as a middle school social studies teacher. Jackson holds a Bachelor of Arts in History from Western Illinois University, USA, and earned her Master of Education in Educational Policy Studies, General Administrative Certification with a concentration in Educational Administration and Leadership, PhD in Educational Policy Studies and her Certificate of Advanced Study obtaining the Superintendent Endorsement from the University of Illinois at Urbana-Champaign, USA. Her research centers on Black women in educational leadership.

Greg Johnson began his career as an English teacher at Urbana High School in Urbana, Illinois, USA, where he taught and coached for nine years. In 2006, he was hired as the Associate Principal at UHS, and in 2010, he was hired as the Principal at Centennial High School to lead the school's restructuring efforts, focusing on addressing achievement disparities, introducing systems of supports, and improving professional development. Currently he serves as Superintendent of Oak Park and River Forest High School in Oak Park, Illinois, USA, where he is leading an effort to de-track the freshman curriculum.

Muhammad Khalifa is Professor of Educational Administration and Executive Director of Urban Education at the Ohio State University, USA. His research examines how school leaders enact culturally responsive leadership practices and authentically engage communities. His most recent book, *Culturally Responsive School Leadership* (2018), inspired the development of the Culturally Responsive School Leadership Institute and academies (www.crsli.org) and he has helped districts perform equity audits as a way to address inequities in school (www.ajusted.org). He is a former district administrator and science teacher in Detroit Public Schools in the USA, and is also a leading expert of educational reform in African and Asian contexts.

Michael Kucera is Teacher and Director of English at Niles West High School in Skokie, Illinois, USA. He has worked as a Teacher and Curriculum Director in a variety of diverse public, private, and charter school high school settings. His research interests include equitable academic access and opportunities for Black and Latinx students and anti-racist leadership. His professional work focuses on schoolwide anti-racist teacher and leadership development, and implementation of culturally responsive curriculum.

Tiffany S. Kyser is a member of the executive team for the United States Department of Education (USDOE) Region III Equity Assistance Center, the Midwest and Plains Equity Assistance Center (MAP Center)—a project of the Great Lakes Equity Center. Her interests focus on critical theories within policy implementation in urban school communities, particularly the interplay between cities and schools. She has published on educational equity, civil rights in education, and the portfolio management model in education. Her most recent publication is a co-authored chapter: "An Initial Exploration of a Community-Based Framework for Educational Equity with Explicated Exemplars" (2017).

Amanda E. Lewis is Director of the Institute for Research on Race and Public Policy, Director of the College of Liberal Arts & Sciences, and Distinguished Professor of Black Studies and Sociology at the University of Illinois at Chicago, USA. She is the author of several award-winning books, including *Despite the Best Intentions: Why Racial Inequality Persists in Good Schools* (with co-author

John Diamond, 2015), and *Race in the Schoolyard: Negotiating the Color-Line in Classrooms and Communities* (2003).

Daniel D. Liou is Associate Professor in Educational Leadership at the Mary Lou Fulton Teachers College at Arizona State University, USA. His research examines the sociological manifestations of expectations in fostering conditions of equity and justice in the educational pipeline. He is an elected school board member at the Los Angeles College Prep Academy in the USA.

Angel Miles Nash is Assistant Professor of Leadership Development at Chapman University, USA. Nash has taught and led in K-12 schools in Washington, DC, California, and Virginia in the USA. Her research includes examining the emboldening of Black girls and women in the K-20+ education, the professional intersectional realities of Black women in education, and the ways that educators and leaders support underserved students in STEM education. Her scholarship has been published in peer-reviewed journals and books, and her funded research projects collectively reify her belief in educators' influence on the historically underserved communities she champions and her development of intersectional leadership.

David Hoa Khoa Nguyen is Assistant Professor of Urban Education Leadership & Policy and Adjunct Professor of Law at Indiana University—Purdue University Indianapolis (IUPUI), USA. His teaching and research interests include the intersections of education law and policy and implications for marginalized and minoritized populations, specifically examining issues of affirmative action, employment discrimination, and organizational change for culturally and linguistically diverse populations. He has a PhD in Education Policy Studies; JD, MBA, and BSEd from Indiana University, USA; and a Masters of Law from Leiden University, the Netherlands. He is licensed to practice law in Indiana, North Dakota, and Texas in the USA.

Dennis Perkins Jr. is an EdD student completing his third year in Education at the University of Pittsburgh, USA. His dissertation in practice is focused on the high attrition rates of live-in professional staff within Residence Life at his current place of practice, at Grinnell College, USA, where he serves as the Director of Residence Life.

Sharon I. Radd is Associate Professor and Program Director of the MA-Organizational Leadership at St. Catherine University, USA. She is also Equity

Fellow with the Midwest and Plains Equity Assistance Center at Indiana University Purdue University Indianapolis, USA, Principal Consultant at ConsciousPraxis, and Senior Partner with The Five Practices Group. Her research interrogates whiteness and re-envisions more equitable, just, and humane leadership. She engages in this inquiry using theoretical, conceptual, narrative, and empirical approaches to the examination of adult learning, organizational change, discursive functioning, leader development and practices, and public engagement of individuals, groups, organizations, and societies.

Meagan Richard is a PhD student in the Department of Educational Policy Studies at the University of Illinois at Chicago, USA, where she currently works as a Research Assistant with the Center for Urban Educational Leadership. Her research centers around emancipatory forms of school leadership in urban settings and her dissertation research examines how emancipatory leadership is shaped by educational market contexts in seven urban school districts across the USA.

Matthew A. Rodriguez is CEO and founder of The Equity Imperative (TEI). Founded in 2018, he and colleagues partner with leaders from diverse backgrounds in redesigning systems to become sanctuaries for justice. TEI provides diversity, equity, and inclusion consultation, professional learning, and strategic planning services. An educator with two decades of experience as a teacher, school and district administrator, Rodriguez is credentialed in educational administration and is currently pursuing a doctorate. He is an acclaimed speaker and leader in designing adult learning, bringing deep intellect and energy to ensure that systems and organizations serve us all well.

Jason Salisbury is Assistant Professor in the Educational Policy Studies Department at the University of Illinois at Chicago, USA. His research focuses on anti-racist school leadership practices in urban settings with a specific focus on culturally relevant instructional leadership, the ways that youth of color engage in transformative school leadership, and the current shortcomings of equity-minded school improvement.

Jeanette Taylor is alderwoman of the 20th ward in the City of Chicago, Illinois, USA. Prior to her career in municipal government, she was a parent leader and community organizer on the South Side of Chicago, Illinois, USA.

Kathleen A. King Thorius is Critical Special Education Researcher and Executive Director of a USDOE-funded educational Equity Assistance Center and educational research center, the Great Lakes Equity Center. Critical whiteness, disability studies, and sociocultural identity theories inform her cultural historical approaches for developing and facilitating teacher learning with white and non-disabled educators toward the goal of inclusive education: a radical social, racial, and disability justice movement. Thorius's work has been published in the *International Journal of Inclusive Education, Harvard Educational Review, Exceptional Children, Remedial and Special Education*, and *Theory into Practice*, as well as other dis/ability-related and interdisciplinary journals.

Rob Timberlake is a graduate student of Educational Policy Studies at the University of Wisconsin-Madison, USA. His research interests include race and class inequalities in education, organizing for social justice, and the politics of educational policy.

Erica O. Turner is Associate Professor of Educational Policy Studies at the University of Wisconsin-Madison, USA. Her research examines the efforts of stakeholders, from school district leaders to students to community members, to challenge racism and inequality in education policy and practice. She is the author of *Suddenly Diverse: How School Districts Manage Race and Inequality* (2020).

María D. Velázquez is a PhD candidate in the Department of Educational Policy Studies at the University of Wisconsin-Madison, USA. Her research examines the structures, policies, and politics that shape inequities in schools, and the ways in which educators and organizing communities seek to disrupt them. Most recently, she published "Reframing Suburbs: Race, Place, and Opportunity in Suburban Educational Spaces" with John Diamond and Lynn Posey-Maddox in *Educational Researcher*.

Anjalé D. Welton is Professor in the Department of Educational Leadership and Policy Analysis (ELPA) at the University of Wisconsin-Madison, USA. Her research broadly examines how educational leaders both dialogue about and address race and racism in their school communities. Her research specific to racial equity and justice also considers the role of student and community voice, leadership, and activism in education reform and transformation. Welton previously had the privilege of collaborating with high school students engaging in social-justice education and youth participatory action research (YPAR).

Erica Young is Restorative Discipline Coach at Jefferson County Public Schools in Louisville, Kentucky, USA. She received her PhD in Education Leadership at the University of Louisville, USA.

Michelle D. Young is School of Education Dean and Professor of Leadership at Loyola Marymount University, USA. Her scholarship focuses on critical policy analysis and the preparation and practice of equity-focused educational leaders. Her research is widely published in academic journals and books and she has received multiple honors and awards, including the William J. Davis award for the most outstanding article published in a volume of the *Educational Administration Quarterly*. Her recent book publications include *Critical Approaches to Education Policy Analysis: Moving beyond Tradition*, the *Handbook of Research on the Education of School Leaders* (2nd edition), and she is currently co-editing the *Handbook of Critical Education Research Theory & Methodology*.

Adam Zang is Assistant Principal at a K-8 elementary school in South Phoenix, Arizona, USA.

Series Editors' Foreword

Discontent and unrest with respect to race, ethnicity, and belonging are enduring societal and global problems—yet despite their importance, these important dynamics remain undertheorized and understudied in the field of education. How education acknowledges, first, and responds to, second, these discontents is as significant as the discontents themselves. Education is a potent force that should mobilize and empower individuals, groups, and societies toward excellence and equity. The Black Lives Matter movement and the pace of global migration have placed increasing focus and responsibility on educational institutions to ensure all who study and work therein feel welcome and ultimately thrive. This series acknowledges that the definitions of race, ethnicity, un/belonging, and even education are contested, and authors will both explain the ways that these concepts are utilized in their works and consider the ways these ideas and their practical application point toward new ways of thinking about these key constructs, and to critique the ways that dominant discourses have shaped them in historical and contemporary educational contexts.

Not all people are treated equally despite repeated worldwide calls for equity in education. In many societies, women and girls are treated differently to men; children treated differently to adults; racially diverse peoples being treated differently from ethnic majority peoples; some people are welcomed into communities with open arms and others shunned or set upon with overt and covert violence. Not only is the treatment of these individuals and groups contrary to international and national laws around discrimination, the treatment of these individuals and groups also goes against what education teaches and promises: the possibility of a better life through increased knowledge, skills, and achievement. This is highly problematic, in particular, where mistreatment originates from everyday processes and practices of educational institutions and/or a lack of courage to change practices. Understanding how students and staff, with a range of characteristics experience education in different international, national, institutional, and disciplinary settings is thus an important issue for researchers, practitioners, and policymakers and aim of this series.

The series focuses on theoretically robust and empirically rigorous studies of students' and staffs' experience of "race" and "belonging" in education/educational settings, where these experiences include a broad range of elements such as student life, student representation, access and participation, curriculum design and delivery, inclusivity of reading lists and assessment, discipline, staff career progression, Anti-Blackness, and political resistance—intertwined with subjects such as populism, colonialism, and imperialism. In this way, the series offer a broad-based approach and view of "race," "ethnicity," and "belonging" which focuses on issues from a multiplicity of lens, and that considers the intersections of these ideas and contexts. The books in the series will be united by the belief that "belonging" (and unbelonging) is an important issue for all peoples, and that it is not possible to understand contemporary educational institutions or the experiences produced therein without understanding the extent to which issues to do with race and ethnicity (in particular, race in/equity) can impact organizational and individual senses' of identity, work, community, values, funding, etc.

The books cover a range of conceptual and methodological approaches to understanding the intersections between race, ethnicity, and belonging in education, educational organizations, and in non-formal education spaces. Books are grounded in—or undergirded by—empirical research, including case studies. Although we have set the main parameters as race, ethnicity, and belonging, we have deliberately not listed particular theories related to race or belonging because we do not want to limit the scope of proposals for this series. Moreover, we intentionally leave space for authors to explain new conceptualizations on the topic that will lead to exciting insights. We use the term race and ethnicity broadly to include individuals and groups from racially diverse, majority, and mixed-race backgrounds in various shifting contexts, and we use the term belonging not to imply that all groups feel they belong but to allow for counter-discourses and evidence that people may feel they belong as well as to acknowledge there may be organizational systems and policies that may create unbelonging.

This series is focused on understanding issues to do with race, ethnicity, and notions of belonging in all aspects, phases, and contexts of education, from early years to higher education and in traditional, non-traditional, formal, and informal settings. The series is international in scope, and open to contributions from all over the world.

Paul Miller, Professor of Educational Leadership & Social Justice, University of Huddersfield, and Educational Equity Services, UK
Jeffrey S. Brooks, Professor and Associate Dean, Research & Innovation, RMIT University School of Education, Australia
Lauri Johnson, Associate Professor and Chair, Department of Educational Leadership and Higher Education, Boston College, USA

Introduction: Strengthening Anti-racist Educational Leaders

Anjalé D. Welton and Sarah Diem

These are certainly turbulent times. There have been a number of signals globally in recent decades that would suggest the sociopolitical moment where we now find ourselves navigating two pandemics, the racial injustice pandemic and Covid-19, would soon arrive. Some of these signals include the rise of white nationalists groups across the globe that now have new tools to mobilize racial hate via social media, a tool that is a new media representation of a white hood given that hate can be spewed while remaining anonymous. And globally these white nationalist ideologies are now in alignment with and used as a mechanism to rile conservative politics and supporters. White fear of increasingly diversifying populations has led to anti-immigrant efforts such as Brexit in the UK, the unprecedented deportation of immigrants during the Obama Administration, and tax dollars dedicated to building a wall along the United States and Mexico border by the Trump Administration (Diem & Welton, 2021). Climate change debates and environmental justice are also issues specific to systemic racism as demonstrated by the Native American Standing Rock protests against the Dakota Access oil pipeline (Lakota People's Law Project, n.d.). And now during the Covid-19 pandemic anti-Asian violence and racism in America is escalating. Yet, this hatred and violence toward Asian-Americans is not a new phenomenon but instead a silenced and ignored part of the country's racial history (Hong, 2021). There have been numerous signals from our world that the pace in which we continue to redress racial injustice has been slow, not enough, and that our global commitment to rectify systemic racism has been waning.

Two and half months after the first wave of the Covid-19 pandemic lockdown, when the world was largely at a standstill trying to make sense of how to navigate an unknown virus, another longstanding pandemic, systemic racism, was laid bare after a senseless killing of a Black man occurred in the United States. On

Memorial Day 2020, a series of videos were posted on social media capturing all of nine minutes and twenty-nine seconds it took for Minneapolis police to execute a modern-day public lynching of a forty-six-year-old Black man, George Floyd. At that point, the Black Lives Matter movement, since its formation in 2013 in response to the acquittal of Trayvon Martin's murderer, had already worked tirelessly to raise global awareness about anti-Black racism in policies, structures, and practice, especially systemic anti-Black racism that is state-sanctioned (Black Lives Matter, n.d.). Even with Black Lives Matter's strategic network of activism, Black, Brown, and Indigenous lives continue to be taken via police brutality and other forms of state-sanctioned violence with such frequency that unfortunately many Americans have become desensitized to the issue. Further, prior to George Floyd's murder, most white Americans were still in disbelief that anti-Black racism was even a problem considering we had eight prosperous years under the leadership of our first Black president (see Bonilla-Silva, 2015). Thus, redressing systemic anti-Black racism was still not a national policy reform priority. Although there is a centuries-long amassing list of Black, Brown, Asian, and Indigenous lives lost due to state-sanctioned violence, watching the video from a smart phone of police brazenly extinguishing George Floyd's life was nightmarishly hard to ignore. It is speculated that being stuck at home because of the coronavirus left Americans, especially white Americans, undistracted to watch the video, witness, and finally acknowledge that anti-Black racism is indeed *still* a very real, present-day problem.

Most white Americans were metaphorically asleep and indifferent to systemic racism prior to Summer 2020, even when they were already familiar with the names Ahmaud Arbery, Atatiana Jefferson, Breonna Taylor, Michael Brown, Tamir Rice, Freddie Gray, and Philando Castile. Sadly, it took the violently public loss of one more Black man's life for the rest of America to finally awaken, which subsequently prompted a global social movement for racial justice. Those who were once uninformed (or before chose to be) to the issue of systemic racism were now hungry to learn about its impact and how they could take action against it. As a result, books on anti-racism were on bestseller lists for months. There was a news and social media cycle highlighting anti-racist organizations and causes to donate to. In this re-awakening the world was finally becoming more attuned to how racism is not only violence enacted by law enforcement, but that racism inhabits every institution from government to business, housing, health care, and *even* schools. But as history has shown us, white supremacy and whiteness is very powerful, and its survival depends on the slow pace in which the world makes progress toward racial justice. As scholars and educators of anti-racism we are conflicted by the possibility that anti-racism could become a buzzword similar to how the concepts equity and social justice became whitened in their meaning and application (Welton, 2020). As we conclude writing this edited book, it is approximately ten months since the initial revival of the global movement for racial justice. However, the world is still enduring and exhausted from the Covid-19 pandemic and, as a result, we fear that the newfound global commitment to anti-racism is already dwindling.

How do we work toward racial justice and equity in a society so entrenched in racism? What does it mean for racial progress at a time when people are still marching, protesting, and demonstrating for Black lives to matter? How might individuals espousing the importance of social justice actually instead be perpetuating anti-Asian, Black, Indigenous, and Latinx racism and how can they unlearn their "well-meaning" actions that actually do more harm to communities of color? Instead of simply reading a book on anti-racism and/or donating money, how are you being critically reflective? Also, stop reading the anti-racist scholarship of just white people as folx of color are the originators of anti-racist change and have written about the strategies for making this revolutionary change for a long time. Moreover, ask yourself, what anti-racist actions are you really taking that are authentic, continuous, and long term?

These are just a few of the many questions we consistently find ourselves grappling with as we engage in anti-racist work, specifically as it relates to schooling and school communities. More so, in this moment of civil unrest and people becoming more aware of the insidious ways racism manifests itself in all parts of society, *and* wanting to practice anti-racism in their homes, places of work, and communities, we worry that it may just be that—a moment, rather than a deep commitment to anti-racist work and all of the challenges it encapsulates. The two pandemics, Covid-19 and systemic racism, were at the forefront of our minds and upended our daily lives as we were in the process of editing this book, and rightfully so many of the book's contributing authors make reference to this unprecedented moment in history.

Defining Anti-racism in Educational Leadership

Yet, even in this ongoing turbulence, how can leaders still stay the course in their anti-racist commitment and actions? Also, how is anti-racism defined and what does it look like in our daily practice as educational leaders? If you are reading a book you cannot simply call yourself anti-racist. Anti-racism is not an adjective that an individual or organization should cavalierly claim to increase their "wokeness" factor. Engaging in the learning is a start but it also involves *actively* dismantling the white-normed racial status quo. This can be done by putting an end to policies, structures, and practices that uphold white norms and by building institutions that restore justice and equity for racially minoritized groups. Thus, anti-racist work requires white people, in particular, to reconcile their role in maintaining whiteness and white supremacy. Anti-racism also involves white-normed institutions like schools to examine their long history of benefiting from racial violence in its many forms against people of color, and right these racial wrongs by committing to designing and implementing policies, structures, and practices that humanize and ensure people of color thrive within organizations. Although racism is viewed by those who are still in denial about its present-day prevalence as more of an individualized and overt act, the most dangerous forms of racism are systemically embedded in the everyday norms and culture of society and institutions that it becomes part of our common sense. Thus, if anti-racism is to be a mechanism for upending racism, it needs to be a strategic, systemic, and an ongoing process. Anti-racism for both individuals and the organization as a whole should be a life-long commitment and journey. This sensemaking around anti-racism stems from our work as scholars and educators (Diem & Welton, 2021; Welton et al., 2018, 2019), but in the subsequent chapters in this book we offer a diverse set of perspectives to define and further conceptualize anti-racism in educational leadership.

Current State of the Educational Leadership Field

Historically, theories on educational leadership centered more "business-like" or managerial approaches to facilitating the day-to-day of districts and schools. However, treating schools as a business failed to address growing inequalities. As such, in the early 2000s there was a growing emphasis on centering equity and social justice in educational leadership research (Tanner & Welton, 2021). Subsequently, by 2015, with the refresh of the Professional Standards for Educational Leaders (PSEL), there was a national campaign led by prominent scholars in the field to ensure that equity and social justice are foundational to the revised standards (Diem et al., 2019; Galloway & Ishimaru, 2015). However, more recently, even the concepts equity and social justice have lost their flair and seem too diluted in implementation to fully address racial inequities in schools, which is why there is now a growing call to apply race-conscious (Gooden & Dantley, 2012) lenses such as critical race theory (Amiot et al., 2020; Capper,

2015; Horsford, 2011; López, 2003) or the focus of this book, anti-racism, to educational leadership (also see Brooks & Arnold, 2013; Gooden & O'Doherty, 2015).

However, the body of research on anti-racist education has been much more expansive in teacher education (de Freitas & McAuley, 2008; Mosley, 2010; Ohito, 2016; Raby, 2004; Ullucci, 2011), with clear research gaps in the field of educational leadership. Consequently, most educational leaders feel unprepared to facilitate anti-racist change in their districts and school communities (Swanson & Welton, 2019). For example, in a national US study, *Education Week* reported that 82 percent of educators indicated receiving no anti-racist professional development in their preparation programs (Superville, 2020). This is unfortunate considering it is educational leaders who are the captain, so to speak, of the ship (i.e., the school). If school leaders are the ones who are primarily steering the ship by facilitating, guiding, and directing the course of racial equity work in school communities, then why are they not provided with significant tools to do this work?

These are key questions we asked and discussed at a small conference we held in early March 2019, thanks to a grant from the Spencer Foundation, where we invited scholars and practitioners to help brainstorm how to expand existent research on anti-racist educational leadership by identifying what type of capacity-building is needed for school administrators to facilitate anti-racist change in their schools. This conference brought together experts including scholars in the field of educational leadership, sociologists of education, school and district administrators, and grassroots community members and activist groups to discuss issues related to anti-racist educational leadership. At the conclusion of the conference we engaged in action workshops to collaborate, plan, and potentially design the type of research that expands anti-racist educational leadership as an ongoing practice in education. One suggested outcome of this conference was to publish this edited book as an effort to expand the knowledge base on anti-racist educational leadership.

As we aimed to further define and conceptualize anti-racist educational leadership, some points of discussion from the conference were, first, that the United States is by default political, especially regarding issues of race and racism. So, for those who reside in nations with a history rooted in white supremacy it is impossible to be apolitical regarding race. For instance, in most Westernized nations Black and Indigenous bodies are criminalized and treated as the "other" even before birth. Schools also implement political ideologies that reinforce whiteness. Hence, we must acknowledge we all have informal and formal agency, and so the individual political decisions we make are manifestations of the political as we co-construct our political realities. Ultimately, *we should understand how policies beyond education shape the experience of educational leaders.* Second, district and school communities are inclined to protect white privilege. Therefore, educational leaders must not only be accountable for working toward anti-racist change but also *hold the responsibility for pushing back against any possible resistance to this more revolutionary change.* Thirdly, the revolutionary change needed to enact anti-racism requires that leaders deeply understand their institutions so that they then know how to use the strength of the system of racism against itself. To upend the racism endemic to their communities, *educational leaders must employ the tools of politicians and activists.* Finally, conference participants *stressed that educational leaders should establish cultures of conflict instead of cultures of conformity or complicity* wherein instead differences are advocated for, frameworks that intersectionally consider race/class/gender are used to inform their leadership, and that complexity and discomfort are embraced when leading anti-racist changes.

Overview of the Book

In this edited book, we seek to expand on the existent research on anti-racist educational leadership by identifying what type of capacity building is needed for school leaders to facilitate anti-racist change in their schools. The book underscores why we need more educational leaders who adopt an anti-racist stance in how they lead and are prepared to face the political complexity and uncertainty that will undoubtedly occur when they try to advance racial equity in their school communities.

Most of the scholarly texts in the field of educational leadership are still in large part written by university scholars/researchers. In this book, we include a diverse set of authors, not just university researchers. Several of our chapters are co-authored by current or former district and school administrators who are engaged in the day-to-day work of being an anti-racist educational leader. Yet, research also shows that educational administrators cannot do racial equity work alone, and community members and activist groups, such as parents, youth, and grassroots community organizers, are equally important to anti-racist educational leadership and serve as a counternarrative to who counts as educational leaders (Rodela & Bertrand, 2018). Thus, we deemed it equally important to invite community members to contribute chapters sharing their experiences as anti-racist educational leaders.

We have organized the book into four sections: (1) the sociopolitical context of anti-racist educational leadership; (2) anti-racist educational leadership preparation and practice; (3) community engagement, activism, and anti-racist educational leadership; and (4) recognizing and accounting for the work of anti-racist leadership. Part I, "The Sociopolitical Context of Anti-racist Educational Leadership," provides an overview of the current social and political landscapes in which educational leaders must navigate race and racism. In Chapter 1, "Anti-racist Leadership in Precarious Sociopolitical Contexts," Anjalé D. Welton, Greg Johnson, and Sarah Diem explore the racial politics associated with doing anti-racist school leadership. Specifically, by examining one suburban school district's efforts to detrack their curriculum, they show the tension of trying to execute an anti-racist agenda in school communities that may espouse to value diversity but are tethered to whiteness and white racism.

In Chapter 2, "Anti-racism as Core Competency for Educational Leaders," Matthew A. Rodriguez and Amanda E. Lewis discuss the need for anti-racist leadership not to be thought of as a radical approach to challenging the racist structures and policies that undergird education systems but rather as the everyday way administrators, leaders, and teachers go about their work. Indeed, Rodriguez and Lewis state that being race neutral when it comes to school improvement interventions can actually do more harm. They use the example of school discipline policies to illustrate how a race neutral approach to policy implementation can contribute to racial inequity and how designing such policies from a place of critical racial awareness, care, and humility, or even doing away with them instead, may create more healing spaces for students to be successful.

Chapter 3, "The Politics of the School–Prison Nexus: Racial Capitalism and Possibilities for Transformation in Schools and Beyond," provides a comprehensive analysis of the political and economic landscape associated with the school–prison nexus. Erica O. Turner, Abigail J. Beneke, Maria Velazquez, and Rob Timberlake assert that this nexus is a result of US racial capitalism that is more interested in protecting and serving profits and people who are white and affluent, while minoritized students, particularly Black students, are subject to constant surveillance and discipline more often than to receiving the quality education that they rightfully deserve. They discuss the actors and organizations complicit in maintaining and even extending the school–prison nexus, as well as the discourses, policies, processes, and events that have contributed to it. The chapter concludes with implications for education leaders on how to challenge and transform the school–prison nexus.

The chapters in Part II of the book, "Anti-racist Educational Leadership Preparation and Practice," outline what type of preparation in university-based endorsement programs, as well as ongoing leadership practices, is necessary to better prepare leaders to be anti-racist practitioners. In Chapter 4, "Considerations for District-level Anti-racist Leadership Preparation," Mary B. Herrmann and Jessica A. Herrmann explore what key elements must be included in district-level preparation programs that are committed to preparing future anti-racist leaders. After presenting eight principles that undergird their evolving vision of anti-racist leadership preparation programs, the rest of the chapter provides a deep dive into three of these principles that they believe should be the main areas of focus in these programs: (1) the personal journey of leaders, (2) the application of scholarly and multi-disciplinary work to practice, and (3) understanding the context of leading for change. The authors' experience as former/current school leaders provides unique and important insights into the work it takes for superintendents to be well-positioned to engage in anti-racist work.

Chapter 5, "From the Inside Out: A Letter to Anti-racist Leaders," looks at what it means to be an anti-racist leader in practice. Marcus Campbell and Michael Kucera frame their chapter as a letter to school leaders, particularly white leaders, as a way to draw attention to the challenges and responsibilities anti-racist school leaders are faced with in their everyday practice. They offer a number of approaches as to what anti-racist leaders can do to address racial inequities, including interrogating the root causes of systemic racism within schools, looking beyond quantitative data to assess student performance, engaging in critical dialogue and group reflection, and examining the hearts and minds of educators and staff members who are responsible for serving students. As the title of their chapter articulates, Campbell and Kucera argue that in order to dismantle racial inequities in education, school systems must be transformed from the inside out.

Situating their study alongside the analytic frameworks of coloniality and the educational racial contract, in Chapter 6, "The Color of Coloniality: White Administrators' Expectations of Black Males in School Discipline," Daniel D. Liou and Adam Zang explore the role of white school administrators in challenging school discipline practices that are illustrative of the larger white supremacist project and how these administrators can disrupt the criminalization of students of color, particularly Black male students, in schools and society writ large. Chapters 2 and 3 highlight problems specific to school discipline; however, this chapter presents a real case of a school leader wrestling with the racial implications of school discipline. The authors focus on the experiences of Adam, who is an assistant principal and manages discipline in an elementary school, and uses a self-narrativization methodological approach that allows Adam to reflect on his disciplinary actions and provide a counter-perspective that can assist in better preparing white administrators to employ anti-racist and decolonial school discipline practices.

In Chapter 7, "Understanding the Racialized Organization: African-centered Leadership and Their Unique Form of Culturally Responsive Leadership," Bodunrin O. Banwo and Muhammad Khalifa explore how, through a process of organizational inquiry, school leaders at African-centered schools are able to shape their practices and culture that eradicate white supremacy in ways that other schools have failed to do so. Specifically, they argue that "African-centered school leaders' anti-racist practice of questioning mainstream culture through a historical and racialized critique creates an organizational process of exploration designed to take up the unexamined social and organizational ideologies formed within western cultural *milieus* of white supremacy." They offer a theory of ethno-cultural responsiveness they believe can assist organizations and leaders in being both aware and responsive to their community's ideal needs and concerns and not just those of the dominant culture.

In the third section of the book, "Community Engagement, Activism, and Anti-racist Educational Leadership," the chapters explore how educational researchers, educational administrators, and community activists work in partnerships to execute research based on problems of practice to address issues of racism and racial inequity, and discuss strategies for forging and sustaining these partnerships. The chapters also highlight the actions leaders must take to support racial equity work in their school communities, and how they can strengthen relationships with community members and organizations in their efforts.

In Chapter 8, "Aligning Frameworks and Identifying Capacities for Anti-racist Advocacy Educational Leadership," Michelle D. Young and Angel Miles Nash discuss the need for leadership to be thought of as advocacy for and with those leaders who serve in their school communities. They offer a conceptual framework for anti-racist advocacy leadership, which includes "anti-racist, equity-oriented, collaborative, culturally responsive, and technically competent instructional leadership practice." This framework builds off of prior leadership models that seek to support diverse student populations (Brooks, 2012; Khalifa et al., 2016; Riehl, 2000), yet centers its focus on the need for leaders to be anti-racist advocates for those directly within their school buildings as well as those in their school communities. School leaders can no longer be thought of as apolitical actors immune from the sociopolitical contexts in which they lead. They must be able to advocate for and with those in their communities, particularly when it comes to seeking anti-racist and more just schooling environments.

In Chapter 9, "Anti-racist Activist Leadership," Jason Salisbury and Meagan Richard explore activist leadership through the experiences of three anti-racist leaders in the Chicago Public Schools district. While each leader focused on issues they felt were important to their school community, they engaged in similar activist practices to push back at the racialized neoliberal policies that are harming their schools. These practices included identifying the community needs, establishing partnerships with organizations in the community, and figuring out how the school can actually help in meeting the desires of the community. The leaders wanted to make sure that their activism was not only helpful and what the community was calling for, but also shined a light on the importance of the school as the heart of the local community. Salisbury and Richard conclude their chapter by offering several recommendations for how school leaders can best engage in anti-racist activism to (re)connect schools and communities.

In Chapter 10, "Toward More Equitable Communities: Leadership Lessons for Systemic Social Change," Rhoda Freelon and Jeanette Taylor, using a life history approach, provide a case study of Jeanette and her experiences as an education and community organizer. They highlight major events in Jeanette's role as a community leader to help illustrate how community-based leadership can assist school leaders and their school communities in advancing more anti-racist and just policies and practices. Community organizing and activism have long been means to push for social change in our society, and in our schools in particular. Indeed, community-based educational leaders are extremely knowledgeable about what is happening in their local schools and are well-positioned to work alongside school leaders to address policies and practices that are racially unjust. Freelon and Taylor posit that "the everyday leadership of families and community members has the potential to not only shed light on critical issues in education, but also to help traditional systems leaders address these concerns for educational justice."

In the field of educational leadership, the literature on university–district partnerships is not robust. Indeed, the research that does exist fails to take into account power dynamics of such partnerships, does not center the community's needs, nor addresses how racism and racial oppression are at the core of these partnerships. In Chapter 11, "(Re)Imagining 'Successful' University–District–Community Partnerships," Decoteau J. Irby, Bradley W. Carpenter, and Erica Young engaged in a building session in which Young served as the interviewer/facilitator of the conversation and Irby and Carpenter reflected on their experiences as university-based researchers and the type of research they want to do that fosters anti-racist university–district–community partnerships. Throughout their conversation, they were able to imagine what ideal partnerships would look like without the constraints of racist policies and practices that are embedded within universities and go beyond how both parties may benefit from them.

The chapters in the concluding section of the book, "Recognizing and Accounting for the Work of Anti-racist Leadership," discuss the work educational leaders engage in and provide specific resources that school administrators can utilize to advance anti-racist work in their district and school communities. In Chapter 12, "The Invisible Labor of PK-20 BIPOC Leaders," Zelideh R. Martinez Hoy, Dennis J. Perkins Jr., and David Hoa Khoa Nguyen present a call to action to organizations and their leaders to immediately address the emotional cost and invisible labor of Black, Indigenous, and People of Color (BIPOC) educators. Specifically, they discuss how critical race consciousness, derived from Critical Race Theory, is essential in any type of approach that is going to result in systemic and sustained organizational anti-racist efforts to support and advance all BIPOC educators. The authors offer powerful recommendations and pose important questions for leaders across PK-20 settings to better reflect upon and engage in the work necessary to change practices and policies that place undue burden and invisible labor on BIPOC educators.

Counter-storytelling, a key tenet of critical race theory, is a powerful and important methodological tool that assists us in gaining more insight into the lived experiences of people of color, experiences, and stories that too often go missing in the dominant educational discourse. In Chapter 13, "On the Backs of Black Women: Examining How the Supporting Administrative Role Is Entrenched in Racism," Asia Fuller Hamilton and Mykah Jackson describe their experiences as Black women and school leaders, and the racism they have endured as they ascended to leadership positions. They specifically highlight attempts that were made to suppress opportunities and "keep them in their place," hold them responsible for maintaining discipline and academic status quo, and use and exploit their Black bodies to serve the interests of white leaders.

Hamilton and Jackson describe their stories "as culmination of warning signs and a bridge that helps make the chasms that exist in the world of educational leadership easier to cross." Indeed, it is through their narratives that we are able to learn more about the challenges Black women face in leadership roles and how we can create a better path moving forward for Black women who aspire to be educational leaders and administrators.

What are white people going to do about racism? In Chapter 14, "Anti-racism for White People: From Inactivism to Activism," Jeffrey S. Brooks explains what it looks like for white people to move from a state of inactivism to activism when it comes to racism, which includes not just unlearning what you have been taught that may actually contribute to racist behavior but to also learn about anti-racist history and contexts through reading, reflection, and becoming informed about your community. Brooks notes how this work must be done at the individual level and collectively with others, and that it requires a commitment to work that will undoubtedly be challenging, nonlinear, and full of mistakes. However, as he argues, if white people want to move from a place of "ignorance to information; from information to intention; from intention to speaking out; from speaking out to standing up, and; from standing up to activism and then to leadership," the choice of whether to engage in this work is pretty clear as there are no neutral positions when it comes to racism.

In Chapter 15, "Sameness and Conformity in Predominately White School Districts," Sharon I. Radd presents the phenomenon she has coined the "homogenous whole," which refers to efforts made by predominantly white school districts to seek to enact equitable and anti-racist practices in their organizations yet do so in a way that does not acknowledge differences. Rather, these districts assert that they are all the same, which on the surface may appear harmless but in reality can hinder any meaningful anti-racist work from occurring as it denies the significance of race in favor of a race neutral approach. By describing the homogenous whole phenomenon, Radd hopes school leaders will be better able to recognize it when it occurs and then act to disrupt its impact so that real anti-racist schooling environments may exist instead.

Finally, in Chapter 16, "Developing Anti-racist Leaders through Equity-expansive Technical Assistance," Kathleen A. King Thorius and Tiffany S. Keyser discuss the equity-expansive technical assistance (TA) provided at the Midwest and Plains Equity Assistance Center they lead, one of four Equity Assistance Centers across the United States, and how this type of TA translates into anti-racist leadership praxis. They describe a theory of equity-expansive TA that grounds the work they engage in, which consists of an explicit examination of the socio-historical and political contexts that have perpetuated systemic issues of racism and injustice, developing relational partnerships where knowledge is shared and support is provided when working toward the disruption of existing inequities, and moving away from technical improvements of policies and practices toward more process-based systemic transformations via expansive learning. Through real-life examples, they illustrate how this theory has guided their work in supporting anti-racist leadership development across school districts.

Conclusion and Acknowledgments

Racial inequities in education persist in part because the solutions that districts and schools choose to employ largely ignore why and how institutional and structural racism is the root cause of inequities in education (Diem & Welton, 2021). Yet, racial inequities in schooling can be redressed if districts and schools have leaders who are deeply committed to combatting racism in their daily practice and structures of schooling.

This book offers a snapshot of anti-racist leadership in schools and communities. Drawing from personal experiences, concrete examples, theoretical and empirical analyses, and even offering new conceptual models and frameworks, the chapters collectively illustrate the many facets involved in engaging in anti-racist leadership. Importantly, the book also provides a more expansive definition of what it means to be an educational leader, which is conceptualized throughout the chapters as anyone who plays a significant leadership role in pursuing racial equity and justice for their district and/or school community. An educational leader can be a school or district administrator, a parent or community member, grassroots community organizers, and even policymakers.

While there are certainly even more viewpoints that we could have included in this book, it is our hope that it will serve as a resource to stimulate new lines of study in research methods for educational scholars, particularly when it comes to partnerships among research institutions, schools, and communities (Coburn & Penuel, 2016; Penuel & Gallagher, 2017). We also hope that by providing a comprehensive perspective on anti-racist leadership in one book, anyone interested in promoting and supporting anti-racist school communities will have a foundational understanding of what this type of work entails.

Finally, we would like to give a special thanks to a number of people who have helped to make this book a reality. Along with the authors of this volume, we would like to thank James D. Anderson, Shannon Paige Clark, David DeMatthews, Mark A. Gooden, Rhoda Gutierrez, Vanessa Puentes Hernandez, Devon Herrick, Jennifer Johnson, Devean R. Owens, Eric Reyes, Rachel Roegman, Nathaniel Rouse, Miguel Saucedo, Rebeca Shick, Daniel Spikes, David Stovall, Joseph Wiemelt, and Irene Yoon for their participation in our Spencer Foundation-funded conference and their contributions to anti-racist research and practice. Thank you to the Spencer Foundation for supporting our conference, which culminated with this edited book. We would also like to thank Bloomsbury Publishing, specifically Alison Baker and Evangeline Stanford, for their assistance throughout the publication process. Thank you to the Race, Ethnicity, and Belonging in Education series editors, Paul Miller, Jeffrey S. Brooks, and Lauri Johnson, for the opportunity to be a part of the series, and to the anonymous reviewers of our proposal for the helpful feedback.

Most importantly, we extend our deepest gratitude to our families and friends for their unconditional love and support. We would not be able to do this work without their encouragement along the way.

Part I

The Sociopolitical Context of Anti-racist Educational Leadership

1

Anti-racist Leadership in Precarious Sociopolitical Contexts

Anjalé D. Welton, Greg Johnson, and Sarah Diem

School Leaders and Sociopolitical and Racial Contexts

On March 17, 2020 school districts across the United States began shutting their doors as a result of the worldwide Covid-19 pandemic (Education Week, 2020). In what seemed like the blink of an eye, school district administrators, school leaders, faculty, and staff were tasked with shifting their brick and mortar schools to remote learning environments. And while the pandemic certainly disrupted how we go about educating students, it further revealed the systemic racism and deep-rooted educational disparities and opportunities available to low-income and Black and Brown students.

Prior to the pandemic, US public schools did not afford equal opportunities to all students. Racially and economically segregated schools are less likely to have access to more resources, teachers with more experience, and more higher-level classes (see, e.g., Orfield et al., 2012; Rosiek, 2019). As the pandemic took hold and schools moved online, these unequal opportunities were exacerbated, particularly in historically marginalized Black and Brown, low-income communities where there is not regular and reliable access to the internet, making it challenging for students to engage in this new learning environment. Indeed, learning just stopped for many students who, along with struggling to access their online classes, are simultaneously dealing with issues such as food and housing insecurity, among others (LaFave, 2020).

A little over two months after schools closed as a result of Covid-19, the nation erupted in protest when on Memorial Day 2020 an approximately nine-minute video was released showing how George Floyd, a forty-six-year-old Black man, was killed while in Minneapolis police custody. While the violence in this video was hard to ignore, this type of violence and dehumanization of Black people and other racially minoritized groups has been a part of the American and global consciousness for centuries. Moreover, Black Americans are more likely to be incarcerated than any other racial group. For instance, there are 1,501 Black prisoners for every 100,000 Black adults, compared to 797 and 268 out of 100,000 for Latinx and white adults respectively (Gramlich, 2020).

Schools are not only a mirror of this larger societal racism but in many ways an indelible starting point for the racism that students of color will then face in their lifetimes. For example, for many Black adults who are or have been incarcerated we must also look back to their schooling to see how their experiences with punitive discipline and policing in school may be tied to their present encounters with the judicial system (Alexander, 2010; Diem & Welton, 2021). This pervasive devaluing of Black lives, or what is known as anti-Blackness, is prime evidence of how the racial hierarchy remains constant. Systematically positioning white people as the preeminent in worth is indeed how whiteness is maintained. Whiteness fuels anti-Blackness just as the devaluing of Black lives elevates white material and non-material interests, privileges, and power (Diem & Welton, 2021).

According to Castagno (2014), "whiteness refers to structural arrangements and ideologies of race dominance. Racial power and inequities are at the core of whiteness, but all forms of power and inequity create and perpetuate whiteness" (p. 5). There is a "possessive investment" in whiteness as white people are rewarded with further accumulated power and privileges if they contribute to the protection of their own interests (Lipsitz, 1998). Also, whiteness situates white as the standard/norm, where people of color are pathologized as the deviation of this norm. "Whiteness is not acknowledged by white people, and the white reference point is assumed to be universal and is imposed on everyone" (DiAngelo, 2018, p. 25). Yet, although white people have the most to benefit from whiteness, people of color should also be mindful that they are not absolved from participating in whiteness, as they can also conduct power plays in the name of whiteness with the hope of somehow benefiting from it (see Castagno, 2014).

In this chapter, we focus specifically on the racial politics associated with practicing anti-racist school leadership. We discuss the need for leaders to understand how whiteness and white supremacy operate within the current educational policy agenda, because only then will they be prepared to upend white racism's efforts to impede their anti-racist policy aims and actions. We focus specifically on one diverse suburban school district's efforts to execute anti-racist policy by detracking their curriculum. One of the chapter co-authors,

Greg, is a leader in the district discussed and shares lessons learned from how they navigated the political tightrope of being anti-racist in values and actions while simultaneously wrestling with the powerful presence of whiteness and white racism in their district community.

The Continued Importance of Detracking in School Districts

In 1985, Jeannie Oakes released a seminal publication on the harmful effects of tracking, *Keeping Track: How Schools Structure Inequality*, in which she analyzed twenty-five schools and almost 300 classrooms to see how tracking "both causes and supports differences in the lives of secondary students" (p. 3). Tracking is used in schools to situate students in classes based on their perceived academic ability (Oakes, 1985). Historically, tracking was used to place students in either "*all* high- or *all* low-level classes" and it was difficult to move into a "higher" class once placed in a "lower" class at any point throughout the K-12 schooling experience, which contributes to furthering academic disparities among students (Yonezawa et al., 2002). The learning experience students receive in different tracked classes is remarkably disparate whereas students in low-level classes are engaged in more passive learning and students in high-level classes are engaged in more active learning (Oakes, 1985; O'Neil, 1992). The belief in favor of tracking, although found to be untrue, is that students in similar academic ability classes would learn better (Oakes, 1985).

While tracking as it was initially conceived is no longer as prevalent in schools, and there may be no specific tracking policy on the books, students are still placed in individual courses based on ability, which are highly segregated by race and income (Venzant Chambers & Spikes, 2016). Low-income, Black, and Latinx students are more likely to be in low-level classes while high-income, white, and Asian students are more likely to be in high-level classes (Stanley & Venzant Chambers, 2018; Venzant Chambers & Spikes, 2016). Furthermore, what is troubling about the segregative nature of tracking is that it is so ingrained in schooling. Indeed, Black students are so "desensitized" to the tracking they experience throughout their schooling that by the time they get to high school, it "seemed very normal to be segregated from their peers" (Venzant Chambers & Spikes, 2016, p. 38). Further, students feel tracking is a practice used to get "the Black students out the way so they [teachers] could teach the white students" (p. 39).

Yet, over the last few decades many schools have attempted to detrack their curriculum to prevent racially segregated classrooms and provide more equitable educational opportunities. In its basic form, detracking involves bringing together students of differing academic ability. However, as Yonezawa et al. (2002) are quick to point out, detracking cannot just stop at this simple act of moving students so that classes may look more equal and less segregated. Instead,

> detracking must involve questioning why we continue to build walls that divide and stratify students based on narrow constructions of students' merit and the value of their lived experiences. … detracking must reconstruct and redefine what these spaces mean by attending to how they shape and codify the identities of individuals within them."
>
> (p. 63)

In a recent effort to detrack schooling, in August 2019, the New York City School Diversity Advisory Group, appointed by Mayor Bill DeBlasio to address issues of diversity and segregation in the city's public schools, released a report that would spur a visceral reaction throughout the community. Among the group's recommendations, one of the most controversial came in the form of eliminating the city's "Gifted and Talented" (G&T) programs and the admissions practices used in selective schools that have existed for twenty years (Shapiro, 2020). The group specifically noted that these programs "do not serve a 21st century educational mission and unfairly block educational opportunities for students who are Black, Latinx, low-income, and who face other challenges, including learning differences, students who are multi-language learners, in temporary housing or face other structural barriers to the educational opportunities they deserve" (School Diversity Advisory Group, 2019, p. 31). New York City Public Schools (NYCPS) is one of the most racially segregated school districts in the United States and students who attend the selective schools are majority white and Asian American (Shapiro, 2019a, 2020). In 2020, out of the approximately 800 students admitted to the city's most selective high school, Stuyvesant High School, only ten were Black students and twenty were Latinx students (Elsen-Rooney, 2020). These numbers are shameful, particularly in a city with such a racially diverse population.

As we discuss in the case presented in our chapter, politics, power, and privilege play huge roles in detracking reform efforts as white and more affluent families, in particular, work extremely hard to ensure their children receive the "best" the education system has to offer (O'Neil, 1992). This is evident in places like the New York City example previously highlighted as parents do whatever it takes, such as paying consultants to inform them of the best admission strategies, to help their children get into the schools they desire (Shapiro, 2019b).

Yonezawa et al. also (2002) discuss the notion of politics and privilege specifically when it comes to tracking, encouraging us to look beyond the actual tracked classes but also what they mean and thus why these classes are considered such a premium by many families. They note, "Tracks are politically and socially significant spaces because we assign meaning to them" (p. 39) much like we assign meaning to any space. When a space is then given meaning, who occupies those spaces and who positions themselves to occupy those spaces can be explained. Yonezawa et al. (2002) argue when it comes to tracking, this is why low-track classrooms are racially and economically segregated and why students in higher-track classrooms feel entitled to these classrooms and act in ways to maintain their positions within the tracking structures despite the impact it may have on furthering educational disparities. As such, Stanley and Venzant Chambers (2018) suggest school leaders need to do a deep dive into how tracking is perpetuating racial disparities in the classroom and work to make sure each class in their buildings represents the demographic make-up of their entire school so that we can dismantle the deficit meanings given to classroom spaces in our schools. Detracking is one anti-racist policy solution if implemented with fidelity that can systemically contest white classroom norms for learning while also improving racially minoritized students' learning opportunities, outcomes, and overall sense of academic belongingness.

Navigating Whiteness in Anti-racist Policy Decision Making

Public education is an agent of whiteness. Access to quality educational opportunities and experiences has always been viewed as property or a material resource. Public education will never be truly public. The question educational leaders should ask is how education is "public for whom?" because in the policy sphere education is increasingly treated as a "private" [white] right or entity (see Diem & Welton, 2021).

Education as an institution was inherently orchestrated to exclude people of color to further the accumulation of white constituents' privileges and opportunities within the educational system. This white supremacy in education is also linked to white accumulated privileges in other societal institutions. Indeed, policies are still intentionally designed to advance white supremacy within these institutions (Anderson, 2016). White flight, gentrification, and housing discrimination via redlining in the United States have led to the ultimate racial and economic isolation of neighborhoods and are why schools are resegregating. Furthermore, the depletion of economic capital and commerce, especially the limited property tax infrastructure, in Black and Brown communities in the United States has created large district and school funding resource inequities between school districts with majority students of color and white affluent districts (Diem & Welton, 2021). This geography of racism that is fueled by educational and other intersecting policies is also coupled with racial inequities in workforce opportunities and disparities in health and wellbeing (Tate, 2008). Thus, education represents just one complex component of the US white supremacist policy infrastructure.

Whiteness also survives and thrives by delaying and often derailing any progress toward righting racial wrongs in educational policy. In this chapter, we use detracking as one example of an anti-racist educational policy that is often never fully implemented with fidelity because district and school leaders struggle to manage the political pushback (i.e., whiteness) from white stakeholders who are concerned with how this leveling in the playing field may take away educational privileges they have long grown accustomed to and expect. Thus, educational leaders must be attuned to the racial politics associated with educational policy and practice, and one method for doing so is by naming and calling out whiteness and white racism in the educational policy decision-making process. Only by understanding how whiteness operates can leaders then ensure that it does not distract from their key purpose, which is systemic anti-racist action.

Even in this current sociopolitical moment where many Americans are now newly enlightened about and conscious to the fact that systemic racism does exist, we are still generally suspicious of whether real action toward redressing whiteness and white supremacy in educational policy will ever happen. As history has demonstrated even when there are global and national social movements and legal decisions that call for racial justice, when it comes to actually carrying out these anti-racist policy changes on the ground, white stakeholders are still hesitant to do so if they feel the said policy change encroaches upon their privileged interests (Bell, 1980).

In the following district case study, we use detracking as a prime example of an anti-racist policy that is often never executed entirely because of overwhelming white resistance. However, we assert that this anti-racist policy solution can be actualized if educational leaders prioritize equity and justice for racially minoritized students over the demands of whiteness and white supremacy.

Example from the Field: Detracking in a Diverse, Inner Ring, Suburban School District

Throughout most of its 150-year history, Oak Park and River Forest High School (OPRFHS), located in an inner ring suburb of Chicago, Illinois, has benefited from what many have considered a progressive and academically strong reputation. Its racially diverse student population routinely and significantly outperforms the state averages in graduation rate, SAT performance, and post-secondary enrollment, and each year its students are placed in elite colleges and universities around the country and abroad. Financially, the district is among the highest in the state, spending almost $24,000 per pupil each year.

At least in part, the school's strong reputation also rests on the pride the community has in embracing its racial diversity. In the 1960s, the Oak Park suburb made an impressive stance against the resegregation that was occurring throughout the Chicagoland area (Lewis, 2019). Redlining was threatening property values in Oak Park and causing white, wealthier homeowners to move to the western and northern Chicago suburbs. Through a combination of visionary leaders and community support, Oak Park took active steps to deliberately encourage an integrated community, a practice that has been largely successful in maintaining both a relatively diverse and financially strong suburb.

This commitment to racial integration in the community, coupled with the resources that come with its per pupil spending rate, has not translated, however, to racially equitable outcomes for the Black and Brown students in its schools. Relative to student performance, the results within the district are stagnant. While a complete overview of student performance data is not the purpose of this chapter, one useful place to begin to examine the school is in how students are currently enrolled in the school's most rigorous classes. Figure 1.1 provides a three-year overview of enrollment in Advanced Placement and honors classes by race and ethnicity. Whereas over 50 percent of white and Asian students are routinely enrolled in high-level classes, Black and Brown students have been routinely under-represented (prior years' data shows similar figures).

When this data is coupled with other marks of student performance, the need for a change becomes evident. However, before moving into steps the district

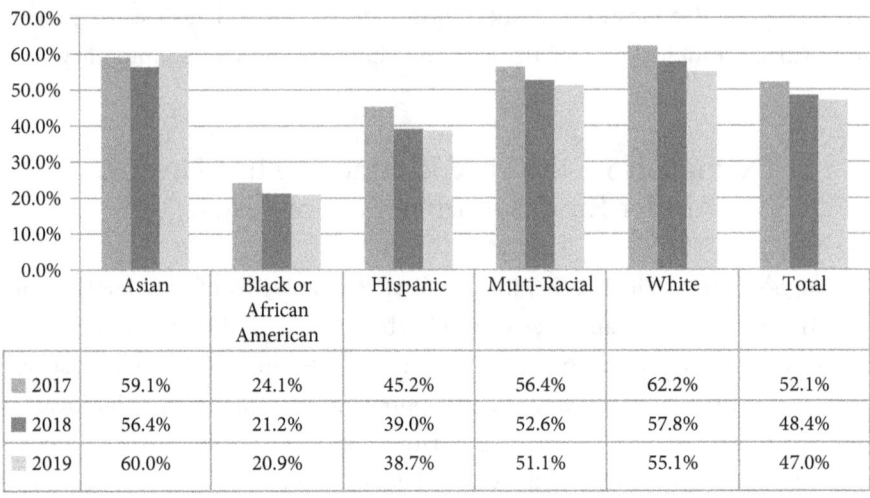

Figure 1.1 Overall AP/honors enrollment by race and ethnicity, Oak Park and River Forest High School.

has recently taken to address some of these disparities, some context into the different communities that make up OPRFHS is necessary.

OPRFHS is the first high school west of the Chicago city boundary, and with a population of approximately 3,400 students, it is one of the largest high schools in the state. Its population (55 percent white, 20 percent Black, 12 percent Hispanic, 9 percent two or more races, 4 percent Asian, and 19 percent low-income) comes from two different communities. Oak Park, the larger of the two, shares a border with Chicago's Austin neighborhood to the east and accounts for approximately 80 percent of the school's total student population. River Forest sits directly to the west of Oak Park and sends approximately 170 students each year to OPRFHS. River Forest's population (70 percent white, 11 percent Hispanic, 6 percent Asian, 6 percent Black, and just less than 5 percent low-income) is less diverse and wealthier than Oak Park. Further entrenching the differences between the two communities is the fact that each has its own elementary school district, only sending their students to OPRFHS District 200 after eighth grade.

Time for a Change

Between the fall of 2016 and the fall of 2019, the district administration experienced significant turnover. The district hired its first Black woman as its superintendent in the fall of 2016, and in the fall of 2017, a white male (Greg) school administrator from central Illinois was hired as assistant superintendent. By the fall of 2019, there were more dramatic changes to the administrative team; the principal had been replaced with an executive director of equity and student success, and the former assistant principal positions had been replaced with directors for student learning and student services, respectively. All three positions were held by people of color.

Other changes were in store for the district as well. During her first year, the superintendent signaled that it was time to take action on several initiatives that had been named but only tepidly implemented over the previous few years. First, she worked with a committee of teachers and other administrators to dust off and revise the district's strategic plan. Once completed, she placed one administrator in charge of each goal, and required each to establish action teams aimed at producing specific outcomes in publicly identified timelines. Each action team consisted of between ten and twenty members and was designed to garner consensus from stakeholders; community membership was required. Additionally, every effort was made to recruit a diverse membership that was racially parallel to the district's student population. After a year of work, these teams established a new range of goals that racialized their aims, refined their timelines for implementation, and developed specific action steps to produce them.

Part of this district strategic plan was the Transformational Teaching and Learning, which was Greg's charge. The initial objective of the team was "to pilot a more inclusive 9th-grade curriculum designed to increase access to honors and Advanced Placement courses, with the goal of increasing by 25 percent the number of students earning honors credit their freshman year." This objective then shifted to implementing "an equitable and inclusive 9th-grade curriculum that is designed to increase access to honors and Advanced Placement courses for students of color such that race ceases to be a predictor of student access to advanced classes."

The first action step of the team was the establishment of a summer research cohort. A total of thirty teachers, six administrators, and two community members joined a team that read school change literature relative to the team's goal. The work, which included an analysis of our students' enrollment trends, performance, and achievement data, resulted in the establishment of problem statements, a causal analysis, and guiding principles to steer the work moving forward. The honesty and rigor with which the team attacked this work were inspiring. The following four resulting Transformational Teaching and Learning

Team problem statements, for example, boldly isolated race as a significant determinant in our students' success:

1. Freshman preparation for academic success is currently perpetuating and exacerbating racial disparities.
2. There is a lack of access/equality for freshman students within all curriculums in the building.
3. White students' achievement improves more rapidly than the achievement of students of color.
4. Our current system places students into tracks that are segregated by race and then highly correlated with long-term academic and economic disparities.

The causal analysis the group engaged in resulted in six root causes—institutional structures/school procedures; ideological/institutional assumptions; curriculum; community, social, and political dynamics; professional development; student academic skills—placing the high school's systemic structures and the ideological assumptions that drive them as the top reasons the racial disparities have continued to persist at our school.

Finally, the team identified eight guiding principles that would provide the necessary vision to the work moving forward:

1. Curriculum needs consistency between sections of courses in terms of standards, sequencing, and common assessments.
2. Courses should allow for multiple pathways for success, allowing teachers to be responsive to students' learning needs.
3. Sorting students by "skill level" is inherently linked to racial inequities in both opportunity and outcomes, and should be reduced and/or removed wherever possible.
4. We must have a growth mindset in all things, for both adults and students, challenging our assumptions about who is capable of doing high-level coursework.
5. Curriculum materials and approaches should be culturally responsive as we work to deliberately disrupt patterns of "doing school" that disadvantage students of color.
6. We should attend to teacher learning at the beginning and throughout the process.
7. Intentional time needs to be carved out to support this work.
8. This change process needs persistence and grit that rewards teacher and team risk-taking.

With this work in place, the school was in position to take meaningful steps toward improving access for students. It was decided to implement the policy with the freshman curriculum. In the fall of 2018, teams of teachers were developed within each division, given an orientation into the work, and embarked on an evaluation of the curriculum within their content area.

At the conclusion of the 2018–19 school year, it was evident that structural shifts were needed in how students were sorted into what were called "college prep" and "honors" courses. As a result, in the summer of 2019 the school was prepared to announce that freshman courses in English, science, history, and world languages would be "detracked," and the number of tracks in math would be significantly reduced. A page on the school's website was developed that detailed the process, cited the research, and made the plans transparent. A meeting was convened with a core group of community advocates that were "key stakeholders," hoping that as community conversations unfolded, they would help to serve as needed advocates for the district's goals. Finally, a series of road shows took place. There are three middle schools that feed into the district, two in Oak Park and one in River Forest, and over the course of a month, evening presentations were given at each to explain the plan, rationale, and approach, and to answer questions and respond to concerns.

Opposition to Detracking

The response both within and outside the organization was immediate. Anonymous letters began to come into the school, addressed to both Greg and the superintendent, declaring that they were wrong minded, ill-informed, and hurting the education of the best students. And while at each presentation there was vocal support for the policy, the dominant voices in the room were critical. During one such presentation some attendees stated that this community "greatly cares about property values," although no explanation or context for the comment was offered. Greg also received an email after another presentation declaring that he "will single-handedly be responsible for driving down property values in our community." Not surprisingly, the causal links between detracking and property values within the community were never articulated in these statements. However, the parallels to this line of criticism and the phenomenon of redlining from a few decades ago are striking. In both, the fear of Black and Brown students existing in spaces that had been largely populated by white students became monetized. Moreover, the color-evasive discourse used both in-person and through anonymous letters demonstrates the pervasiveness of whiteness in education and who (i.e., white students) "should" be afforded opportunity (Diem & Welton, 2021). Additionally, and not surprisingly, the anonymous comments shared with the district were less civil and direct in tone as there was no way in identifying who provided the comments. However, similar comments were still expressed, albeit in "nicer" ways, during in-person presentations about the detracking initiative (Zirkel & Pollock, 2016).

Over time, it became clear that criticisms of detracking began to coalesce into a more or less consistent message. Most frequently, those who challenged the plan professed an academic open-mindedness (i.e., white liberalism) to it. However, the group's primary concern was that any step toward detracking would lower the rigor of the curriculum, hurting the academic achievement of all students, "regardless of race." According to some dissenters, only a longitudinal study that made it clear that detracking would not hurt the top students would warrant their support.

By the late fall of 2019 the opposition began to organize. A group had formed to challenge the detracking plan, calling themselves the E3 Group, to highlight their commitment to "excellent, equitable education." Most notably, the group took steps to place a nonbinding question on the November 3, 2020 ballots in both River Forest and Oak Park asking, "Shall Oak Park and River Forest High School eliminate separate, standalone freshman honors courses in English, history, and science?" In light of the death of George Floyd and the protests that ensued during the summer of 2020, the E3 Group eventually withdrew their question from the ballot, stating that in such a time of civic unrest, "fostering debate on what specifically is the best course of action to reduce the opportunity and achievement gaps at this time may end up causing further pain and trauma within the community."

At the time of writing this chapter, the district's work continues. The curriculum teams are writing, action research and pilot units are being planned, and with the teachers union support the period for professional learning to support the rollout date has been extended and is now planned for the fall of 2022. The community continues to be engaged in conversation about where the district is headed, and why it is necessary.

Conclusion

For most white people in America and even globally, it took the public lynching of a Black man to finally recognize that systemic racism is still a problem endemic to society. And it is indeed unfortunate that in the district highlighted in this chapter it took the cost of violence against a Black body for the naysayers in the community to withdraw their campaign against an anti-racist policy such as detracking. However, the district leadership did not let the white racism from community stakeholders thwart their plans for structural changes that prioritize racial equity and justice for their students of color. The steps district leadership took to critically research and eventually implement a new detracking policy are parallel to an anti-racist policy decision-making protocol for educational leaders designed by two of the chapter co-authors (Anjalé and Sarah) that consist of the following six phases: (1) assemble the appropriate team, (2) set expectations for the team, (3) understand the sociopolitical and racial context of the district and community, (4) conduct a critical policy review, (5) conduct a critical leadership review, and (6) summarize, (re)assess, and take action (Diem & Welton, 2021). For the purpose of this chapter, we will focus our attention to step 6, as this is akin to the phase where the planning team for detracking in our district example is working toward presently.

Step 6 of the anti-racist policy decision-making protocol involves summarizing findings from the previous six steps and then planning on how to best communicate the findings to the rest of the district community, as well as getting feedback from the community on which plan of action best aligns with anti-racist change. Once the anti-racist plan of action is decided team members then discuss who will be accountable for each aspect of the plan, and subsequently the policy should be (re)assessed and recalibrated throughout the implementation process. For each phase Diem and Welton (2021) include a list of guiding questions and key recommendations for teams when using their protocol as a guide in the policy process. Since community members in our district example were very vocal in their disfavor of detracking, which was the more racially equitable policy decision, we suggest leaders in this case emphasize the following guiding questions from phase six of our protocol: *What types of risks are you willing to take when taking action? How will you respond to pushback and resistance from some members of the school community based on the team's decision* (Diem & Welton, 2021, p. 148)?

Racial justice in districts and schools can only happen if educational leaders prioritize repairing the systemic harm done to minoritized community members (students, educators, and families) over the white dominant voice's efforts to make their privileged demands known in order to maintain the racial status quo. Staying true to this anti-racist mission will require educational leaders to adopt an activist stance. An activist is an "individual who is known for taking stands and engaging in action aimed at producing social change, possibly in conflict with institutional opponents" (Marshall & Anderson, 2008, p. 18).

If you are a district- or school-level leader who aims to be anti-racist, you must first understand how the very educational system in which you lead was designed to maintain whiteness and white privilege. Once educational leaders understand how whiteness operates, they can then begin to dismantle the longstanding policies, structures, norms, attitudes, and practices that sustain whiteness. However, being an anti-racist leader extends beyond dismantling whiteness but is also a willingness to restructure and rebuild an educational system that humanizes and sees students of color as the basis for educational success, not as a mere accessory to white normative schooling.

2

Anti-racism as Core Competency for Educational Leaders

Matthew A. Rodriguez and Amanda E. Lewis

Introduction

One of the challenges for educators who want to think about schools as places where we enact our commitment to a better world, to a place where all children have the opportunity to thrive, is reckoning with the reality that that is not what they were designed to do. At the macro-level, when we consider historically how school systems were designed and developed, it was often hand in hand with the architects of systems of racial exclusion, racial control, and racial hierarchy (Anderson, 1988; Litwack, 1998; Takaki, 1993). Obviously these forces were contested—there is a long record of organized efforts to the contrary—but the point of starting with the recognition of the limits of the school systems we have is to understand that many of the structures put in place "long ago" are still with us and still limit our efforts today, particularly if we are not thoughtful, knowledgeable, and critical. Examples of this are many—how we fund schools (at the state level, locally); how we set the boundaries on school districts (which are still contested); how we organize students within schools through tracking systems; how we think about and deploy standardized testing in schools (Darling-Hammond, 2007; Epstein, 2011; Frankenberg, Knoester, & Au, 2017; Lewis & Manno, 2011; Liu, 2007–08; Oakes, 2005; Steele, 1997). These structures and practices don't even include all the ways that racist ideologies pervade schools and shape educators' expectations, disciplinary practices, and curriculum. The reality of this can be daunting. It can lead some to question the enterprise of schooling altogether.

Yet, for many of us, our paths into education were laid by our own experiences with amazing educators, sometimes wonderful schools, and through the acquisition of critical knowledge that together lead us to think that education as an enterprise is a necessary (if not sufficient) ingredient to a racially just future. Not only that young people need critical knowledge about the world around them, how it came to be and how it might be different, but that they need the skills of literacy, critical thought, and numeracy to deploy in making the world better. Their brilliance needs to be nurtured, polished, and unleashed. We know this *can* happen in schools. We have seen it for ourselves. The question is, how do we advance this as the regular order of things for every student, rather than just for the exceptional few?

To be sure, some of the structural constraints are overwhelming. A school building leader cannot change how districts are funded or how district boundary lines are drawn. These kinds of examples of structural racism make the work of education harder and harder particularly in places where kids' needs are higher. However, we will suggest that rather than being disempowering, knowing the full reality of the structural barriers we and our young people face is helpful. In part because it helps us to have a critical eye about what our work is. It is also important because beyond the structural constraints, there is also much that happens within schools that make things worse. Even if principals can't change school-funding structures, it is helpful for them to understand their origins, to have a foundation of structural competency (Metzl & Roberts, 2014). This would facilitate a shift in their analysis from a deficit framing of students to a structural one that understands the impact of racism in schools, where students are honored and supported through leadership action that addresses problems by understanding their structural root, instead of seeing young people as the problem that needs to be fixed.

We know that not only do young people need access to a robust and "high-quality" education, but the world needs these young people. We mourn the Black and Latinx genius lost to low expectations and dehumanizing education. We are all in. And we work in schools because we love these young people and want to be a force for ensuring public systems live up to their stated commitments and do better.

This chapter is written for "anti-racist" leaders, for those who aspire to "anti-racist" leadership. Some might understand anti-racist leadership as being a vanguard of some kind, educational leadership on the margins, a radical venture that departs from the mainstream. We want to suggest that that is a fundamental problem. This orientation to leadership must become mainstream, be seen as a core competency of leaders, administrators, teachers. It must involve not just a set of ideas, but a set of practices that involves challenging much of what seems normative. In a society like ours imbued for hundreds of years with racist ideas, built on racist laws and practices, none of us are free from its reaches. There is no "neutral" non-racist position. In the context of schools, with regard to school leaders, one is either challenging the racist structures and practices that have dominated school for centuries or enacting them.

In this chapter we will begin by discussing why the move toward "race-neutrality" in school improvement interventions is problematic. We then turn to a brief discussion of how white supremacy has become institutionalized in schools historically and spend some time on one example of what this looks like on the ground and what it might look like to challenge such practices. In doing so, we draw on our experiences leading schools and in working with school leaders to make change. We do not have the space to be comprehensive but instead offer ideas about how to critically engage, how to be reflexive about implementing policies that do harm to young people. Building from this example, we suggest that anti-racist school leaders should regularly ask themselves and their staff a core set of questions: What current policies and practices contribute to racial inequity? How might we do school differently?

The Problems with "Race-neutrality"

In this chapter we are advocating for the necessity for school leaders to have a clear and explicit race analysis and explicitly anti-racist commitments. In a broad context in which colorblind ideology often reigns supreme, leaders may want to suggest that the ideal stance for a leader is as a "race-neutral" champion for all children (Bonilla-Silva, 2003). Aspiring to a colorblind or race-blind leadership style, they believe such a seemingly "neutral" stance will allow them to nurture all children to be their best selves. As we and others have written about extensively, this kind of colorblind ideology typically functions in the world as colorblind racism. It ignores that we do, in fact, see race, that seeing race has consequences, and that pretending not to see it just makes us blind to its effects (Bonilla-Silva, 2003; Forman & Lewis, 2006; Lewis, 2003). As many scholars thinking about racial justice in schools have pointed out, we must confront head on the ways that racist ideas are part of daily life in schools not only because they are harmful to people's identities but because they are harmful to their school experiences and outcomes. For example, John Diamond (2018), writing about the legacy of white supremacy in schools, argues,

> Because of the dominant white supremacist and anti-black ideology in the United States, when someone is identified as "black," there is a semi-automatic set of negative beliefs that are triggered in most whites ... [these] stereotypes about gender, race, and intelligence are productive of structural inequality.
>
> (p. 350)

Challenging racist ideas not only is about challenging *explicitly* racist ideas (e.g., that some are better at math), but includes the need to challenge "ideologies ... steeped in deficit thinking" (Kohli et al., 2017, p. 184; O'Connor et al., 2009; Solorzano & Yosso, 2001; Tuck, 2009; Valencia, 2010), colorblind racism that denies that race matters, and racialized performance expectations (Ladson-Billings, 2014; Lewis & Diamond, 2015; Stack et al., 2020; Valencia, 2010). Without affirmative insistence on the full humanity and capacity of all children, widespread racial mythology will fill the void with significant consequences.

Beyond just actively challenging racist thinking, and in some ways perhaps more important than the work to change educators' thinking, is the need to be explicitly anti-racist in changing policy. If we look at school discipline, for example, we know there are widespread and deep race and gender disparities in disciplinary outcomes in schools beginning as early as preschool (CRDC, 2016; Skiba et al., 2011). Recent research shows that these disparities are not so much about disparities in rule-breaking, but about disparities in student–teacher interactions with, for example, Black and Latinx students more often punished for perceived violations of subjective (e.g., defiance) as opposed to objective rule-breaking (e.g., truancy) (Gregory et al., 2010; Gregory & Weinstein, 2008; Losen & Gillespie, 2012; Skiba et al., 2011). Collectively, this research demonstrates that disciplinary practices are far from "race-neutral" with lots of evidence that young people's behavior is viewed and interpreted differently by adults (Ferguson, 2000; Goff et al., 2014; Morris, 2016). Qualitatively, this work shows how racist ideas and stereotypes continue to shape Black and Latinx children's experiences in schools.

Importantly, even when educators acknowledge these kinds of troubling racial patterns in outcomes, too often reform is undertaken in such a way that does not directly confront the role of racial dynamics. In a recent review of research on disproportionality in discipline practices, for example, Welsh and Little (2018) found that many interventions designed to address racial disparities in discipline are "race-neutral" reflecting a "mismatch" between what is generating disciplinary disparities (e.g., biases and cultural clashes) and what is being implemented to address them (e.g., behavior management through conformity). They find that when schools implement "raceblind" interventions they may reduce punishment overall, but do not reduce disparities in who is being disciplined.

Part of the challenge of trying to be "race-neutral" is that it ignores the reality that schools are not and never have been. Schools have been a key part of the formation of the racialized social system in the United States (Anderson, 1988; Bonilla-Silva, 2003). Those trying to enforce racial boundaries, build racial hierarchies, and control low-wage laborers have always recognized controlling or limiting education as a key part of their work (Anderson, 1988; Chesler et al., 2005; Takaki, 1993). As Kohli, Pizarro, and Nevarez (2017) put it in a recent review, "schooling in the United States has a history driven by racialization and racism. From [the 19th century] … students of Color have been subjected to institutionalized conditions that contradict their interests and their humanity" (p. 184). This has not been just a side effect but a core part of the development of these structures. As Carter G. Woodson (1933) discussed almost a hundred years ago in his *Miseducation of the Negro*, much of this was done with the recognition of the possible power of education to disrupt racial hierarchies, "when you control a man's thinking you do not have to worry about his actions" (p. ix).

Today, our struggle to make education a source of liberation must contend with the legacy of this history in our current school systems, structures, norms, and practices. Racism is different today and the mechanisms of racial hierarchy inside and outside of schools are different (Bonilla-Silva, 2003; Lewis & Diamond, 2015). But many of the practices and policies put into place in an earlier era of formal and explicit racism never went away. We may have a different explanation for their use today, but they still need deep interrogation.

Formal school discipline policies and the accompanying set of related practices are just one example of apparently "race-neutral" school routines that have racially disparate effects. In the next section we offer a glimpse of how discipline of students plays out in school settings and a brief description of how and why "race-neutral" discipline practices need to be reconsidered. This example is intended to illustrate not only what is problematic about these practices but what it would mean to try and rethink them in ways that put children at the center of our work. It also provides an illustration of how to confront and dismantle racially inequitable practices. As we discussed above, to be an actively anti-racist educator requires that we recognize not only the ways in which societal structures have distributed access to opportunity along racial lines historically, but how they do so currently. This requires educators to take a close look at the day-to-day functioning of schools, including the regular classroom, hallway, and school-wide routines, procedures, practices, and policies that may be contributing to racially disparate results year after year.

Seemingly Race-neutral Practice: Classroom Behavior Management Plans

Ask any teacher to share with you their ladder of consequences, and almost immediately they can outline the four to eight steps they take with students in their classes before sending them out of the room with an office referral. Regardless of the number of steps, the general sequence is the same:

- Teacher starts with a nonverbal or verbal warning to a student who is considered off-task.
- If student's behavior remains off-task or worsens, so, too, do the consequences transitioning from the level of warning to intervention which could include a conference in the hallway, a demerit, a seat reassignment, a detention, or a combination of those.
- The escalation of classroom consequences often culminates with a phone call home, an office referral, or both.

In comparison to the various tasks a teacher or school administrator is responsible for, the construction and execution of the ladder of consequences are given scant thought. Arguably, however, this aspect of a classroom is more significant in shaping the daily experience of youth than, for example, a district's formally adopted Student Code of Conduct which is given much more time and attention. The lack of pause and reflection about the functioning of the ladder is tied to it being part of our "common sense" understandings of how a positive and productive classroom culture is set and maintained. However, there are at least two aspects of how the ladder of consequence plays out that potentially contribute to racial inequity:

- Institutional authority is imposed upon students in both the design and execution of the ladder in a way where students have no voice.
- Enforcement of the ladder of consequence is unfair, as teacher bias against Black and Latinx youth is manifested in these seemingly small interactions (as we discussed above).

There is a logic and set of assumptions embedded in the ladder of consequences that are so normative, that to call them into question feels as though the entire system of education is being scrutinized. One major assumption is that school personnel have a perspective that is more important than that of any youth. This is true for both in design and implementation where school staff unilaterally define "appropriate" and "inappropriate" student behavior and regularly use discretion in deciding on consequences to ensure that students receive the message of who is in charge.

While teachers and administrators couch adherence to ladders of consequence in the language of rigor, high expectations or standards, and even tough love, students on the receiving end, especially those most marginalized, often feel alienated, ostracized, and even pushed away by these practices (particularly when they are meted out in ways that feel capricious or unfair). The holding of high expectations is not in and of itself problematic. In fact, history shows how low expectations contribute to a separate and unequal educational experience for students of color (Kohli et al., 2017). Instead, high expectations become problematic when they are not coupled with an understanding and strategic wrap-around of the systematic supports that students need based on their circumstance both in and outside of school.

In classroom behavior, teachers are the law-makers, law-enforcers, the jury, and the judge. They can remove a student from their classroom without once reflecting on any role that they may have played in creating the conditions that eventually "required" discipline. This arrangement is also organized around the principle that what teachers deem as important is what matters in a classroom setting and anything else is a distraction, deviant, and in possible need of intervention.

Imagine a sixth-grade student, named Mariela, who transfers into a school district at the middle of the year. She repeatedly refuses to engage with classwork. Over the course of a few weeks, her behavior slowly deteriorates the level of engagement of other students around her. The teacher attempts to uphold their high standards and utilizes the intervention strategies they normally would. Starting with non-verbal, and then transitioning to a verbal warning, Mariela snaps back with, "I hate this class and this stupid work!" The teacher writes a referral slip, hands it to Mariela, and sends her to the office to think about what she has just done. In a matter of minutes, Mariela experiences the full ladder of consequence and finds herself sitting in an office with strangers probing her understanding of the value of high expectations, and the need to be prepared for college and career.

What the teacher and administrators did not know was where Mariela came from, why her family moved, and what Mariela is faced with in her life outside of the school environment. This is where the development of racial consciousness is key, and anti-racist practices can positively impact the teacher–student interaction. The racist history of the United States of America, for example, positions Latinxs as 2.6 times, and Blacks as 2.8 times more likely than their white counterparts to be in poverty (Valencia, 2015). For students like Mariela, that reality impacts their lived experience, frequently requiring the adults in families to work multiple jobs, leaving students like Mariela to take on more responsibilities at home, which limit their ability to complete school assignments. This may also mean that food is limited at home, and students like Mariela decide to feed their siblings instead of themselves, which keeps her hungry throughout the day. These circumstances, born out of societal inequality, would make anyone irritated, let alone an adolescent learning to navigate the world.

When a teacher removes a student from their classroom under the guise of "holding high expectations" for appropriate behavior, and neglects to engage in any discussion with the student outside of the rearticulation of classroom routines, procedures, goals, and expectations for good behavior in class, they uphold a racist structure that turns a blind-eye to the history that influences the moment, a history wrought with inequality. By not being open and understanding to the story and context of Mariela, the teacher and administrators lose an opportunity to reach her and, in the process, limit their own ability to help her heal from the wounds of racial injustice. Consequently, their blindness contributes to, instead of subtracting from, the factors that push Mariela away. With the best of intentions, they are unable to see how the unilateral execution of the ladder of consequence can become the equivalent of holding a twelve-year-old individual, like Mariela, personally accountable for the way historical racial oppression manifests in their behavior. In this context, teachers and administrators become numb to the notion that high expectations must be coupled with a deep understanding, care, and active work to imagine the kinds of supports that a student like Mariela may need in order to achieve at high levels.

So, why do we use the ladder of consequence, and how might we do things differently? While classrooms need ground rules for engagement, scholars recently have called for a different approach to their creation. Crystal Laura (2014) and Angela Valenzuela (1999) have argued that a focus on care and relationships is critical to the school engagement and success of Black and Latinx students. Similarly, in his advocacy for a healing-centered approach to the engagement of youth, Ginwright (2016) argues for a shift from a technical focus to a more relational one. Such an orientation shifts the focus on classroom management away from order and "consequences" to building relationships and community.

This work is not simple. While teachers sometimes engage students in brainstorming rules and expectations, those discussions are frequently used by teachers to define the ways that students agree for their own behavior to be restrained. Doing something different means either eliminating the ladder altogether, or approaching both the design *and* delivery of the ladder from a place of racial awareness and humility. Designing and delivering a ladder of consequence with a critical racial awareness require that educators understand the role that healing must play in the educational process, especially for marginalized students. Black and Latinx students, navigating the geography of social inequality, need a school environment that is supportive of who they are, not one designed to goad students into compliance (Steele & Cohn-Vargas, 2013). This is not to reproduce a stereotype that all Black and Latinx students are marginalized. Instead, it is to challenge educators to design practices from the margins, keeping students at the center and forefront of the work we do. Returning to the guiding questions, how might this practice contribute to racial inequity, and how can we do things differently? Research shows that when this kind of design takes place, all students can truly thrive (Blankstein et al., 2016).

Executing this work through humility involves teachers and administrators "listening to all that come to us" (Freire, 2005, p. 72). Akin to the techniques recommended in restorative circles, this kind of listening would allow for a meaningful discussion between students and educators to build an accountability system focused on mutuality, something that students of color rarely experience. In fact, within schools in the United States, students of color are more likely to have to contend with the opposite—more teacher authority and "fewer opportunities to fully express themselves" (Valencia, 2015, p. 289). Recognizing that students of color voices matter is a critical step in the direction of anti-racism. Thus, discussion about the ladder of consequence might broaden to include not only descriptions of student behavior but listening to what students have to say about the behavior and establishing a mechanism by which students can give adults real-time feedback. Accountability here is mutual and about accountability to the broader community rather than to the adult "authority." In this new frame, a ladder, for example, instead of being seen as a mechanism to escalate consequences and control behavior, can be viewed as a set of steps in creation of a learning community that serves all members.

Conclusion

For education to become the site where every student, especially those most marginalized, thrive and reach their fullest potential, leaders must act proactively with explicit anti-racist commitments to interrupt and eliminate the way racism manifests in thought patterns, beliefs, and values as well as in language, informal practices, and policies. As Carla O'Connor (2020) has written, we must pay attention even to those practices that seem the most mundane and routine:

> In fact, the consequences may be particularly intractable and reproductive as per their articulation in everyday and mundane interactions and circumstances that have become routinized and systematically structure school inequality … the singular preoccupation with macro-level dynamics and reforms leaves underspecified microlevel production of racialized and gendered oppression and how individuals are culpable in the maintenance and, by implication, the disruption of racism, sexism, and oppression more generally.
>
> (p. 3)

As anti-racist educators reckon with the reality that schools have historically been a part of the construction of racial hierarchies, they learn to face and name that history. The goal here is to put this knowledge to work, to eradicate any remnants of past structures that remain embedded in policies, tied to routine decision making, and interwoven within the normative daily practices of school life. Only in this way can we begin to transform schools into liberatory spaces.

Anti-racist educational leadership ought not to be considered as some revolutionary set of understandings and practices. Instead, it must become part of the normative fabric that makes up who we are as educators and that informs our daily work. It is our duty to hold ourselves and the school systems accountable for the multiple ways that we continue to perpetuate inequities in our beliefs, our actions, and our policies. As we stated at the beginning, with regard to school leaders, one is either challenging the racist structures and practices that have dominated school for centuries or enacting them. It is our job to ask ourselves regularly and rigorously, what current policies and practices contribute to racial inequity? How might we do school differently?

3

The Politics of the School–Prison Nexus: Racial Capitalism and Possibilities for Transformation in Schools and Beyond

Erica O. Turner, Abigail J. Beneke, María Velázquez, and Rob Timberlake

Over the past six decades, harsh and exclusionary school discipline policies, surveillance technologies (e.g., metal detectors, video cameras), and school policing have become increasingly commonplace in schools serving low-income Black and Latinx students (Bahena et al., 2012; Kafka, 2011). Such policies and practices criminalize students of color, low-income students, and dis/abled students, subjecting them to harmful and unnecessary surveillance and policing that frequently entangle students in the legal system making schools de facto prisons (Nance, 2015; Nolan, 2011). Links between schools and the legal system can also put undocumented immigrant students on the radar of Immigration and Customs Enforcement (ICE) and be used against them in detention and deportation proceedings (Dillard, 2018). The tightening linkages between schools and prisons have contributed to a "school–prison nexus" that incorporates all the "policies, practices, and informal knowledges that support, naturalize, and extend relationships between incarceration and schools" (Meiners, 2007, p. 4), including denying access to rigorous, engaging curriculum and caring adults in schools (Winn & Behizadeh, 2011), in addition to experiences in criminalization in their schools and communities (Shedd, 2015). The school–prison nexus reveals a callous disregard for the lives of the students who are disproportionately ensnared in it. Though many aspects of the school–prison nexus are billed as ensuring safety in schools and communities, it is tremendously harmful for these groups of students.

In this chapter, we map the political and economic terrain of the school–prison nexus, an expansive task which includes the relatively recent turn toward school discipline reform and the maintenance of academic tracking within schools.[1] As one of the first such efforts to do so, this is an important, yet initial picture. We draw on racial capitalism, a framework for understanding society as mutually constituted by racism and capitalism, as well as by patriarchy and other systems of oppression (Robinson, 2000). Racism has provided the justification for capitalist exploitation. Likewise, racial capitalism has depended historically upon violence—including slavery, imperialism, and genocide—as a means of controlling people at the margins of capitalism and white supremacy, and of ensuring the racialized accumulation of wealth and property. Today, surveillance, policing, and mass incarceration serve those same ends (Davis, 2011). Even as they have suffered under it, groups subject to violence and exploitation have also carved out spaces of transformation and possibility (Kelley, 2002). Through the lens of racial capitalism, we identify and analyze the systems of white supremacy and capitalism that provide fertile ground for the school–prison nexus and we focus on the material, institutional, and discursive elements of racial capitalism in and beyond schools.

In what follows, we offer education leaders an overview of the political and economic context of the school–prison nexus, including the elements noted above that have played a part in its development and may contribute to its continuation, expansion, transformation, and/or elimination. Throughout we note how racial capitalism plays out in this context and indicate serious challenges and new opportunities for eliminating the school–prison nexus. We end with a few lessons for education leaders who wish to challenge the school–prison nexus.

Racial Capitalism and the School–Prison Nexus

A constellation of shifting and contradictory actors, groups, discourses, policies, initiatives, processes, and relations intersect to allow for, alter, transform, and challenge the school–prison nexus. While some of these convergences are expected, others might seem unassociated with the school–prison nexus, but consistently these are shaped by white supremacy, capitalism, and other systems of oppression. We illuminate this expansive and complex terrain to provide education leaders with a map of the contemporary construction of the school–prison nexus, including the serious challenges and potential opportunities for transforming the school–prison nexus.

Economic Recession, Poverty, and the Shrinking State

Once a robust manufacturing-based national economy, deindustrialization, capital dispersal, and economic recessions over the last seventy years (Sugrue,

2014) have contributed to an increasingly unequal US economy and fewer middle-class jobs. Black and Brown communities have been more vulnerable to the ravages of deindustrialization and unemployment, including food and housing insecurity, lack of health care, poor health, and stress related to racism and poverty, all of which can manifest in behaviors that are criminalized and punished in schools and in the legal system (Morris, 2016) and can make it difficult to learn. At the same time, a shrinking tax base for many state and local governments has precipitated cuts to education, law enforcement, corrections, health, and social services budgets, and resulted in layoffs and furloughs (or threats of these). Funding for corrections and law enforcement has been prioritized at the expense of education and other social services (Western, 2006), leaving fewer resources to serve a growing population of young people living in racialized poverty.

In an earlier era, those exploited under capitalism had their demands and discontents addressed, minimally and unequally, through food benefits, welfare, public schooling, and other forms of redistribution (Lipsitz, 1998). However, recessions and economic crises since the 1970s helped usher in neoliberal economic theories and policies that opposed a government role in ensuring social welfare (Harvey, 2005). Instead, neoliberals envision government as a means to bolster business (corporate welfare). Coupled with economic pressures, neoliberal theories have contributed to efforts to dismantle the public sector, make dramatic cuts to social welfare spending, and embrace low-cost educational policies like high-stakes accountability that operate using business logics.

Racial Advancement and the Crime Control Turn

As economic insecurity has deepened and social welfare programs have been eviscerated, white fears of a growing population of people of color who were demanding their rights helped usher in a parallel punitive turn in crime control (Garland, 2001). The 1970s and 1980s brought a massive rise in Black imprisonment (Western, 2006) and Black juvenile incarceration (Ward, 2012). Crime control discourses have helped fuel this growth by positioning incarceration as the only way to keep people safe and as both necessary and inevitable (Nolan, 2011). While grounded in deeply rooted discourses of the "dangerous other" that position Black men and other people of color as criminally inclined (Garland, 2001), crime control discourses are purportedly "race neutral," which allows racist policies to gain traction even as discriminatory practices have been outlawed (Bonilla-Silva, 2018). Today, we see the consequences of this purportedly race-neutral shift in crime control. More than 2 million people are incarcerated in US prisons, jails, and detention centers; the vast majority are Black and/or Latinx (Hernández et al., 2015).

Discourses and policies in schools have mirrored those of the broader society and make schools "look, sound, and act more like criminal justice institutions" (Hirschfield, 2018, p. 81). Most notably, zero-tolerance policies that emerged in the 1960s and gained traction again in the 1990s prescribed automatic punishments for particular behavioral infractions (Kafka, 2011; Skiba & Peterson, 2000). Mirroring the turn toward mass incarceration in the legal system, zero-tolerance policies rely upon exclusion, such as suspension and expulsion, and disproportionately impact Black and Latinx students (Skiba et al., 2011). In schools serving Black and Latinx students zero-tolerance policies have been accompanied by surveillance through security cameras and metal detectors (Advancement Project, 2010) and close collaboration between schools and law enforcement, including School Resource Officer (SRO) programs that station police officers in schools and make it more likely that students will become entangled in the legal system (Nance, 2015). Even in schools without a physical police presence, students of color are still disproportionately surveilled, labeled, and punished (Annamma, 2018).

Through his xenophobic, racist, and anti-Muslim rhetoric and punitive immigration policies, Donald Trump followed in the path of earlier politicians by criminalizing people of color (Bonilla-Silva, 2018). Teachers report that immigrant students and students of color now express increased fear, anxiety, and difficulty concentrating on schoolwork, as well as increased bullying and hateful speech from peers (Ee & Gándara, 2020). These experiences may very well fuel the school–prison nexus.

As suggested above, the political context of the school–prison nexus is closely tied to the broader US political economy. Those connections are particularly clear when we examine the business of incarceration.

The Political Economy of Punishment

The enormous growth in US incarceration—and the criminalization, surveillance, and policing that help drive it—is a product of the formidable edifice known as the Prison Industrial Complex (PIC). The PIC links the prison system to the economic and political spheres through "a set of symbiotic relationships among correctional communities, transnational corporations, media conglomerates, guards' unions and legislative and court agendas" (Davis, 2011, p. 107) that help maintain the prison system by contributing to its seeming inevitability and expansion (Gilmore, 2007). For example, rural communities, many of them white, have turned to prisons to provide jobs and tax base. This economic development strategy depends upon urban crime control that incarcerates low-income people of color as a solution to poverty and unemployment. Moreover, as prison populations grow, these rural prison communities gain political influence due to the practice of counting incarcerated people as residents of the municipalities where prisons are located for purposes of electoral representation (The Problem, n.d.). These communities are now invested in prison expansion, including the growth of an immigrant detention and deportation system run by private prison corporations that profit from federal contracts and from prisoner labor (Hernández et al., 2015).

Similar to the PIC, a series of relationships between federal actions on "school safety," law enforcement, a corporate security industry, and others work together to expand the school–prison nexus. Federal legislation such as the Gun-Free Schools Act of 1994 and No Child Left Behind of 2001 nationalized school adoption of zero tolerance policies and held schools accountable for school safety (Hirschfield, 2018). The US Departments of Education and Justice have also promoted security systems and law enforcement methods like threat assessments and crisis management plans as responses to highly publicized school shootings (Casella, 2006). These federal actions, and others, have responded to a corporate security industry seeking further profit in schools (Casella, 2006) and law enforcement seeking a way to avoid layoffs and shore up their finances against ongoing state and local budget cuts (Koon, 2020). All this has contributed to growth of the security technology industry, of police presence in schools, and of training and consulting services to assist schools with implementing federal recommendations (Casella, 2006).

In 2011 the Obama Administration launched an effort to disrupt racial disparities in school discipline. They clarified students' civil rights with regard to school discipline; added funding and data reporting aimed at eliminating disparities in discipline; and stoked civil rights investigations and enforcement (Hirschfield, 2018). These moves compelled districts to seek out alternative discipline approaches and, through the Supportive School Discipline Initiative, the administration created opportunities for philanthropists, researchers, law enforcement and counseling professionals, and nonprofit and for-profit organizations to develop, research, and advocate for products and services like Positive Behavioral Intervention Supports (PBIS) that are marketed as teaching students "appropriate" (read: white, middle-class) behavior; meanwhile, restorative justice and implicit bias training, which may more explicitly name and address racism as a problem, received relatively little support (Koon, 2020).

Illustrating both the fragile nature of school discipline reforms and overall consistency in federal action on "school safety," the Trump administration has rescinded Obama-era efforts to reduce racial disparities in discipline while Congress responded to the 2018 mass school shooting in Parkland, Florida with continued promotion of school policing and surveillance technologies, as well as the behavioral intervention approaches advanced under Obama (STOP School Violence Act of 2018, 2020).

In short, through federal backing predominantly white, male actors—law enforcement, the security technology and gun industries, and the politicians who work on their behalf—have expanded policing that disproportionately impact Black and Latinx students and their schools.

Neoliberal Education Policy

Although discussion of the school–prison nexus has often focused on school discipline, the second-class education of low-income students, dis/abled students, and students of color is also a central aspect of the school–prison nexus. Neoliberal education policies like high-stakes accountability and charter schools are contributing to the surveillance, punishment, and second-class education of these students, current manifestations of a longer history of exclusion, and white supremacy in schools (Ladson-Billings, 2006; Lipman, 2011).

Since the 1980s, US schools have been subject to high-stakes accountability policies that ostensibly aim to improve educational achievement by testing students and punishing schools and/or students who fail to meet "proficiency" goals or show improvement. The strongest supporters of this approach were Southern governors, including future US presidents George W. Bush (Texas) and Bill Clinton (Arkansas), and corporate executives through organizations like the Business Roundtable, who viewed this as a low-cost approach to increase student achievement, address workforce needs, and boost stagnating economic conditions in their states (Vinovskis, 1999). By 2001, Congress passed the No Child Left behind Act (NCLB) with bi-partisan support, spreading the model nationwide.

Justified as countering teachers' "low expectations" for children of color and ensuring they are not "left behind," these approaches leave predominantly low-income students and students of color in poorly resourced schools, often with a stripped-down, test-preparation-focused curriculum, and then punish them for failing to achieve despite federal and state-sanctioned policies that ensure their failure (Ladson-Billings, 2006). High-stakes accountability is also a form of punishment that further erodes quality education for low-income children by labeling their schools as "failing." This, in turn, has justified school closures and opened education up to marketization (Lipman, 2011) and "no excuses" charter schools that enact harsh disciplinary regimes in order to produce high test scores (Goodman, 2013).

White and Privileged Families and the Hoarding of Opportunities

Historically and in the present, predominantly white, middle-class and upper-middle-class families have also been central to upholding academic tracking, segregation, and other mechanisms for sorting low-income students, students of color, and dis/abled students into second-class education (e.g., Welner & Oakes, 2005). These families use their social networks, cultural capital, and threat of exiting schools to hoard resources and to maintain systems of sorting and stratification that advantage their children (e.g., Lewis & Diamond, 2015). Similar dynamics are evident at the district level where leaders, who share social networks and neighborhoods with these families, fear the financial repercussions of these families leaving the district (Turner & Spain, 2020). In these ways, racial capitalism functions to achieve and reinforce the school–prison nexus as the familiar practice of predominantly white, middle-class and upper-middle-class families leveraging their resources to maintain tracking ultimately punishes marginalized students for the conditions of racialized poverty while elevating the status and opportunities of those who are already advantaged by their class position and benefit most from white supremacy and capitalism.

Organizing and Advocacy against the School–Prison Nexus

Civil rights groups, community-based organizations, and racial justice activists have been organizing for years against both the school–prison nexus and racial injustice in schools and society. Civil rights organizations like the American Civil Liberties Union, the Advancement Project, and the UCLA Civil Rights Project, along with networks like Dignity in Schools, have raised awareness about the "school-to-prison pipeline" and succeeded in getting it on the policy agenda (Koon, 2020). In addition, youth active in the Movement for Black Lives and the immigrant rights movement have connected the aims of these larger movements with the criminalization, policing and punishment, and the denial of education they experience. These youth have been active in reframing notions of "safety" and "criminality" that justify the punishment of their communities. For example, Black youth from Oakland to Philadelphia have highlighted the harms of school police on dis/abled students, immigrant students, and Black students, and they have reframed student behaviors as a result of the harms of poverty, racism, and related trauma, rather than as criminal behavior (Advancement Project & Alliance for Educational Justice, 2018). However, Turner and Beneke (2020) found that school district policymakers largely disregarded Black youth activists' testimony about the harm and fear they experienced due to school police, and their ideas about alternative reforms to policing were largely ignored.

At times, these groups' demands were met. Civil rights organizations and community-based groups have taken advantage of rising doubts about the costs and efficacy of incarceration to press policymakers to act on the school–prison nexus. Under pressure from these groups, a smattering of schools, districts, and states have taken actions like limiting out-of-school suspensions, collaborating with families on disciplinary policies, providing holistic student supports, adopting restorative justice, and establishing a school district's authority over police intervention in schools (Advancement Project, 2010). However, state and school budgets have never fully recovered from Great Recession-era budget cuts, and these initiatives have been limited to places where leaders are able to secure funding from private philanthropies or states (Hirschfield, 2018).

Black youth activists have used nationwide mass protests against anti-Black violence, including recent responses to police killing George Floyd in Minneapolis to renew their demands for police-free schools. In a matter of weeks, school boards from Portland to Minneapolis announced they would end their school policing programs. In Los Angeles and Chicago, proposals to remove police from schools remain stalled by debate about reforming, rather than ending, school policing (Goldstein, 2020), but advocates for police-free schools have been successful in gaining broader support. These developments have been possible because social movement actors organized to end school policing before it seemed possible. While their recent successes are promising, many of these groups' more transformative demands have yet to be met.

Teachers' Shifting Relations with Communities of Color

Teachers and teachers unions historically have been instrumental in lobbying for zero-tolerance policies and police in schools (Kafka, 2011). In highly racialized moments, such as Black migration (Kafka, 2011), school desegregation (Arum, 2003), and Black students' assertion of their culture, autonomy, and liberation (Sojoyner, 2013), a largely white, female teaching force has largely assumed disorder in schools is due to the presence of Black students rather than a result of conditions such as racist policy or under-resourcing of their schools. In response, teachers have lobbied to codify punishments for various infractions and to transfer responsibility for discipline to other school personnel or law enforcement.

Teachers have also played a central role in upholding academic tracking and other forms of labeling and sorting that disproportionately funnel low-income students, dis/abled students, and/or students of color to low-quality, low-track classes that are correlated with being disproportionately subject to school discipline (e.g., Meier et al., 1989). These classes are ultimately insufficient for helping students access social opportunity and they directly facilitate student contact with the legal system (Winn & Behizadeh, 2011). Teachers who support tracking tend to view students in low tracks—typically low-income students, students of color, and/or dis/abled students—as pathological (e.g., dangerous, culturally deficient, and/or dis/abled) (Annamma, 2018) and see sorting students by "innate ability" and weeding out the "bad kids" as an easier and/or more effective way to teach (Oakes, 2005). Moreover, veteran and credentialed educators are more likely to teach higher tracks and to work in better-resourced schools, exacerbating the inequality inherent in tracking and making it more likely that teachers assigned to high-track classes will resist untracking and the loss of advantage and status that entails (Kelly, 2004).

Recently, some teachers' unions have begun organizing against elements of the school–prison nexus such as accountability policies, harsh school discipline, and school policing. For example, since 2012, the Chicago Teachers Union has aligned their agenda with the working-class families of color they serve and they have included in their contract negotiations demands for less standardized testing, more counselors, and enforceable sanctuary for immigrants. Today, several teachers' unions which had been previously silent on the issue or had advocated for school policing, including the CTU, have joined the campaign for police-free schools and called for replacing school policing with care and resource support for students and teachers (Day, 2020). Such support adds new impetus to struggles against the school–prison nexus. However, teachers' support for police-free schools has been predicated on schools providing emotional and material support for students with behavioral issues (UTLA, 2020); without such resources, teachers' backing for ending school policing and harsh discipline may wither.

Conclusion

There are considerable challenges to achieving deep change to the school–prison nexus and ultimately to a more just world. In this chapter we have laid out the formidable and multifaceted political and economic terrain of the school–prison nexus. We show how the nexus is shaped by US racial capitalism that privileges and serves corporate profit and people who are well-resourced and white, while multiply marginalized students of color, especially Black students, are offered surveillance and punishment more often than a quality education that will help them navigate through the world. While there has been attention to racially disproportionate school discipline, this chapter reveals the multiple actors and organizations (e.g., law enforcement and school security businesses) and deep relationships, politics, processes, discourses, policies, and events which maintain, reproduce, and extend the school–prison nexus and thus the links between students and futures of under- and unemployment and/or imprisonment. We have pointed to places where challenges to the school–prison nexus have the potential to be nourished and grow, but substantial elements of this political and economic context are likely to maintain the school–prison nexus and contribute to its continued expansion.

There are several implications here for education leaders. While we reaffirm the importance of adopting strategies that address school racism (e.g., confronting anti-Blackness; diagnosing how tracking and discipline perpetuate racial inequities; hiring more educators of color; and adopting schoolwide discipline reforms) (DeMatthews et al., 2017; Diem & Welton, 2021; Lewis & Diamond, 2015), our analysis suggests that educational leaders should be prepared for resistance to transforming school structures that have granted some privilege over others. Moreover, some reform efforts may be co-opted by those who benefit from elements of the nexus or may inadvertently reinforce the school–prison nexus. Transformation of the school–prison nexus will require race-conscious analyses of the implementation and outcomes of school reforms, strategies for dealing with resistance and co-optation, and attention to how such reforms move us toward an alternative system of social care and investment in marginalized youth.

In highlighting the role of racist, capitalist forces in producing the school–prison nexus and the groups and dynamics that are working to challenge it, our research also suggests educational leaders must work to dismantle the racial structure of society beyond the schoolhouse doors. Educational leaders are in key positions to build coalitions among those who are most marginalized by racial capitalism and to support the social movement activity that is fundamental to changing racial inequalities (Bonilla-Silva, 2018). As Wilson et al. (2020) note, "the system that produces dehumanizing labor conditions for teachers is the same set of structural conditions that reproduces the dehumanization of Black families" (p. 154). There are opportunities—not without challenges—for nurturing a collective movement for transforming schools and society across groups that are currently fractured by race, ethnicity, dis/ability, class, and labor. Following Meiners (2007), we call on educational leaders to create and sustain collective action by supporting others in their efforts to transform the school–prison nexus and by fostering in their schools and communities the caring and authentic relationships needed to act collectively. For example, education leaders can learn about, support, and collaborate with community-based organizations, civil rights organization, unions, social movements, and other actors working in their communities and nationally to disrupt the racial capitalism that maintains and expands the school–prison nexus, including student activists and activists-to-be in their own schools (Diem & Welton, 2021). Our hope is that the racialized political and economic terrain we have outlined and the challenges and opportunities that we identified, though necessarily incomplete, will help education leaders identify who and what must be challenged and point the way to allies and opportunities to work collectively to disrupt the school–prison nexus in their schools and districts.

Part II

Anti-racist Educational Leadership Preparation and Practice

4

Considerations for District-level Anti-racist Leadership Preparation

Mary B. Herrmann and Jessica A. Herrmann

It is humbling to write about preparing anti-racist leaders. As white women, we (the authors) have each experienced immeasurable forms of privilege throughout our lives, some of which we can recognize and some of which we have not yet discovered. This reality certainly shapes our perceptions, experiences, and credibility in profound ways. We acknowledge that simply caring deeply and being committed to an anti-racist and just world are not enough. We cannot be bystanders, complicit in continuing to enable oppression and racism. We have much to learn, and many difficult choices to make, regarding what we do with our learning. We are grateful for the opportunity to embrace this inquiry as we face our own implicit biases and experiential limitations with great humility.

We have learned and continue to learn from others. We have been particularly impacted by those whose stories of injustice give voice to the personal toll of racism and oppression. We have also learned from those who have acted courageously in working to disrupt the status quo and embed anti-racist principles and practices in all aspects of their leadership.

Specifically, this chapter has been greatly informed by district leaders who have invested deeply in embedding equity within the fabric of all their district work, and who were highly reflective regarding their own preparation as leaders. We extend a special thanks to superintendents Dr. Margaret Clausen (personal communication, May 5, 2020) and Dr. Jennifer Cheatham (personal communication, May 13, 2020) who shared their challenges, experiences, and personal frameworks for conceptualizing their leadership work.

As educators we know that context greatly influences one's learning experiences. With this in mind we want to make explicit the beliefs, assumptions, and operating principles that underscore our evolving vision of an anti-racist leader preparation program:

- Leadership matters. Racism and white supremacy are systemic and institutionalized within our society; therefore, the role of leaders must be to proactively disrupt and ultimately dismantle the status quo.
- Leadership is a work in progress. Deep ongoing learning, both on an individual and organizational level, is essential to continuous growth.
- Both superintendent preparation programs and the position of district administrator continue to be dominated by white males. This domination has shaped the conceptualization of both preparation programming and the position itself. This must change.
- Leadership programs must be intentionally designed so that anti-racism principles and practices are core. They are systemically integrated into all aspects of the program and deeply embedded within the institutional culture itself.
- Effective leadership preparation programs prepare leaders with the multidisciplinary knowledge and skills needed to perform both the technical and adaptive aspects of anti-racist work and provide ongoing professional learning opportunities and coaching to leaders in the field.
- The beliefs, mindsets, and dispositions of those who prepare and those who enter leadership preparation programs matter greatly. Those who prepare aspiring leaders need to invest in their own ongoing personal learning and growth. In addition, they need to ensure that those candidates who enter preparation programs are committed to personal learning and transformation.
- Leadership preparation programs must ensure the extensive recruitment, selection, and support of racially diverse faculty members and candidates. Faculty should be hired from diverse backgrounds and include those with expertise in teaching about race and inequality from multidisciplinary perspectives. Faculty members, as well as the leadership candidates themselves, should reflect the diversity of the students and communities they serve.
- Advancing anti-racist leadership preparation requires an action-oriented investment individually, collectively, and institutionally.

Grounded in these eight principles, this chapter is organized to encompass three main areas of focus for anti-racist district-level leader preparation. These areas include the *leader's personal journey, the application of scholarly/ multidisciplinary work, and the understanding of context and strategies for leading change*. A focus on these three areas fosters the balanced integration between thought and action, which is essential for anti-racist work. Jal Mehta, a professor of education and co-director of the Deeper Learning Dozen at Harvard University, asserts that "change comes when actions and beliefs move in a reinforcing cycle. In this view changes in actions, lead to changes in belief, which stimulates demand for further change" (Mehta, 2020, p. 3).

The Personal Journey

Leadership preparation programs (particularly those preparing superintendents) are only a brief and momentary intervention in one's journey as a leader, but effective programs have the potential to shape the journey in significant ways. Programs that make an impact appreciate that leadership is a personal journey and above all else a work in progress. These programs recognize that "personal learning requires us to continually revisit who we are and to regularly address our contradictions. Essentially learning brings us back to the role of novice again and again" (Herrmann, 2020, p. 13).

In order to support leaders along this personal journey, effective preparation programs focus on the *mindsets, dispositions, and behaviors* necessary for anti-racist work as well as on the *personal characteristics and attributes* that facilitate anti-racist action.

Mindsets, Dispositions, and Behaviors

Ibram X. Kendi, anti-racist scholar and author of *How to Be an Antiracist*, states, "To be an antiracist is a radical choice in the face of this history, requiring a radical reorientation of our consciousness" (Kendi, 2019, p. 23). To develop anti-racist leaders, then, preparation programs need to provide the space and resources to facilitate this shift in consciousness among faculty and students alike.

With a significant focus on personal growth and development, effective preparation programs support deep, ongoing learning that is propelled by a moral imperative and grounded in anti-racist mindsets and dispositions. However, these mindsets and dispositions are not frequently cultivated in traditional educational settings. Because anti-racist work requires us to re-envision our world and challenge the very systems and structures from which many of us—particularly white males—benefit, there are significant paradigm shifts that are essential in order to begin developing an anti-racist mindset.

These paradigm shifts are critical for all individuals invested in this work, but they may be particularly challenging for white people. Paul Gorski, founder of the *Equity Literacy Institute*, offers several paradigm shifts white people must experience in the development of an equity-focused mindset. These paradigm shifts include:

- From Human Relations programming to Social Activism;
- From Racism as a People of Color Problem to Racism as a white People Problem;
- From Color Blindness to Self-Examination;
- From Racism as Individual Acts to Racism as Institutional Oppression;
- From Racial Harmony to Racial Equity; and
- From Focus on Intent to Focus on Impact (Gorski, 2020).

These paradigm shifts do not happen quickly, coherently, or painlessly. A challenge for leadership preparation programs, which have traditionally catered to a "customer satisfaction" orientation, is to insist that candidates experience and learn from pain and discomfort rather than avoid it.

Strategies that help with this effort further advance the development of personal dispositions and behaviors that are critical for enacting racial equity and justice reform. These dispositions/behaviors are essential for those who are recruited and selected into leadership programs as well as for all who prepare practitioner scholars for leadership work.

We recognize that many scholars who study leadership acknowledge the importance of identifying leader dispositions and behaviors that have an impact in leading equity work. In an effort to be succinct we have chosen to highlight, as an example, the *Leadership Academy* compilation of the work. The Leadership Academy, formally the NYC Leadership Academy, is a nonprofit research and training organization that works with educational leaders to disrupt systemic inequities and create the conditions necessary for all students to thrive.

Further described on their website, https://www.leadershipacademy.org/, the following dispositions/behaviors are integral to the Academy's *Culturally Responsive Leadership Framework*:

- reflecting on personal assumptions, beliefs, and behaviors;
- publicly modeling a personal belief system that is grounded in equity;
- acting with cultural competence and responsiveness in interactions, decision making, and practice;

- purposefully building the capacity of others to identify and disrupt inequities in the school;
- confronting and altering institutional biases of student marginalization, deficit-based schooling, and low expectations associated with minoritized populations; and
- creating systems and structures to promote equity with a focus on minoritized populations.

Demonstrating each of these dispositions and engaging in ongoing anti-racist work require continual learning. As Kendi states, "being an antiracist requires persistent self-awareness, constant self-criticism, and regular self-examination" (Kendi, 2019, p. 23). Therefore, leadership preparation programs must also focus on the personal characteristics and attributes that will cultivate these critical paradigm shifts and dispositions.

Personal Characteristics and Attributes

"No one becomes a racist or antiracist. We can only strive to be one or the other" (Kendi, 2019, p. 23). Knowing that this work—this journey—is ongoing, preparation programs have the responsibility to help faculty and scholars develop personal attributes such as courage, agility, and resilience.

Specifically, preparation programs must acknowledge the discomfort and fear associated with leadership and prepare leaders to lean into this fear rather than avoid it. The significance of courage in anti-racist leadership cannot be understated. We believe that courage is a learned attribute that can be strengthened with the right mindset and practice, and leadership preparation programs need to foster these types of opportunities.

In the book, *Everyday Courage for School Leaders*, Cathy Lassiter (2018) describes the following four dimensions of courage and provides tools to help assess and grow one's capacity to courageously lead an equity-focused agenda:

- Moral Courage—Standing up and acting when injustices occur, human rights are violated, or when persons are treated unfairly.
- Intellectual Courage—Challenging old assumptions and understandings and acting on new learnings and insights gleaned from experience and/or research.

- Disciplined Courage—Remaining steadfast, strategic, and deliberate in the face of inevitable setbacks and failures for the greater good.
- Empathetic Courage—Acknowledging personal bias and intentionally moving away from it in order to vicariously experience the trials and triumphs of others (Lassiter, 2018, p. 13).

A more comprehensive understanding of the complexity of courage can help leaders appreciate the significance of employing courage in all aspects of one's leadership behavior to ensure a more coherent and far-reaching approach to dismantling systemic racism. Leader preparation programs can assist leaders in growing their capacity to act courageously daily and consistently by providing routine exercises and ongoing coaching.

In addition, to transform complex organizations into socially just, anti-racist communities, leaders must remain open to new ways of thinking and constantly make meaning from their experiences. This concept of *learning agility* is significant in both the selection and development of school- and district-level leadership candidates. In a *Center for Creative Leadership* white paper, the authors state:

> When discussing the issue of long-term potential an individual's current skill set is of secondary importance to their ability to learn new knowledge, skills and behaviors that will equip them to respond to future challenges ... Leaders who refuse to let go of entrenched patterns of behavior or who do not recognize the nuances in different situations tend to derail, whereas successful leaders continue to learn and develop throughout their careers.
>
> (Mitchinson & Morris, 2014, p. 2)

Learning agile leaders question norms, challenge the status quo of white supremacy, and put themselves "out there," which is critical for anti-racist leadership. They learn continuously by stretching themselves outside their comfort zone and generating deeper insights into themselves, others, and the complexities of leading change.

The Center for Creative Leadership and Teacher's College, Columbia University have developed a learning agility assessment instrument (LAAI) to measure what they believe to be the five facets of *learning agile* behavior. Of these five facets of behavior the following four enable one's learning agility:

- *Innovating*—not being afraid to challenge the status quo
- *Performing*—remaining calm in the face of difficulty

- *Reflecting*—taking time to reflect on their experiences
- *Risking*—purposefully putting oneself in challenging situations

The fifth facet of behavior, *Defending,* actually frustrates or impedes learning. *Defending* refers to being closed to new learning and/or acting defensively when challenged (Mitchinson & Morris, 2014, p. 3).

When considering learning agility relative to anti-racist work, each facet of behavior is critical. It is especially important for white leaders to engage in innovating and risking behavior that disrupts, rather than defends, status quo white norms and behaviors.

Leader preparation programs can help develop and strengthen learning agility in their candidates by intentionally, routinely, and strategically focusing on personal learning and challenges to racism that, for white candidates in particular, move them well beyond that which is familiar and comfortable.

Courageous and agile leaders also exhibit greater resilience. Resilience is essentially the ability to manage stress, accept setbacks, learn deeply from one's struggles, and stay strong and focused on the mission. In many ways, resilience is a personal act of defiance. It is personally persisting in the fight against racism and injustice and requires an extensive repertoire of intentional strategies and behaviors to sustain the work over time.

Leader preparation programs can help candidates build their personal resilience by structuring their learning in ways that help ground the leaders in their sense of purpose and mission, manage their personal stress and energy, and control how they perceive what is happening by reframing their perspectives. For example, if leaders can reframe their perception of themselves from *compliant defenders of the status quo* to *rebels who need to disrupt it*, they are more able to align their values and behaviors and sustain the continuous battle against racism over time. Leaders must rebel in order to abolish unjust systems and drive positive change.

Candidates developing their capacity to become anti-racist leaders also need ongoing opportunities to personally grapple with the types of complex equity issues superintendents face. For example, as a superintendent, how will you confront the systemic racism that is endemic to the traditional Board governance structure? How will you work with your Board in advancing an *equitable* rather than *equal* allocation of resources? How will you lead and support your administrators in ensuring bold actions related to dismantling inequitable practices such as tracking and disproportionality by race in school discipline procedures? What will you do to give voice to, and build connections with, families who speak languages other than English? Through case studies, simulations, and field experiences relating to these types of questions, candidates can further strengthen their own personal dispositions and leadership skills around anti-racist work.

Intellectual and Multidisciplinary Focus

To advance anti-racist work, leaders need to have a strong and evolving intellectual and multidisciplinary understanding of the complexities related to race and structural racism. Bettina L. Love, author of *We Want to Do More than Survive: Abolitionist Teaching and the Pursuit of Educational Freedom*, writes that professional education programs often serve to perpetuate—rather than dismantle—stereotyping around students of color and their families (Love, 2019, p. 127).

In order to address this problem, Love posits that educators must study theory. Love writes, "Theory does not solve issues—only action and solidarity can do that—but theory gives you language to fight, knowledge to stand on, and a humbling reality of what intersectional social justice is up against" (Love, 2019, p. 132). According to Love, theories such as critical race theory, settler colonialism, Black feminism, dis/ability, and others also help educators understand the broader societal implications of educational justice. "Educational justice can happen only through a simultaneous fight for economic justice, racial justice, housing justice, environmental justice, religious justice, queer justice, trans justice, citizenship justice, and disability justice" (Love, 2019, p. 12).

This understanding is especially critical for school leaders. In this chapter, we provide a very small sampling of potential theories, frameworks, and resources that may be helpful in strengthening one's knowledge base around anti-racism and leadership. It is essential that whatever content and resources are selected be thoughtfully embedded and integrated throughout the program in a way that essentially transforms the traditional, white-centered construct in which candidates conceptualize and develop as leaders.

An understanding of the tenets and underpinnings of an array of theories is critical for transforming the "traditional" constructs many of our candidates—and instructors, for that matter—have developed about education and leadership. For instance, Feminist and Postmodern perspectives offer the potential for reconceptualizing how we consider the position of superintendent itself. These theories challenge us to consider the role of gender in leadership and suggest that female leaders resist the images that have been traditionally reserved for them and reinvent the superintendency on their own terms. "These terms imply a commitment on the part of the superintendent to ask tough questions, to consider issues from multiple perspectives, and to put himself or herself on the line. In sum, it means taking a stand on issues of social justice (and communicating that stand to others) that reinforces an active inquiry into what is happening in a district" (Grogan, 2000, p. 133).

Leadership preparation programs must also integrate content and leadership models that use the intersectionality of racial, gender, and other elements of personal identity in providing a more comprehensive historical context for educational leadership that can inform leadership practice today. Sonya Horsford, in *This Bridge Called My Leadership: An Essay on Black Women as Bridge Leaders in Education*, writes about Black women "serving as a bridge for others, to others, and between others in multiple and often complicated contexts over time" (Horsford, 2012, p. 17). She suggests that *bridge leadership* can be a model for leading diverse school communities across the country where there are large numbers of poor, Black, Latinx, and immigrant children and youth. A further examination of *bridge leadership* and the intersectional identities of Black women and how they model these qualities will increase our understanding of the full potential of school leadership that is centered on working for "diversity, equity, and social justice" (Horsford, 2012, p. 19).

In addition, since effective leadership is essential in all sectors and areas of life, programs that prepare leaders must position themselves in ways that ensure programming that fosters multidisciplinary and multi (counter) narrative approaches to understanding the contextual and complex nature of leadership itself. A thoughtful and critical integration of multiple perspectives requires that programming extend beyond an education-centric professional credentialing focus to a broader multidisciplinary approach that captures a wide array of conceptualizations and strategies for leading change. This programming, therefore, must be led by deeply invested, highly reflective, and knowledgeable faculty members whose collective learning and expertise cuts across multiple disciplines.

Context and Leadership in Practice

Enacting theory into practice is an ongoing challenge for leadership preparation programs. For those who help prepare leaders to change the world, there are many contradictions and challenges. Leadership preparation programs exist within a broader authorizing environment that requires compliance to the rules and standards required for administrative certification or licensure. At the same time, effective programs need to prepare leaders to rebel against the "authorizing" systems and practices that are systemically racist and inherently unjust. The technical aspects of learning the job through field embedded and clinical experience is often contradictory to the type of "breaking the rules" experiences that are necessary to disrupt an unjust system and ultimately make an impact. Essentially, leaders need to be prepared to work within the system, while rebelling against it.

As author Muhammad Khalifa states in *Culturally Responsive School Leadership*, "when educators enter a school, they will assume control over systems that have been oppressive to students, particularly minoritized students. They will either reproduce oppression or they will contest it" (Khalifa, 2018, p. 19).

Ensuring that leaders are well positioned for anti-racist work requires a significant shift in leadership preparation. Specifically, preparation must move away from traditional "schoolcentric" perspectives of leadership to culturally responsive, community-based perspectives. This has significant and far-reaching implications for all phases of leadership preparation. The traditional experiences of educators who "work their way up the ranks" to become school administrators are often grounded in an insulated and colonized version of schooling. Khalifa (2018) asserts,

> School leadership models were situated in colonial schooling, which meant that schools were meant to build good citizens who would contribute to the economic viability of the society. This was particularly problematic for Native American, Black, and Latinx communities because while the government prospered, these minoritized communities (and their resources) fell further behind … Schools were crucial in this exploitation and school leaders often led this charge … Because of this legacy, school leaders have difficulty breaking out of a colonizing mold.
>
> (p. 51)

Leaders therefore need to live with paradox. They need to actively disrupt a system they have been hired to defend.

Navigating the Community Context for Anti-racist Leadership

Repositioning the context of leadership preparation, from the school as the central institution to the community as the focus and driving force for change, requires significant transformation. This begins with an appreciation for the complexity of the position of the public-school superintendent within the context of the community.

According to Mark Moore and Andres Alonso from the Public Education Project at Harvard, school superintendents are somewhat unique among executive leaders in that they use collectively owned assets granted to them by the community as a whole to achieve publicly defined goals. Thus, "the important arbiter of the value (superintendents) produce is the community that gives them the money and authority they need to operate—not so much the clients (students and parents) who benefit from the enterprise" (Moore & Alonso, 2017, p. 3).

This conceptualization of the role has tremendous implications for how superintendents think about and lead change. It suggests that the skills and competencies required by school district leaders to leverage and impact broader communities are far more reaching and complex. Leadership preparation programs, therefore, have a responsibility to prepare leaders to understand their community-based position and context and to develop the capacity to explicitly assess and impact their environment to advance change.

Sharing different conceptual frameworks that help leaders better understand complexity and meaningfully frame and reframe issues is critical to any leadership development program. One possible lens for district-level leaders to use to assess environmental conditions and complexity is the *Strategic Triangle Framework* (Moore & Alonso, 2017, p. 34). We are sharing this as just one example of a conceptual framework that can be used as a tool in helping superintendents analyze key contextual elements when leading anti-racist work. The *Strategic Triangle* consists of the following environmental elements:

- *Public Value:* Produced when people's lives are improved as a result of services provided by the district. Leaders must consider, *what is the public value I am trying to create?*
- *Legitimacy and Support:* The "authorizing environment" describes the group of people who are in positions that could confer legitimacy and support (or the opposite) on the service. Leaders must consider, *what/who authorizes and supports my efforts to produce that value?*
- *Operational Capabilities:* This relates to sufficient resources, correctly allocated. Leaders must consider, *what operational capacity must I build and deploy to produce the desired result* (Moore & Alonso, 2017, p. 34)?

To effectively lead change all three of these environmental elements need to be understood, assessed, and aligned. For example, when considering just one dimension of the *Strategic Triangle*, legitimacy and support, one quickly discovers that the "authorizing environment" for a superintendent is vast, messy, and complex. "It includes political actors and forces such as: local school boards; mayors, city councils and public agencies; interest groups; media; citizens, voters, taxpayers; parents and students; educational foundations; and State legislatures and departments of education, as well as, the incredible power of the status quo" (Moore & Alonso, 2017, p. 17).

This means that superintendents are dealing with demands for accountability that come from many different directions with no clear focus, and few shared priorities, among the many divergent and often competing groups. The complex authorizing environment alone makes equity work extremely challenging. This is especially true when one considers that change for racial equity typically occurs only when it aligns with the interests and priorities of white people.

It is imperative that leadership preparation programs use an anti-racist lens in grappling with questions related to public value, legitimacy and support, and operational capabilities. They also need to cultivate, through intentional, cross-disciplinary, and job embedded experiences, the essential skills, competencies, and strategies needed to leverage community assets. According to Moore and Alonso, superintendents need to develop skills and acquire strategies in the areas of *entrepreneurial advocacy, managing processes of policy development, negotiating value, orchestrating processes of public deliberation and learning, and public marketing* (Moore & Alonso, 2017, p. 20).

These areas of focus are critical to anti-racist work. By strengthening leadership skills in these areas, superintendents will be better equipped to organize collective processes of decision making that have the support of all stakeholders. They will also feel more confident in promoting public deliberation and adaptive learning about anti-racism, recognizing that such deliberation is likely to include fear and the perception of loss of white privilege and power for many within the community. In essence, they will be better prepared for doing the important work of deeply engaging others in efforts to advance equity and improve conditions through their own independent actions.

According to researchers Welton, Owens, and Zamani-Gallaher (2018), "implementing long-lasting anti-racist change is impossible for a single leader to facilitate ... Building the capacity of others to lead and shoulder the responsibility for facilitating anti-racist change only increases the number of those throughout the institution (and community) who are accountable for and committed to accomplishing the institution's goals for racial equity" (p. 12).

It is also crucial that leadership preparation programs prepare leaders for sustaining the work by being realistic about the challenges and approaching it with high, but measured, expectations. In *Learning to Lead for Racial Equity*, Gislaine Ngounou and Nancy Gutierrez share that the potential for setbacks increases when leaders overestimate their own competency to lead this work; underestimate the time and effort that this work requires; and assume that everybody is equally ready and willing to discuss these issues (Ngounou & Gutierrez, 2017).

According to Ngounou and Gutierrez (2017), leaders need to be ever mindful of the long-standing history, biases, and deep-seated effect of inequities in American education. They remind us that professional learning related to race and equity requires a systems-thinking approach and a willingness to experience discomfort, requires people to tell their stories, and rarely leads to closure.

Conclusion

Preparing anti-racist leaders to change the world is a challenging and continuous process. The significance of the work necessitates an ongoing investment in all aspects of leader preparation and practice, from the active recruitment and selection of diverse students and faculty, to post-degree continuous, multidisciplinary professional learning, networking, and coaching that directly support all leaders in anti-racist work in their communities.

As we shared in the beginning of the chapter, we are humbled by how much more there is to learn, and how much we need to do. As we strive to better prepare ourselves and our leaders for advancing anti-racist work, we recognize that waiting until we feel more confident with our knowledge and skills is not an option—we need to act now. As author Ijeoma Oluo (2018) so eloquently reminds us, "no matter what our intentions, everything we say and do in the pursuit of justice will one day be outdated, ineffective, and yes, probably wrong. That is the way progress works. What we do now is important and helpful so long as what we do now is what is needed now" (p. 187).

From the Inside Out: A Letter to Anti-racist Leaders

Marcus Campbell and Michael Kucera

Introduction

Historically, a lack of proficient racial equity leadership has led to racially based achievement gaps among students of color. Increasing access to honors-level coursework for students of color enhances their potential to excel, but implementing such changes presents a substantial challenge to the status quo because the inequalities are integral to an institutionally racist social structure from which white students and staff benefit (Ladson-Billings, 1994b). To undo racial injustice in schools, race and racism must be addressed inside and out. School leaders must address their own racism, biases, and unpack their own social narratives if they want to do this work well. Also, in order for school districts to move their work forward, leaders must be willing to confront the racism that lives within their upbringing and shows up in their thinking. Too often school leaders feel passionate about the task of eliminating racial achievement disparities without looking at the racism in the school or the racism within themselves. This confrontation with the past and present can be daunting, even embarrassing, but it is necessary at modeling the types of practices leaders will need to ask of staff to address racial disparities. Without an internal examination of themselves, as well as an external examination of the institutions, departments, and classrooms they lead, school leaders will attempt to unsuccessfully program the way out of addressing these racial inequities directly. There is a level of programming required but these programs must emerge from a way of thinking that only comes through the pain of unpacking racism (Singleton, 2014). Schools aren't in need of reforms but they must be transformed.

One of the most important keys in leadership is knowing oneself and being reflective about one's habits, thoughts, and relational interactions (Boyatzis &

McKee, 2005). Leading for racial justice is no different. It requires a level of honesty about race that many white school leaders are often afraid to admit. Those who wish to lead for racial justice can have the passion and the moral conviction to address what has been an inadequate schooling experience for students of color, but they can lack the courage to deal with the implicit bias that frames their thinking. Some leaders may not want to acknowledge how the impact of racist language, attitudes, and beliefs shaped their worldview. These leaders would need to unpack how they began to unlearn those frameworks and how they systematically should begin to undo their own racial bias. You can't lead for racial equity if you don't have the skill or capacity to talk about race. Therefore, leaders should unpack how certain social constructs and worldviews compel them to hold onto their white privilege, especially since this tendency is self-contradictory or antithetical to what it means to be an anti-racist leader that ultimately compromises their leadership praxis. If leaders are unable to acknowledge social privileges, acknowledging racism may be far-fetched (DiAngelo, 2018). As current practitioners and school leaders, we understand anti-racist work is as challenging as it is urgent, and our aim in this chapter is to highlight both what it means to be an anti-racist leader and what it means to lead anti-racist work.

A Call to White Leaders

The acknowledgment of privilege by white school leaders is important for a couple of reasons. First, although our student and family populations are becoming more racially diverse, the racial demographic of teachers and school leaders remains primarily white. Ten percent of students currently enrolled in K-12 settings are Black and 27 percent are Latinx, whereas 80 percent of the total teaching population, 78 percent of school principals, and 71 percent of all school administrators are white (United States Department of Education, 2019). Although the overrepresentation of white educators is not a focus of this chapter, this can become problematic and, in fact, does damage to students and staff of color if school leaders do not develop and implement anti-racist competencies within themselves and their practices (Horsford, 2014).

For leaders to be considered "anti-racist," they must acknowledge that the core of schools and school systems is deferential to whiteness and white supremacy, and that school systems deliberately or inadvertently exclude students and staff of color from wholly reaping the benefits of structures and programs that grant them access to more rigorous curriculum, and consequently, access to more desirable opportunities beyond high school (Welton, 2013). Further, anti-racist leaders actively work to dismantle racist ideologies and infrastructures that exclude or inhibit the growth of people of color within the school community. However, school leaders often avoid confronting those racist structures head-on because they are ill-equipped to address implicit biases within their institutions, or because they fear backlash from white stakeholders (Castagno, 2014).

Unfortunately, it is still difficult in this country to talk about race. It is even more difficult to talk about owning one's racism (DiAngelo, 2018). The sociopolitical climate that emerged in the post-Civil Rights era made racism socially unacceptable. A moral shift occurred in this country which made being openly racist problematic. The challenge occurs when racism and those who harbor it go underground and only speak openly privately in their homes, offices, and where it is socially acceptable. Being called a racist implicates a flaw in one's moral fabric and character; people should not be working to not be racist, they should be working to be anti-racist (Kendi, 2019). Racism can be spoken about in historic terms but should also be addressed in more contemporary terms (DiAngelo, 2018). Moreover, race was created to divide and dehumanize others and continues to do so today. Ta Nehisi Coates (2015) notes, "But Race is the child of racism, not the father" (p. 7). Working through what race means as a social construct for leaders is critical to reclaiming one's humanity and it is also helpful for modeling to staff about how to reclaim theirs.

White leaders have a lot of learning to do as they acknowledge race and their own racism and come to an understanding of how this social construct has impacted our history and current events (DiAngelo, 2018; Stevenson, 2014). The historical trauma inflicted on communities of color over many generations cannot be addressed by singular disconnected book studies, race avoidance, and denial (Singleton, 2014). These challenges must be faced with bold courageous reflections of the self and how the self is implicated in today's social and academic realities. If leaders cannot engage in this reflective process, they cannot be trusted in the work. The process without these types of personal confrontations only produces more of the same, and we need something different. One's personal racism has to be addressed.

It is important for leaders to model the behaviors they want staff to engage in (Brooks, 2012). This level of vulnerability is necessary for building relational trust with staff who will also have to be vulnerable. There is no learning without vulnerability and humility. It takes practice to be able to have these conversations and leaders must create spaces for staff to practice. These rehearsals mean hitting the wrong notes and keeping the wrong tempo. People of color are always the most vulnerable, the most at risk, and are the ones who have been impacted by generational racial trauma, racial trauma in their communities, and their own negative experiences with race. Yet, if the work is being done correctly, race never leaves the table. Working on racial inequities through the process of modeling vulnerability is how systemic transformation for racial equity is achieved. There must be rehearsals before there is ever a performance. There must be trial and error in practicing the conversation before the skill and capacity are developed for leadership. The conversations are high-stakes in that leaders don't want to sound racist or be perceived as racist (Singleton, 2014). The point here is to hit those wrong notes of racism in order to learn, heal, and grow. This process is essential for racial justice. Leaders who try to function within cultures of academic perfection will struggle with this concept of vulnerability and normalizing mistakes. It is important that adults see themselves as learners, function as learners, and cultivate a culture of learning among staff. Having and maintaining a sense of curiosity and empathy is essential for getting this right.

This work isn't just about having the right vocabulary or saying the right buzzwords, it is more than that. Many white leaders feel they are actively engaging in the work because they are able to talk about the work. They have the "right" vocabulary to be able to fully engage in a conversation about racism. This places them ahead of many other white people who don't have the vocabulary and are afraid to say the wrong thing, but it unfortunately also gives them a false sense of security. Because they can talk the jargon, they think they are proficient in leading the work. This may or may not be the case. There could be other white educators who don't have the vocabulary, but are genuinely empathic in the work; they truly want to own their racism and want to be anti-racist (Kendi, 2019). While other white educators who seem more astute in these conversations may still not necessarily display empathy and own their racism. Thus, white people who can talk about the work but can't do the work are the most problematic in leading for racial equity. The racism that undergirds their supposedly anti-racist talk can be lethal to the work and can feel burdensome to those who are actually practicing the work.

White colleagues and colleagues of color alike can become confused, angry, and frustrated with these paradoxes in leadership. These inconsistencies have the potential to set back and fracture the work, and the relational trust needed to move the anti-racist work forward can become compromised. It is important that white people leading this work understand that their racism may be visible; they must own and not be afraid of that. It is the only way to build trust and model the learning process.

White people who believe they have truly conquered racism cannot lead this work. White people who look down on other white people for what they do not know cannot lead this work (Payne, 2008). White people who have not understood their own guilt and fragility cannot lead this work. But white people who see themselves as unlearning their racism, those who have capacity for grace and care and those who understand their humanity in this process and are on a journey, can build the capacity to lead this work (DiAngelo, 2018).

It is also important for leaders who want to do the right thing in this work to actually commit to doing the right thing. The right thing usually means doing what is politically unpopular: sending more resources to Black and Brown schools and Black and Brown kids, creating racial affinity spaces for students and staff, asking/answering tough questions about race, talking openly about white supremacy, asking white staff to confirm and not to deny their racism, creating spaces for white people to examine race without the labor of people of color. This list is not exhaustive by any means. They must also recognize the blind-spots provided by their social privilege that inhibits them from seeing the right thing and consequently doing the right thing. This is no one's fault but a part of the healing and growing process. Far too many times leaders will talk about the right thing to do but never get around to doing it. They will also commit to doing the right thing but aren't willing to make the tough choices in clearing the path to actually doing it (Collins & Hansen, 2011). They allow the subtle and sometimes larger complexities of school bureaucracy to stop the work or they argue for incremental change. They fail to realize that the system that we work within was born and bred in white supremacy and the ideologies that aren't congruent with that thinking don't fit. Building more culturally responsive practices and more healing-centered schooling is not consistent with the manner in which schools are currently managed and run. The commitment to leading for racial equity is larger than one programmatic project. It is more complex than a one and done PD session. It is also more nuanced than any one single effort. It requires a systemic approach, systemic thinking, and systemic responses (Senge & Sterman, 1992). Racial equity leadership demands a commitment of courage and requires a long-term commitment. The criticism and backlash from all sides will be strong, consistent, and swift. Those who aren't ready for such change will resist, those who feel that change isn't coming fast enough will push, and those who don't understand and disagree will retreat and sabotage.

Racial equity leaders who start one project begin to realize that there is always more to be done, and with it make the mistake of engaging in incremental change. The change that racial equity leadership requires is self-examination that evolves as the work evolves; and as the leaders and the organization evolve, the work becomes more racially just. One can only implement the levels and standards of justice that matches or supersedes one's own conceptual understanding of justice. Change is adaptive, not fixed or static (Fullan, 2008). Engaging in this work correctly is just as any other work; the more you know and have the courage to do, the better it gets. The more courageous the leader, the better and the further the organization can go (Boyatzis & McKee, 2005). Those who say we should "take our time" or "we aren't ready" haven't engaged a series of questions.

The Political Nature of Anti-racist Work

Leaders have to be ready to do the work of anti-racism, knowing that the work will evolve and get better as they move the organization along. Decisions to put off and start later are simply one of the ways in which white supremacy is maintained and justice is denied. The work is politically toxic yet morally pure; it isn't for the faint of heart or for those who simply use leadership for personal gain. Change management in general is hard work (Fullan, 2008). However, change management with the goal of eliminating white supremacy is *extremely* hard work. Aspiring racial equity leaders can be sure that political allies will fade but new ones will come, and they can expect to lose friends yet build new partnerships in the process. They should assume that those who have been their closest advisors may not support their efforts for racial justice. There are no political maneuvers that will build blind trust and move the organization along. There are no tactics that will build instant "buy-in" and collaboration. The politics of whiteness are to blame.

Race and racism have a long, complicated, and dark history in this country that must be confronted (Kendi, 2019; Stevenson, 2014). This history is often painful and tough for those who currently live under the burden of racism, and so there is often a large gap between people of color and white people in understanding the current complications of racism and its impact (Kendall, 2013). This disconnect is often a major challenge in leading the work with staff and students. Oftentimes the experiences of people of color are too painful as they relive racist encounters while white people are unfamiliar with the weight of the burden of race. Too often people of color are asked to relive their trauma for the education of white people (Leonardo & Porter, 2010). This is not to say that people of color should not share their experiences, but naming the tension in this work is important. Why should staff and students of color relive racial trauma to educate white people? Elevating the perspectives of people of color is important to moving the work forward, but exploiting their voices for the benefit of white people can be problematic.

The adults in schools can often seem more concerned with politics and not the lives of the children (Payne, 2008). It is important for racial equity leaders to realize that the lives and humanity of students are what they are fighting for. The leadership calculus cannot ignore the current need for action and desperate change. One way in gathering support is by building a coalition of those who are willing to do the work and believe there is a need for change. Creating this broad base leadership team is important for spreading the need for anti-racist change. It is the leader's responsibility to build support for anti-racist change from the inside out. In this case, it means from teachers, staff, support staff, and anyone who believes in the need for understanding race in the organization and how to go about finding the solution, this is the nature of adaptive work.

Heifetz and Linsky (2017) speak about technical challenges and adaptive challenges. The problem of race in school is an adaptive challenge in that it requires an adaptive solution. An adaptive solution involves creating teams of stakeholders who can come together to strategize and implement anti-racist changes. It involves an adaptive communication strategy that can speak to multiple issues and concerns that may arise where leaders may not know the answer. Thus, leaders modeling a learning space and process are also adaptive and healthy for staff to experience with leadership at the table. For anti-racist change efforts, the journey of learning is equally important to the destination. However, it is okay for the sake of racial equity if the destination needs to shift at some point, as this adaptability is all part of the learning journey (Fullan, 2008). The journey is adaptive; the learning is adaptive which makes this process fluid and not fixed.

Approaches to Addressing Racial Inequities

Anti-racist leaders seek critical approaches to changing culture and addressing racial inequities. Although no one-size-fits-all model of a systematic approach to personal reflection and development in leaders exists, a key lever in informing, understanding, and raising awareness of an individual leader's thought processes involves collecting and looking at data with a critical lens (Skrla et al., 2009). For example, a perusal of internal data will likely reveal, even with similar achievement on standardized tests, Black and Latinx students are less likely to be placed in advanced coursework and more likely to be taught in lower-tier, skill-driven coursework, and are disproportionately disciplined. Examining racial demographic data often highlights an "inadvertently racist system" within the school and gives leaders a starting point for systemic change (Theoharis & Haddix, 2013, p. 12). But inadvertent racism is racism, nonetheless, and racial segregation via tracking masked as a well-intentioned "meeting students where they're at" strategy is still racial segregation. Anti-racist leaders have the responsibility of not only naming the practices that lift up one set of students while diminishing the others, but also removing the practices entirely. This section highlights some essential components of leading anti-racist, systemic change.

Interrogating Root Causes

One way to dig deep into better understanding the root causes and impacts of systemic racism within schools is by conducting an exhaustive racial equity audit of both systems and people. If the goal is to address racial inequities head-on, it is imperative that school leaders not only consider the needs of minoritized students, but also identify and remove long-standing systems that perpetuate the minoritization of people of color (Hill, 2017). Coded language, tracking, deficit ideologies, whitewashed curriculum, and policies are all too often unchecked but well-within the immediate control of school leaders and personnel. Conducting racial equity audits allows leaders and learning communities a formalized system that gathers data and seeks to identify the broader, systemic issues, like those above, that prevent students from accessing the resources provided by the school.

Looking beyond Numbers

There is ample research that supports critical examination of numerical data. It is tempting, and frankly easier, to limit data collection to things like test scores, enrollment in advanced coursework, grade distribution, and disciplinary data. Numbers do not have names or faces and allow white school leaders and educators to point fingers and depersonalize racism rather than considering their role in perpetuating it and the profound effect it has on communities of color (Stevenson, 2014). Consequently, it is essential that leaders invite and listen to the voices and stories of students, parents, and staff of color who have been marginalized by systemic racism (Skrla et al., 2009). After all, it is difficult to advocate for racial equity without knowing and engaging the necessary stakeholders and centering conversation on the voices of the individuals who are most adversely affected by racist systems within a school.

Counter-narratives are important data as they lift up and recognize the experiences of people of color and accurately and necessarily challenge the narrative of white supremacy in and outside of school communities. Thus, counter-narratives as data are important and powerful because they quell white voices by requiring white leaders and educators to do more listening than speaking, which further challenges white educators to hear and see patterns of racism and deficit mindsets within the building and themselves (Flores & Kyere, 2020). It is also imperative that leaders work to heal relationships with those who have been consistently and disproportionately affected by racially unjust educational practices (Khalifa et al., 2016). This healing process should begin by prioritizing the voices of the marginalized in the discussion that targets solutions (Brooks, 2012).

Collective Reflection and Dialogue

Within the school walls, there are often elements related to racial equity that are discussed in pockets, rather than in public. The avoidance of critical dialogue about racial inequity feeds a culture of politeness, ignores the role of power and privilege, and defers to the status quo of maintaining schools as white spaces (Castagno, 2014; Horsford, 2014). When it comes to addressing racial inequities in school settings, the conversation can and should be uncomfortable because discomfort is part of the work (Singleton, 2014). But a school leader leading public reflection and transparency is essential, because doing so conveys an urgency to acknowledge inequitable systems and a desire to take action (Jean-Marie & Mansfield, 2013; Khalifa et al., 2016).

Effective school leaders prioritize time and spaces for group reflection, where staff members can have opportunities to examine whiteness, white privilege, racism, and the role of those components within school climate and student perception. If leaders are unwilling to address the fact that racism in all forms is ever present in their school community (Singleton, 2014), then it becomes difficult to lead meaningful change. In order for school staff to become aware of these systems, they must be empowered by school leaders who share, encourage, and engage in conversations and provide ongoing professional development that seeks to address and rectify harmful racist systems (Brooks, 2012; Jean-Marie & Mansfield, 2013).

One practice that is communicated as well-meaning but is anything but is the employment of colorblindness in any arena. Colorblindness is problematic because it allows educators to apply race neutrality in both personal practice and systemic policies (Flores & Gunzenhauser, 2019). Additionally, colorblindness prevents leaders and staff both from seeing people of color in their work and from planning and reflecting on how their own perspective and actions (or inaction) perpetuate racism within the institution. For instance, colorblind decision making in the form of tracking, access (or lack thereof) to advanced curriculum, disproportional discipline, and decisions that fail to reflect and honor the diversity of the school's student body, let alone the diversity of the world, are symptoms of school systems with undercurrents of racism (Castagno, 2014; Welton, 2013). Yet, examining both quantifiable and qualitative data highlights inequities and, in doing so, brings the issues of race and equity to the forefront of the conversation. The unfortunate benefit of numerical data with regard to racial demographics is that they often show trends of marginalization of students of color, especially Black and Latinx student populations. However, a hopeful outcome is that, once aware of the racial inequities that data uncovers, staff members are more likely to engage in a dialogue of professional inquiry and action toward redressing the problem (Skrla et al., 2009). For example, when seeing racial disparities in higher-level course enrollment, staff would question and identify those who are playing the role of gatekeeper by marginalizing students in accessing a more rigorous curriculum. Ultimately, staff members would identify and address the adult behaviors as root causes of the problem. This outcome, however, is often not the case. When looking only at numbers, it is easy to intellectualize and explain away the data and put the onus on students of color. Making room for students' personal stories, experiences, lived realities pushes educators to consider how their current practices promote or reduce marginalizing conditions. It is the role of the school leader to not merely present data to staff and expect that alone will allow for school-wide reform; they also need to engage staff in the practice of seeing and understanding the many, well-established faces of racism within the system (Brooks, 2012).

Ultimately, the work of racial equity is the work of community (Lightfoot, 2004). Collective and reflective dialogue that addresses systemic racism should also involve students, families, staff, and those who want to help build a better and brighter future for all youth. Anti-racist work cannot be done in silos. This work must be done in classrooms, houses of worship, and community centers. It must be done in the cafeterias, bleachers, and parks. The solutions must be community-centered and therefore involve the community. It takes civic leaders, community partners, and their teams to coalesce around a vision for racial equity. Schools and its leaders cannot do this in isolation, apart from other members of the proverbial village. It is a vision that can be written and embraced by all, worked on by all, and achieved by all.

Examining Hearts, Minds, and Practice

Too often, school leaders and personnel get bogged down in the talk of inequity without really addressing the deficit mindsets and practices that exist within the school community (Skrla et al., 2009). In the context of school, most deficit mindsets and practices on the parts of teachers, counselors, and school leaders are unintentional and surface in seemingly innocuous ways: externalizing students' challenges (e.g., blaming parents or socioeconomics), racially coded language, fearing the material is too challenging, and blind adherence to an oppressive curriculum. In each of these cases, deficit practice places the burden of failure on the students without requiring the adults to reflect and change their own practices. Practice, however, is as much at the core of change as mindset. Although there are external factors that can negatively affect student performance that cannot be controlled by school personnel, there are internal factors that schools indeed have control over and can change. School leaders have the power to lead change insofar as exposing systemic racial inequities and changing mindsets and practices through ongoing development (Castagno, 2014). Additionally, school leaders have the power to both assess teacher mindsets and see practice in action, and with that, have the power to make decisions as to which teachers have the right mindsets for the school community and students (Brooks, 2012). What is needed, however, is an ongoing commitment to actually develop staff and programs, assess attitudes and behaviors, and act when attitudes and behaviors of leaders, teachers, or staff members adversely affect the experiences or outcomes of students of color (Khalifa et al., 2016).

Conclusion: Leaders' Commitment to Anti-racist Work

Coordinating anti-racist change takes a lot of work, talk, and constant commitment. It takes coffees and seminars. It takes trial and error. It takes votes, candidates, policy, and procedure. It takes lunch and learns, speeches, and data. It takes personal narratives and vulnerability. The work takes book groups, documentaries, and tears. The work involves reflections and sharing. It takes long curricular conversations and redesign. The work demands holding oneself accountable and being called into account. The work involves the past self and the present self. It involves learning the racial history of our country, the racial history of our schools, and the racial history of our neighborhoods. The work demands that we truly see ourselves and what we can become as human beings, reclaiming our humanity as we seek to humanize others. If leaders cannot model listening and be impacted and moved by the lived experiences of those they hear or those they read about, the work cannot be done. The respect of listening and leaning into that discomfort is the first step toward humanity.

Leaders must remember this endeavor isn't simply about student data and research outcomes. This work is about the potential of beautiful kids of color whose potential and promise get extinguished under the hands of an oppressive system. If we truly want to change the world today and not to repeat the horrific racial injustices of our past, school leaders must reach and teach for racial equity in all of what they do, which goes beyond afterschool programs and once-a-year assemblies. School systems must transform themselves from the inside out.

6

The Color of Coloniality: White Administrators' Expectations of Black Males in School Discipline

Daniel D. Liou and Adam Zang

Introduction

Several years ago, we had the opportunity to meet Dylan (pseudonym), a high school junior in good academic standing, through a research partnership that explored the role of teachers' expectations in establishing conditions of equity to address the long-standing racialized opportunity gap. Dylan was charismatic, liked by his peers, and considered college-bound by his teachers. We remember Dylan vividly due to his personality and intelligence, but we were also troubled by our observed treatment of him in his Chemistry classroom.

Over the course of a year, we sat in the back of Dylan's Chemistry class to document teacher–student interactions. From the beginning of our observations, we could tell that Dylan was deeply invested in the subject, as he regularly expressed his enthusiasm through raising his hand to either ask questions or engage in discussions. His questions were often complex and insightful, showing his propensity to learn. Dylan's teacher, Dr. Alexander (pseudonym), was a white woman with a PhD in chemistry who was teaching high school for the first time. As a new teacher, Dr. Alexander did not have a system of mentorship and support from school administration. It was also clear to us that she did not know much about her students prior to teaching that course. Despite Dylan's demonstrated enthusiasm, Dr. Alexander rarely called on him except for the few times when her brief answers were not enough to deepen the discussion.

Initially, we thought Dr. Alexander's reluctance to engage with Dylan might be due to her weak classroom management skills. On average, Dr. Alexander's instructional time only took around twenty minutes of the fifty-minute class period, leaving students with a significant amount of unstructured learning time. During this lack of instruction, the noise level in the classroom would increase. Despite this, Dylan showed resilience and continued to engage with course content on a daily basis, frequently needing to shout from the back of the room in order to get Dr. Alexander's attention.

At first, Dr. Alexander actively ignored Dylan, creating a situation that forced him to shout louder in the hopes that the teacher would hear him. Soon, Dr. Alexander began to reprimand what she perceived as Dylan's disruptions by repeatedly sending him out of class with disciplinary referrals. Upon returning to class, Dylan was much more compliant, but he gradually stopped engaging in classroom activities and instead turned to his cell phone. By the middle of the semester, Dylan's grades in chemistry had fallen precipitously. We soon realized that Dylan's experiences were reflective of the larger patterns at the school, wherein the higher suspension and expulsion rates for Black males corresponded with schoolwide disparities in grades and test scores. We interviewed Dr. Alexander after she submitted her resignation at the end of the semester. She shared with us that she "did not have any expectations for these students."

From a social contract perspective (Mills, 2014), issues such as school safety are generally agreed upon as good and necessary for all students. However, Dylan's story shows that these contractual agreements often are not extended to protecting the identity, intellect, and physical safety of Students of Color (Steele & Cohn-Vargas, 2013). Dylan's administrators repeatedly doubted his innocence, despite his attempts to explain his classroom behavior. Some researchers point to the lack of diversity in the teaching force as a major contributor to this problem (Hughes et al., 2005). This mismatched argument is further exacerbated by many teachers' deficit ideologies of Students of Color, which firmly deny their racialized history and experiences with school safety measures, even as these disciplinary actions heighten these students' awareness of race and racism (Noguera, 2003). Mills (2014) points out these different standards of treatment in his concept of the racial contract, which debunks the social contract thesis that assumed laws, policies, and social institutions to be race neutral, and forms of common good equally applied to all citizens. He argues that the dominant social contract is written as an exclusionary contract to benefit white Americans and has never been equally applied to People of Color. Dylan's story illuminates the salience of the educational racial contract (Leonardo, 2013), wherein Black Americans are viewed with suspicion and guilt even when they have socially conformed to Eurocentric standards of conduct.

For these reasons, we invite school leaders to contemplate the following questions: (1) What role should white administrators play in challenging the white supremacist practices of school discipline? (2) How should white administrators deconstruct and transform their expectations to stop the criminalization of Black males in schools and society? To answer these questions, we draw on the experiences of the second author, Adam, a white assistant principal who recently completed his first-year managing school discipline at an elementary school in Arizona. Through critical analysis of disciplinary cases that involved Students of Color, the goal of this self-study is to reflect on his preparation prior to his first leadership assignment and to describe how he enacted expectations associated with anti-racist leadership and school discipline. We chose Adam's elementary school as the site for this self-study because student–teacher relationships in the early grades have the strongest influence on students' trajectories, especially for racialized populations and those who have been negatively impacted by societal inequities outside of school (Hughes et al., 2005).

Racializing Crime: A Case of Coloniality and the Educational Racial Contract

White administrators continue to be the numeric majority in the educational leadership pipeline (Smith, 2016). Many of these white administrators subscribe to race neutrality and avoid race-conscious responses to race-based inequities in their schools. In response, we draw on the traditions of coloniality and the educational racial contract to describe disciplinary practices applied to Black students at different levels of schooling and society.

Race and Discipline at the Societal Level

At the societal level, research has shown that the stratifying effects of school discipline are a byproduct of zero-tolerance policies across the country that have disproportionately impacted Students of Color (Skiba, 2014). The enforcement of these policies has prioritized pedagogical brutality in the form of control-oriented models of education, legitimizing the notion of criminality amongst Students of Color through suspensions, expulsions, and arrests (Delgado, 2020). Importantly, these zero-tolerance policies have militarized schools by increasing security personnel and police presence (Delgado, 2020). The well-worn framework of disproportionality in school discipline has minimized the role of white supremacy in its deployment and implementation, especially in contexts where disciplinary actions and achievement outcomes co-construct white superiority and the inferiority of racialized populations.

The racial construction of the criminal also inversely fabricates the concept of white innocence. This good/evil dialectic is a part of how coloniality plays out in constructing a knowledge system for how Black males should be seen by school personnel, which often leads to self-fulfilling prophecies of criminality. Such modes of knowledge production are conditions of the coloniality of power, defined in this chapter as the psychological classification of races that provides the norms and reasonings to differentiate the human from the subhuman, the innocent from the criminal, and the victim from the predator (Quijano, 2000). This coloniality of power requires governing knowledge systems, such as schools, to socialize people to categorically construct biological race as a probable cause for criminalization and incarceration.

When these expectations of racial difference are carried over to adulthood, they become knowledge systems that justify how citizens are treated by society. Statistically, Black Americans are five times more likely than white Americans to experience traffic stops, brutality, and incarceration (Wagner & Kopf, 2015). The recent police killings of Black Americans without cause have sparked global outrage, galvanizing the Black Lives Matter movement (Rickford, 2016). In 2020, many white people joined widespread protests to challenge the racist police treatment of Black people (Harmon & Burch, 2020), creating urgent conditions for white administrators to respond to a historical moment with anti-racist leadership.

Race and Discipline at the School Level

At the school level, the divergent application of safety and disciplinary measures for differing populations can be explained through Leonardo's (2013) concept of the educational racial contract. In this contract, white students are provided an education that recognizes the importance of their intellectual and physical safety, while racialized populations are educated through exclusionary discipline. In schools, the educational racial contract perpetuates the superiority–inferiority dialectic through ability classifications, test scores, and school ranking to hierarchically delineate deserving students from undeserving substudents, despite schools' codes of conduct and disciplinary policies appearing race-neutral, fair, and universally beneficial on the surface.

As managers of the educational racial contract, white school administrators need to breach the contractual expectations that subjugate Students of Color to the school-to-prison pipeline. McMahon's (2007) study indicates that white administrators often conceive social justice uncritically, believe that racism is an individual act without understanding its connection to settler colonialism, and prefer celebrations of diversity to interrogating and transforming the existing racial structure. We have also observed similar patterns with aspiring school administrators in educational leadership programs, which often conceive race as a social category, a data point for reviewing student achievement, or an indicator of different origins and cultures. Seldom do these administrators see themselves as raced or understand how their personhood is defined and redefined over time "in opposition to and conjunction with other races" (McMahon, 2007, p. 687).

Race and School Discipline at the Classroom Level

At the classroom level, research shows that teachers frequently attribute white students' "behavioral problems" to mere situational factors while treating those of Black students as innate and dispositional (Jackson, 2002). Further, teachers are more likely to exaggerate Black males' verbal and physical expressions, subjugating them to lowered educational expectations and harsher punishments than white students, females, and other racialized populations (Gregory et al., 2010). In a study involving first-grade students, researchers found that teachers were more likely to hold negative perceptions of Black students and their families, influencing their perceptions of those students' intellectual capabilities (Hughes et al., 2005) and sowing distrust between families and schools (Delgado, 2020). Such classroom practices tend to escalate hostility and perpetuate anti-Black learning environments (Gregory et al., 2010). Despite recognizing these persistent dynamics, white teachers often minimize the role of race and racism in police brutality (Alvarez & Milner, 2018).

Race and School Discipline at the Student Level

At the student level, the literature reveals that young people often perceive their teachers' disciplinary practices as racist and inequitable (Carter Andrews & Gutwein, 2020). These racialized expectations subjugate a disproportionate number of Black students to a substandard education, wherein the system imposes a structure and culture of disbelief about these students' academic capabilities (Liou et al., 2019). As adults, Black Americans later encounter similar expectations with the criminal "justice" system (Nadal et al., 2017), reinforcing the multiple ways they are criminalized as a population in a racialized society.

It is clear that the zero-tolerance policies are untenable in serving the interests of Black males. Vavrus and Cole (2002) contend, "Removing a student from class is a highly contextualized decision based on subtle race and gender relations that cannot be adequately addressed in school discipline policies" (p. 87). Students who frequently face disciplinary actions are more likely to be placed in low-expectation classrooms or pushed out of school in ways that further subjugate them to the possibilities of juvenile detention and adult incarceration (Okonofua et al., 2016). Though some administrators may insist that the intent of these actions is not race or gender related, it is important to consider how students interpret and experience the patterns of such expectations and practices (Weinstein, 2002).

As a part of the white supremacist knowledge system, deficit assumptions about Black males are epistemic distortions that many white Americans have come to internalize. They manifest these distortions by becoming agents for the educational racial contract, denying the salience of race and the construction of whiteness. To work toward decoloniality, we posit that white Americans must internally examine their history and socialization as white people, decenter Eurocentric beliefs, and abandon posts of colonial administration. Recent research with liberatory stances has called for epistemic justice through community-centric leadership (Liou & Liang, 2020), illuminating the importance of administrators establishing conditions of confidence and compassion to reinforce the humanity of all students (Lomotey & Lowery, 2015).

Palomino Elementary School: The Case Study

Palomino Elementary School offers services from kindergarten to the eighth grade and is located in a predominately Latinx neighborhood in a large city in Arizona. There is a history of racial and economic stereotyping about the level of safety in the community, despite more recent neighborhood gentrification. The mission of the school is to provide innovative learning opportunities, family engagement, and community partnerships through technology, with the support of safe and nurturing environments to promote student success. Of the 643 students, 574 are Latinx, 30 are Black, 3 are Native American, 2 are Pacific Islander, 6 are multiracial, and 19 are white. The school district provides guidelines for disciplinary actions that categorize different behaviors and offenses, plus procedures for repeated violations. Individual schools can also impose additional consequences through site-based disciplinary programs.

Adam is a white male who grew up in rural Michigan. As a child, he became aware of the role of race and racism after seeing how the very first Black student in his elementary school was treated differently than other children. Years later, he started working toward anti-racist education through his role as a teacher and curriculum leader. As a first-time assistant principal, his primary responsibility was to manage school safety and discipline at Palomino, which is known for racial disproportionality in discipline actions. During his first year as an assistant principal, the school had a total of forty-five disciplinary incidents in a year shortened due to the Covid-19 pandemic. Of the students involved in these incidents, thirty-two were males, nine Black and twenty-three Latino. In the next section, Adam describes his leadership experiences and how disciplinary actions were implemented at Palomino.

As a white person, I (Adam) strive to acknowledge the salience of white privilege in society and have been actively working to develop my own race consciousness. My experiences in the university-based educational leadership program helped formulate my view that anti-racist leadership is not a destination but a journey, knowing that I am far from perfect in putting my beliefs into action. As an aspiring anti-racist, I am sharing my story to challenge pervasive assumptions of race-neutrality among white administrators and to open myself to suggestions for growth from other anti-racist leaders.

In all disciplinary cases at Palomino, I intentionally examined each scenario through a lens of race consciousness, especially since Palomino's majority white and Latinx teaching force uses racially coded words to describe students. As I soon learned, Aaron a Black eigth-grader had previous disciplinary incidents, enough that the former administrator wanted him expelled. Aaron's family felt that these actions were racially motivated and not transparent, as they were never notified or consulted about their son's education until they received a certified letter reassigning him to the district's alternative school.

On my first day as assistant principal, Aaron and his parents came to discuss his school reassignment. I listened carefully and tried to understand how Aaron had been unfairly treated in the past. I then explained my beliefs and values and committed to a fresh start with Aaron remaining at Palomino. From there, I introduced Aaron to other Black educators who helped plan to reintegrate him, and they eventually developed sustained relationships with his family. Mr. Chambers, a white male first-year principal assigned to Palomino after a long history working in the district, joined me to meet with Aaron and his parents for the next few months. We had honest conversations about race and talked through how they, as a Black family, had reached their breaking point with how

Aaron and his older brothers had been treated unfairly by white and Latinx members of our staff and community. I made efforts to connect with Aaron about video games, and we bonded over the fact that we were both introverts. Despite this fresh start, Aaron's teachers continued to doubt him and questioned his return to campus.

A few months into the school year, I was approached by a student named Maria, a seventh-grade Latina who had just finished serving lunch detention. She reported that Aaron, who had been in the same detention, had threatened to shoot her with a gun he had brought to school. I quickly scanned the area for Aaron, pulled Maria to the side, and contacted the school principal. As Maria described the situation, we saw Aaron and followed him into a classroom. We requested that he join us in the hallway and discovered a handgun in his belt.

During the previous four months, Aaron had never displayed any aggressive behaviors at school and only had two lunch detentions for incomplete homework. In fact, Mr. Chambers and I felt that Aaron was fully cooperative, and we also trusted that Aaron was not going to hurt us. The situation deescalated quickly due to the relational work we had committed to prior to the incident. Since the three of us knew and trusted each other, we intuitively understood the most productive way to work with Aaron.

Per district protocol, the police were contacted and came to the school to investigate. The district also instructed us to wait for the police to arrive before contacting Aaron's parents. During this time, Aaron's feeling of isolation magnified, as he repeatedly expressed his fears about being misunderstood as a school shooter. Aaron was eventually charged, convicted, and served time in juvenile detention. After serving his time, the district did not allow Aaron to return to Palomino. Aaron and his family were then presented with several options to continue his education in the district, and eventually he was reassigned to the alternative school. It was not until then that we learned that Aaron had brought his father's gun to school to "look cool" after Maria and her friends made him feel excluded as the racial Other.

In retrospect, Aaron's story is a classic tale of coloniality and the educational racial contract. Since the district's disciplinary policies and procedures are based on society's laws and values, the incident quickly escalated into a criminal case. Once the district was notified that there was a gun on campus, the situation rapidly spiraled from a relationship-based intervention into a practice of zero tolerance without regard for Aaron's needs and right to due process.

By activating the educational racial contract through the disciplinary protocol, the assumptions made about Aaron's criminality minimized any concern for his wellbeing, as he was treated to a pedagogy of enforcement, brutality, and isolation. As he observed the reversion to the educational racial contract, Aaron seemed to become fearful of the adults who purported to care for him. Importantly, Aaron's fear appeared to infer his awareness about the consequences of being perceived as a school shooter with a probable cause for criminalization and incarceration. As society has repeatedly demonstrated, it only takes one phone call to determine the criminality of Black people. These social agreements are conditions of coloniality, where racist ideologies are deeply embedded in the criminal justice system.

In the principal's office, Aaron was questioned by the police without parental or legal representation. These actions took place after Aaron had already handed over the gun without incident and in the presence of two administrators who did not consider him an imminent threat. By negating due process and allowing the police to talk to Aaron prior to his parents being contacted, the system funneled Aaron to a substandard contract as an undeserving substudent. This disciplinary procedure was punitive instead of restorative, creating the same self-fulfilling prophecy that profiled Aaron into the same mold as society uses for other Black males.

The system's racial construction of Aaron's criminality also inversely fabricated Maria's innocence, which perpetuated society's raced and gendered expectations regarding who has a greater propensity to commit crime. The educational racial contract reproduced the good and evil narrative, as Maria was able to work with a social worker to overcome her distressing experience. However, the good and evil narrative never accurately described the situation, as this case neglected to deconstruct the complexity to rewrite the decolonial educational contract. For example, without further investigating Aaron's motives, it was unclear whether there were other instances in which Aaron was teased and bullied. It was also undetermined whether he had had prior experiences with Maria or if there were unresolved issues with the teachers who did not want him to return to school. The focus on Aaron's single action without examining the larger socio-emotional context that led to his arrest is a prime example of the educational racial contract delineating a hierarchy between him and Maria.

One of the district administrators wanted to use this incident as a case study with other principals. Questions were raised by some principals about whether the school should have been locked down before approaching Aaron, in order to minimize the risk of someone getting hurt. To effectively use Aaron's story as a case for professional development, a series of discussions concerning the reality of coloniality and the educational racial contract would need to take place, drawing on restorative frameworks to reconstruct a justice-based, decolonial educational contract with students and families. Since then, the district has revisited the idea of having anti-racist professional development for the school community. However, Adam and the school principal felt the district's approach would reinforce zero-tolerance policies and teachers' and staff's deficit conceptions of Black students. For this reason, they steered the district away from having such discussions in the school and are now navigating the system to address these issues from critical perspectives. Without these professional development sessions, Palomino is currently stuck with the status quo, sustaining the educational racial contract.

Despite Adam's efforts to acknowledge Aaron's painful experiences and set high expectations for Aaron to do well in school, Aaron still bumped up against the educational racial contract. Through this process of dehumanization, Aaron was also denied an education, as he spent an excessive amount of time away from the classroom, including the time he served at the juvenile detention center. The denial of access to an equitable education is a condition of coloniality that racialized populations continue to experience. The combination of disciplinary actions and loss of instructional time co-constructed the power relationships between the district, the school administrators, the police, and Aaron.

Implications for Leadership Preparation and Practice

This chapter presents the story of a white administrator and his interactions with Aaron as the basis to explore how white anti-racist allies can confront white supremacy in sincere and explicit ways. We learned that there were multiple factors that contributed to Aaron's disciplinary outcomes, shaped by societal expectations of Black males bestowed upon them at an early age. Aaron's story is far too common. Despite the best intentions of the administrators in this case, their expectations at the individual level bumped up against the expectations of the system. We acknowledge that administrators are often only the managers and not always positioned to rewrite the system. However, we believe that a critical mass of anti-racist administrators can help to enact a different reality with students that is restorative and humane.

Through Young and Laible's (2000) notions of anti-racist leadership, we contend that breaching the contractual expectations of race and criminality requires school administrators to attend to whiteness as a social system, understand the inner workings of each person's participatory role in white supremacy, and commit to actions that oppose the perpetuation of the educational racial contract. We emphasize that there must be an epistemic transformation in the ways administrators decenter colonial methods of enacting discipline and punishment. In retrospect, Adam wishes that he had had more in-depth training on ways to be an anti-racist educator at the university. He reflects:

> My teacher education program never talked about issues of race, deficit thinking, and low expectations of students. My school principal used to tell me that Ruby Payne was the best. Reflecting on Aaron's case, I realized that I need to be a catalyst in starting anti-racist dialogue and action at all levels of Palomino.

As a starting point to challenge the coloniality of power in the system, decolonial and anti-racist leadership must reposition students' humanity at the center of disciplinary practices through political sympathy and solidarity. At the core of these leadership practices are four expectations serving as the basis for school discipline: (1) develop intimate knowledge of students and their race, class, gender, and immigration history; (2) enact sympathy as a condition of political solidarity to facilitate caring relationships and students' community cultural wealth; (3) form connections based on relational equity and political empowerment to counteract the realities of white supremacy; and (4) utilize positive expectations to prepare students for a more equitable future through academic rigor (Liou & Liang, 2020).

School administrators should recognize that disciplinary actions are systems of racialized representation of institutional values and priorities. To truly rewrite the educational racial contract, we believe families should be key participants in the construction of school disciplinary policies. School administrators need to utilize the expertise of families in communities of color to develop a range of asset-based, restorative practices for school discipline. Families should be fully involved in the decision-making processes leading to the restoration of classroom practices that move us toward higher forms of educational expectations. Family members' presence on campus can help to support students in ways that are humanistic and culturally reaffirming.

Understanding the Racialized Organization: African-centered Leadership and Their Unique Form of Culturally Responsive Leadership

Bodunrin O. Banwo and Muhammad Khalifa

When viewing the position of schools as social institutions of society, it provides a lens to explore the theory behind the legal and organizational realities we are asking children to participate in. Handel (2006) observes these systems as agents of socialization that are used by communities to "shape the behaviors and values of the less powerful members of our society" (p. 400). Additionally, scholars like Handel view this process as a foundation for the social construction of cultural identity, theorizing that social institutions are tasked with transmitting traditions and values the broader society deemed necessary and vital for preservation. Take, for example, Berger and Luckmann's (1967) idea of social constructionism and its understanding that societies organize themselves through intimate relationship formations defining and limiting the boundaries of what is acceptable behavior.

For us, we see a failure of leaders to grapple with how ideologies of racial expropriation and culture enter our formal systems and define how students experience its cultural productions (Wilderson III, 2018). Watkins (2001) and Apple (2004) are among the many scholars who regard the concealment and underestimation of ideology as our society failing to see or care about how notions like "social constructionism" are operationalized as an apparatus to control weaker members of our community. Moreover, particularly for Watkins, this concealment serves as the machinery by which the dominant members of our society reproduce and influence the social roles Berger and Luckmann (1967) see playing out. For example, **Social Scripts**, "A series of behaviors, actions, and consequences that are expected in a particular situation or environment" (Linton, 1936; Mead, 1934), and **Inequality Regimes**, "interrelated practices, processes, actions, and meanings that result in and maintain class, gender, and racial inequalities within particular organizations" (Acker, 2006, p. 443), are both critical theories scholars like Apple believe must be acknowledged and challenged.

At the center of the discourses around social constructionism and race is a series of "why" ideas that function as jumping-off points for leaders and thinkers interested in taking up the mantle of anti-racist educational leadership. How does society reproduce race? Why does society reproduce race? Most notably, for school leaders, for whose benefit is to racialize productions occurring? These questions of "why" are equally picked up and advanced by leaders of organizations that have taken a critical perspective of society, principally how harmful cultural practices and attitudes are privileged, constructed to harm, and determinant of marginalized peoples' life outcomes. Suppose we know from Berger and Luckmann's (1967) research that cultural practices and ideas are replicated, defined, and passed down to future generations. In that case, we also know from researchers like Handel (2006) and March (1991) that social learning and memory can survive through many generations of organizational participants. Then we can assume that organizational "learning" can occur through system practices like "best practice frameworks and historical memoing." If we take this notion from another viewpoint, it can also be seen as a school's capacity to historize saved actions and behaviors into practices, traditions, and ideas as systematic memories (Cyert & March, 1992).

Therefore, we view this chapter as a tool for practitioners to examine how leaders of ethnic schools ideologically shape their practice and culture through a process of *Organizational Inquiry*. Moreover, these leaders view these political inquiries as a method to root out negative histories and practices of institutional white supremacy found in many of our formal organizations. African-centered school leaders' anti-racist practice of questioning mainstream culture through a historical and racialized critique creates an organizational process of exploration designed to take up the unexamined social and organizational ideologies formed within Western cultural *milieus* of white supremacy. Cultures of bigotry and exclusions are not spontaneous phenomena for these leaders; on the contrary, culture is planned, replicated, defined, and passed down to future generations, who are then socialized into it as a societal project. This belief requires African-centered leaders to take up the mantle of social constructionism and confront race within systems through a public-facing political project of acknowledging people racialized and marginalized into particular life experiences.

We explore African-centered leaders' anti-racist approach to learning in two sections of ethnographic vignettes (from the first author's perspective) and a conclusion. The first section will consider a new organizational and leadership concept entitled *Ethno Cultural Responsiveness*, which we see as a hyper-focused leadership practice approach that is purposefully responsive to an ethnic or social community's needs and problems. This theory will help mainstream leaders understand how their leadership is a form of *Cultural Artisanry* that gives them an ability to cultivate and construct their organizational culture from an ideological lens—similar to how an artist cultivates art from an idea in their imagination. This section demonstrates how African-centered school leaders create organizational inquiry processes designed to root out harmful social practices of white supremacy that they find entering their unique school organization from the outside dominant cultural *milieu*.

Section two will examine the uniqueness of centering Africana ideology as the imagined ideal of an organization, mainly how a public political and ideological inquiry can help mainstream school leaders understand how ideology can be disrupted and repackaged for everyone. Much of this work will be done within the Asantain (1991) notion of "Afrocentricity," which we conceive as a process of authentic Black cultural development. For Asante and this chapter, culture is a social-relational development based in history and ideology, requiring Afrocentricity practitioners to begin and proceed with Africa as the center and not on the periphery of learning (Schiele, 1994).

What makes Asante's Afrocentricity concept in education so potentially liberating for anti-racist practitioners is the notion of examining alternative histories, cultures, and communities at the organizing center of schools. This work is not about the efficacy of Black Nationalism and Pan Africanism, which we feel is a promising educational model for healthy Black socialization; it is more about how non-mainstream educational leaders examine and alter their organizational culture and transform it into an instrument of social liberation. Although African-centered schools concentrate on facilitating healthy Black social bonds, their governing practice can still be useful for leaders interested in unmasking harmful values and practices that regulate the experiences of their marginalized students. There is much knowledge in African-centered schools when it comes to an understanding of how to combat harmful social histories and practices. We can learn from this model if only we are willing to listen.

Organizational Artistry as Social Exploration and Disruptive

During one of my last visits to an African-centered school, we entered the school gym where Baba Nicholes was talking to the second- and third-grade students after their morning ritual. I would come to understand that this flexible time in many African-centered schools (time between morning rituals and the start of their formal education day) was a time used by teachers and staff to have conversations with students about Black life. In the schools I visited, this time was used to discuss bullying, loving, and caring for each other, healthy ways to disagree, community violence, healthy social responses to neighborhood concerns, police brutality, and many more concerns that affect the students. However, today, the students were discussing their upcoming science fair.

Baba Nicholes asked the students if they had brought in glass jars for the science fair. Most had not. He would later tell me during one of our conversations that *"we wanted to demonstrate to them (the students) that this science fair was their project, and they were responsible for the items that were needed."* He would in the moment, reiterate to the students the importance of how this event was a celebration of their intellectual work, that it was their opportunity to demonstrate Umoja (Unity) ending with, " ... *We either win together, or we fail together, either way, we will be together."*

(Banwo, 2020, p. 210)

Ethno-cultural Responsiveness

When we present this work to audiences who are not familiar with African-centered schools, we get comments about how multiethnic and multiracial schools are unable to center race and differences in the way African-centered schools can. Although this may be true for some, the question we put to these leaders is to think about how their school engages currently with marginalized students. How would they, if they could transform their organization into a place that focuses, like a laser beam, on students they view "most at risk?"

Mazrui and Levine (1986) describe cultures on the African continent as a trinity of cultures (ways of being) and values that emphasize "closeness to nature, familial ties, and religion" that have served to bind populations and ethnic groups throughout greater Africa. Furthermore, Mazrui and other Africana scholars perceive these African cultural connections as extending beyond Africa's physical landmass into the broader African diaspora. These scholars viewed this extension as a bridge that creates an imagined cultural connection, similar to Anderson's (1983) conceptualization of an Imagined Community. We contend that the *Imagined African-centered community* is a cornerstone and theoretical framework for approaching the phenomena of African-centered schools and is the basis and rationale needed to understand how and why African-centered leaders do what they do.

Ethno-cultural Responsiveness is our understanding that an organization can be both hyper-focused and responsive to an imagined community's needs and concerns. We understand these organizations as hyper-focused on cultural practices that socialize younger members into an imagined community with goals and ideology. Moreover, we regard it as the instrument by which agents of the imagined community reproduce their ideological and political projects through intentional organizational cultural artistry (picking and choosing what will enter the organizations). For example, the democratic school model seeks to incorporate emancipatory practices in its pedagogical approach or single-gendered schools aim to make right past gendered wrongs, and African-centered systems desire to grapple with a search for care and belonging that many Africans in the West find themselves undertaking.

African-centered schools have an emphasis on groupness. Look back to the earlier story of Baba Nicholes, "*We either win together, or we fail together, either way, we will be together.*" This is the ideology driving the political goals and operation of the organization. The Baba and his school are using the organization's apparatuses to socialize the students into a position that best encourages healthy Black social relations, a fundamental goal for the school. Everyone involved, students, teachers, parents, and administrators, has to be a voluntary member of this organization because it is so politically and ideologically different from the individualist ethos governing mainstream schools and society. Mainstream schools are also acting out this process; however, we contend their political ideology is obscured as normal or "just the way WE do business here." Moreover, we theorize that since each organizational participant in mainstream schools tacitly accepts the ideological rules, like in ethno-organizations, leaders can claim Europeanness as normal and thus blunt true cultural responsiveness because fundamentally, the leaders are acting on pressure from the most dominant social members of the organization.

Space for the Marginalized

Khalifa et al.'s (2016) framework of culturally responsive school leadership (CRSL) and the idea of "responsiveness" occurring in four areas of the framework (critically self-reflects on leadership behaviors, develops culturally responsive teachers, promotes culturally responsive/inclusive school environment, and engages students, parents, and indigenous contexts) speak to how school leaders who are interested in creating room for marginalized students have to undergo an organizational process that seeks to create a space for the marginalized. If we look at African-centered schools, transformational actions are occurring through leadership that centers marginalized students' culture and traditions in a space that is customarily dominated by European-centered ways of doing.

However, like Khalifa et al.'s framework suggests, African-centered leaders' process of deep ideological and system inquiry is the only way a school can discover and learn how European-centered ways of doing inform traditions of education and organizational ecology. If you look at Figure 7.1, you can see how we envision Ethno-cultural Responsiveness playing out in an organization. The figure is a closed cultural network, represented by a solid lined box surrounding its activities. At the core of the chart is a porous box representing the *Imagined Cultural Ideal* for organizational participants in the closed system. You can see by the arrows how culture radiates out from the center into every aspect of the organization.

This imagined ideal is the prototypical (or normative) "way of being" for the organizational citizens and is defined by the imagined community's ideological and constructivist feedback work. Khalifa et al. are correct that multiracial systems are being controlled by a dominating ideology, which is indeed serving as policing agents and gatekeepers to organizational resources. However, what do you call a closed, homogenous system, where leaders are hyper-vigilant and aware of cultural concerns and issues? We theorize these leaders are practicing a

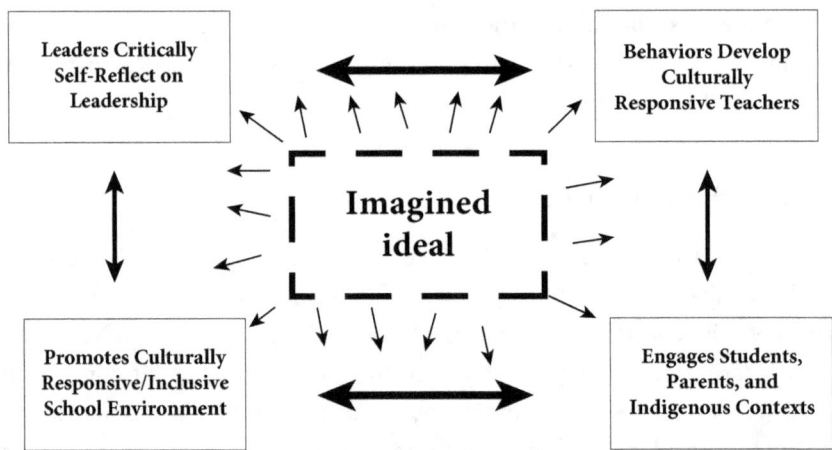

Figure 7.1 Responsive school leadership defined by the imagined cultural ideal.

form of *Ethno-culturally Responsive School Leadership* that is being used to adjust the organization in directions that serve to erase interpersonal concerns among the network participants and broader social concerns entering the organization from a dominant outside force.

Let us return to the school featured at the beginning of this section. We spoke to a student named Justin, who described participating in two days of an all-school and community conversation about bullying and familiar relationships during our research. What was unknown to Justin was that this stoppage in academic learning was not a random occurrence. On the contrary, it was a deliberate and focused community-building practice intentionally implemented by his school's leadership. The leaders of Biko Charter (the school featured) sensed their "organizational culture" required intervention because of what they saw as troubling social behavior entering their organizational culture. Remember, for African-centered schools, building healthy Black social bonds around collectivism is a fundamental goal for Black liberation. So when a breakdown in interpersonal relationships happened, the school had to pause for the day and address that organizational concern because in the words of one school leader, "we cannot permit a pattern of harmful and traumatizing behaviors to interfere with our goal of healthy Black connections and building healthy black communities."

According to Lomotey (1993), there is something dynamic happening with Black educational leaders and their ability to utilize their unique cultural positionality to display culturally responsive school sensitivity. However, and more to the overall topic, the Black leaders in Lomotey's research were able to use their historical and cultural awareness of organizational shortfalls to improve marginalized students' lives. As we close this section, we want to reiterate that mainstream schools are awash in obscured and normalized political behaviors that serve to reproduce the system we are currently living in (May & Finch, 2009). Conversely, we believe that multiracial and multiethnic system leaders can enact *Ethno-cultural Responsiveness*.

However, we regard this process as fraught with challenges because mainstream leaders will have to navigate decades of marginalization, social attitudes, and pushback from dominant organizational members. Nevertheless, if they can construct a culture that unites their disparate cultural constituents into a shared "imagined culture and ideal," we believe they can achieve this organizational state. So, in the end, when we are presenting this work to audiences who are unfamiliar with ethno-cultural responsiveness, we tell them to unite around a culture that imagines everyone as equal, loved, and cared about through having clear political and ideological goals centered in their organizational ideal.

Ideological and Organizational Inquiry for Leaders

The construction of an *Imagined African-centered community* as a framework helps us understand how these schools exist in contradistinction to mainstream schools, particularly in how they ideologically approach marginalized students' social development. Moreover, the context of an *Imagined community* allows leaders to see how the unmasking of society's social cleavages (marginalized students being *othered* in mainstream schools) can abstract forms of difference to highlight racial trauma and organizational violence. For instance, each leader interviewed for this chapter has a unique morning ceremony that serves to open their institutional day.

Although morning traditions and rituals are not new to education systems, they are, in the case of African-centered schooling, an intentional organizational praxis constructed and shaped wholly to socialize students into a particular ideological outlook. Leadership uses their intentional morning rituals and traditions as a tool of ideological orientation and group care, helping to connect students to their teachers, elders, and to a broader notion of what Anderson (1983) described as an imagined community. The students see themselves as a family and understand themselves as community members with responsibilities for the larger group's success. Take another example, Justin, the student from section one, realizing that his school is a place he can be vulnerable in a world that traditionally socializes Black males to avoid feelings of vulnerability or feelings altogether (Curry, 2017).

Organizational Inquiry

There are ideological and structural questions leaders can ask themselves when shaping their organizational culture around ideas of healthy social relationships and social bonds. African-centered leaders have to engage in a battle to combat histories and echoes of oppression through a political and ideological doctrine. We are often frustrated working with mainstream school leaders when they cannot conceptualize that within their organization is an intentionally crafted idea of community and place that has significance in the broader society. Indeed we regard mainstream school leaders' lack of intervention through "a systematic examination" into every aspect of their organization as leaving their marginalized members at risk for continued social harm (Asante, 1991; Monteiro-Ferreira, 2014).

We call this intervention an *Organizational Inquiry*, and it is here African-centered leaders define their political, social, and ideological doctrine into the more extensive system. Moreover, it is here where African-centered leaders intentionally decide, with an ideological and political goal, on school structure, language, and culture. They ideologically see all the critical ideas and practices as essential to rooting out historical harm from Black children's schooling experience. We contend this practice for African-centered schools is intentional; however, for mainstream schools, we submit these practices are unintentionally happening because of leaders' lack of deliberate focus on ideologies and politics (power and resource distribution) of histories of white supremacy. In other words, the dominant culture from outside of the organization is allowed to enter the formal organization uncontested with its racial baggage and hangups, further defining how racialized and marginalized people are to be treated without any pushback.

We further argue that the social reproduction of white supremacy (Social Scripts and Inequality Regimes) is mainstream schools mimicking their surrounding social doctrines. African-centered schools have a unique perspective because their model calls for a process of (de)Europification, which is undertaken through an intentional practice of organizational inquiry. This deliberate political practice allows educational leaders to fully gauge and process how pervasive practices and ideas of white supremacy have entered and embedded itself into their system. There are ideological and structural questions African-centered leaders ask themselves when shaping their organizational culture around ideas of healthy Black social relationships and social bonds.

They understand that the Black community's familial bonds in the United States have been defined by horrifying histories of capitalist exploitation, from slavery to convict leasing to Jim Crow to now the foster care and mass incarceration systems. Moreover, leaders of Black organizations that are defined and centered around healthy Black social relations have to ask themselves a series of questions that help them define how their organization will necessitate the disruption of race and racism. Although there were countless items asked, we found these three general themes leaders used to frame their organizational inquiry.

They ask,

1. Why are we doing this practice or technique? Where does it originate?
2. How will this help in the liberation of African peoples?
3. Moreover, how will this improve Black social relationships?

For African-centered leaders, schooling is not just about learning academically. It is also about coming to terms with the history and the harm that has echoed through the ages. History for African-centered schools is seen and used as a tool to demystify racialized jargon and practices. Students who attend African-centered schools have no illusions of the Black historical experience and how that experience connects to Black America's current position (Piert, 2015). There are no myths of America being taught here, only the hard truth of what Blackness has meant in the United States, and most critically for the leaders, what Blackness was before Blackness was even a racialized concept.

Cultural Responsiveness through Organizational Inquiry

Let us look at Figure 7.2, which we have created as a visual conception and framework of an organizational inquiry, core, and imagined cultural ideal. Figure 7.2's components are informed by Bills et al.'s (2017) research on school leadership surround the organizational core, containing the imagined ideal. The ideological and political work of the imagined ideal is, in turn, released into every aspect of the school's operations. In the organizational core, leaders wrestle with the fundamental ideological and structural questions (organizational inquiry) that radiate out into school. Below is a brief description

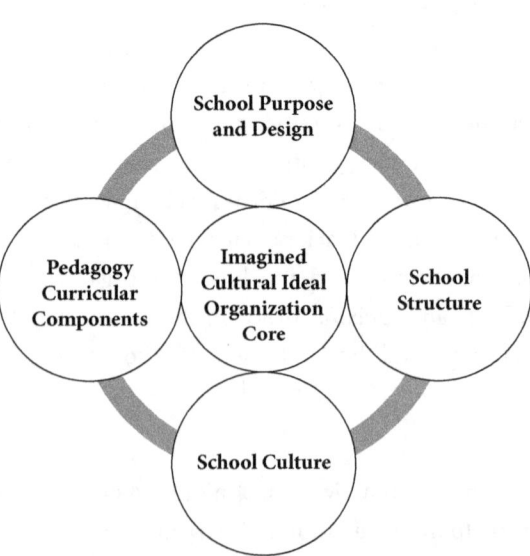

Figure 7.2 Responsive school leadership defined by the imagined cultural ideal.

of how we observed African-centered leaders' thinking and conceptualizing of their leadership, using Bills et al.'s framework components from interviews and observations.

School Purpose and Design

The purpose of African-centered schools is to address a particular historical wrong with a reimagining of schooling coupled with the politics of Black Nationalism. When looking at the communities that conceive these institutions, we see places grounded in a type of Black radical tradition that acknowledges the political nature of Black childhood, Black socialization, and the communities' desire for political and social agency.

School Structure

We witnessed in African-centered schools that organizational culture is grounded in methods that value collectivism and social cohesion. These schools serve to socialize Black children into a healthy sense of self and self-efficacy. Sounds of children collaborating, drums playing, and familiar African rhythmic cultural sounds permeate the halls. The students address adults as "Mama and Baba"; every day, the schools perform rites and rituals that help to develop the organizational identity. For example, one of the schools we visited has an open school model. According to the school leader, this model allows the school to reinforce their ideological goal of students' relationship-building through collaboration, spontaneous conversation, and learning. During this institution's conception, the leadership intentionally selected this structural model because it best paired with their central goals of healthy Black social relations.

School Culture

While observing a class, we witness a teacher connect her math lesson on integers to twentieth-century Black female mathematicians. According to the teacher, racism and sexism prevented both mathematicians from fully excelling in their chosen careers and fields and "should serve as a reason" for the students to understand how bigotry and sexism can put up walls to success, but because these women had a strong community backing them, they were able to overcome dead ends. The teacher with this lesson was demonstrating to the students that they were not "just" individual actors in the world, and racism and bigotry should not exempt or prevent anyone from not aiming to be successful or helpful to the larger community.

School Pedagogical/Curricular Components

You can see in the earlier section that the teacher's pedagogical approach to the classroom and school culture formulation centers on strengthening and privileging social-relational development. In our opinion, classroom time is the most valuable thing a teacher possesses, and, interestingly, during the lesson featured, the teacher connected the academic instruction to the significances of healthy Black social relationships. This intentional organizational practice and leadership demonstrate how the African-centered approach to education uses their role as crafters of pedagogy and curriculum to develop within students a deep affinity for camaraderie and partnership between Black students, history, and community.

Conclusion: Anti-racist Leadership That Disrupts

The social challenge that ethnic schools raise in our society is that of radical social democracy in the sense that it shines an unwanted light onto Western understandings of the humanity of people with dark skin. These schools are critiques of Western organizations and their inability to forcefully and healthily create inclusive and caring locations for all children. In our opinion, the social challenge of our time is to confront the complicity of our formal systems in institutionalizing social scripts of harm. For us, as scholars interested in the process of how leaders shape organizations, we pay care to how odious practices of tradition, normality, and just "plain and simple" organizational inertia forward social scripts that continue tendencies and trajectories of racialized social realities.

Scholar Julius Nyerere (1961) spoke about African communitarian power as an ancestral inheritance going back millennia on the African continent. Moreover, he also believed the communitarian power of care is also the inheritance of all peoples. We all can trace our lineage back to communities of communitarians concerned with the broader community's survival and justness. Forging collectivist practices requires us to reexamine how our social systems constitute adverse ways of comportment for some people. Moreover, African-centered thinkers believe for true multiculturalism to arise, the universality of eurocentrism must be challenged. They believe that marginalized cultures must assert themselves into the space reversed as a social commons.

Multiculturalism means "many"; yet for many students of color in schools, this truth fails to materialize, which directs them to what we see as "harm and danger" of passively participating in a system that does not value their cultural contribution to the fabric of America. Ethnic educational scholarship is an unmasking of race's hiddenness in our racialized culture by emphasizing the deconstruction of society's underlying premises and its formalized organizations. It is a way for minority members to take their place in the community on an even ground, which, in the end, is what culturally responsive leadership is asking for understanding and space for the complexities of lived experience and culture to flourish.

Part III

Community Engagement, Activism, and Anti-racist Educational Leadership

8

Aligning Frameworks and Identifying Capacities for Anti-racist Advocacy Educational Leadership

Michelle D. Young and Angel Miles Nash

The American school-age population has always been diverse across race, cultural background, language, gender, socio-economic status, religion, and additional differences. Furthermore, our nation's school leaders have long struggled in their attempts to meet the social, educational, and developmental needs of students who are not white, protestant, and middle or upper class.

Many models have been put forward for effective school leadership, including models focusing on effectively supporting diverse student populations. In 2000, Riehl theorized about the practice of multicultural leadership and identified three key leadership tasks: fostering new meaning about diverse student populations, promoting inclusive instruction, and building connections between schools and communities. More recent conceptualizations of inclusive, social justice, and culturally responsive school leadership argue for shared, distributive, collaborative, and community-based leadership practice (Brooks, 2012). In their effort to define and refine the notion of Culturally Responsive School Leadership (CRSL), Khalifa et al. (2016) emphasized the importance of critical self-reflection, development of culturally responsive teachers, promotion of culturally responsive and inclusive school environments, and engagement of students, parents, and indigenous contexts. It is our contention that these leadership capacities, while essential, are not sufficient for supporting the education of diverse student populations in today's schools. Leaders must be culturally responsive, dedicated to excellence and equity, and must be anti-racist advocates for their students, schools, and communities.

Anti-racist advocacy leadership is an approach to leadership that is practiced by, for, and with one's school community, including students, educational professionals, parents, and community members, especially in low-income communities and those that are stratified by race, language, culture, and social class (Anderson, 2009). The overused image of educational leaders who can make everything right for all student populations regardless of the challenges put in their path, merely by sheer will and moral fortitude, does little to advance equity, social justice (Young, 2019), and anti-racist environments (Diem & Welton, 2021). Research affirms that moving equity-oriented practice from the margin to the center is hard work, requires an infusion of resources, and is often ignited and sustained by a school or district leader who capitalizes on and develops collaborative capacity and leadership toward this end (Theoharis, 2009).

Like Anderson (2009), we intentionally use the term advocacy leadership because we believe a more politicized notion of leadership is needed that acknowledges leaders' responsibility to understand and act in the best interest of their students, staff, and broader school community. To be clear, we are not talking about an occasional trip to visit elected officials or members of the department of education. Anti-racist advocacy leadership is a human-centered, proactive, and collaborative approach to fostering equity and excellence.

In this chapter, we present a conceptual framework for anti-racist advocacy leadership, which is built from a foundational understanding of effective, equitable leadership that includes: anti-racist, equity-oriented, collaborative, culturally responsive, and technically competent instructional leadership practice. Subsequently, we delineate the critical capacities that leaders require in order to embody the characteristics of anti-racist advocacy leadership, including critical reflection, capacity building, strategic thinking, seeing the system, and bricolage. Finally, we discuss the implications of this form of leadership for preparation programs that center anti-racist practices.

Coalescing Frameworks for Anti-racist Advocacy Leadership

Drawing on normative, empirical, and critical literatures, the following integrative review explores the role of advocacy leadership in responding to diverse students' needs and advocating for the resources, school conditions, and supports needed for each and every student to be successful. Specifically, we take a constellated approach to framing anti-racist advocacy leadership, mapping the alignment and overlap between two leadership frameworks—the Ontario Leadership Framework (Leithwood, 2012) and Culturally Responsive School Leadership (Khalifa et al., 2016). We chose these two frameworks in

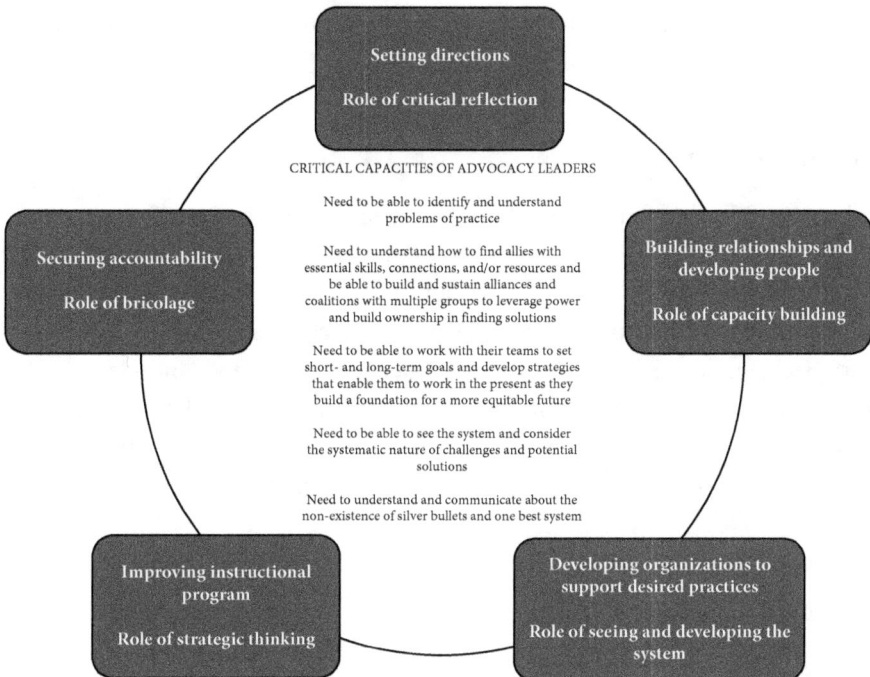

Figure 8.1 Critical capacities of advocacy leaders.

this amalgamation because we believe advocacy should include an integrative approach of strategies that progress an anti-racist agenda. These connections support the subsequent articulation of five critical capacities of advocacy leaders (see Figure 8.1).

Rooted in foundational research explicating the work of school-level leaders, the OLF (Leithwood, 2012) offers data-informed practices for individuals and organizations to improve student outcomes. Of particular importance to advocacy leadership, the updated 2012 OLF acknowledges the importance of: situated and social contexts in which leaders serve; relationships, temperaments, and climate across organizations; flexibility in leaders' responsiveness to events and challenges; leaderships' collective nature; and production of research that demonstrates the connections between leaders' actions and outcomes. Accordingly, the five OLF domains—setting directions, building relationships and developing people, developing organizations to support desired practices, improving instructional program, and securing accountability—were expanded to highlight leaders' actions. The following subsections explore the framework in light of CRSL tenants and the critical capacities of anti-racist advocacy leadership—critical reflection, capacity building, strategic thinking, seeing the system, and bricolage.

Setting Directions

Educational leaders influence schools' student outcomes by setting directions (Hallinger & Heck, 1998). Investigating the relationship between students' reading scores, school context facets, administrators' instructional leadership, and the climate of instruction across eighty-seven elementary schools, Hallinger and Heck found a specified connection between distinctive and clear school missions and the instructional leadership of principals. Further, distinct missions impacted the opportunities to learn that students were afforded and teachers' perspectives on students' academic achievement.

Role of Critical Reflection

A leader's understanding of their positionality and the cultural standing of those with whom they interact influences their ability to establish a well-defined vision for a learning environment (Gooden, 2005; McKenzie et al., 2008). CRSL asserts that developing an in-depth and meaningful command of one's self, and further locating one's work in critical and anti-racist work, requires an honest and continuous exploration of the personal biases, presumptions, expectations, and principles one holds (Gooden & Dantley, 2012; Young & Laible, 2000). Likewise, employing critical self-reflection in an analysis of educators', students', and families' needs and assets, while also acknowledging how leaders' positionality does and does not mirror that of their learning community, helps leaders identify how they need to develop followers' capacities to that all community members are able to work for change from a place of critical self and organizational awareness.

Building Relationships and Developing People

Research demonstrates that principals influence student achievement through engagement with teachers (Hallinger & Heck, 1998; Witziers et al., 2003). This indirect relationship (Hallinger & Heck, 1998) implies the paramountcy of school leaders investing in educational professionals' knowledge and skills (Bredeson & Johansson, 2000). The development and maintenance of healthy engagement promote teacher self-efficacy (Hipp, 1996), reinforce collective efficacy (Kurt et al., 2011), encourage teachers' professional satisfaction (Anderman, 1991), and build the trust needed for educators to engage in collaborative and distributive leadership (Wahlstrom & Louis, 2008).

Role of Capacity Building

Developing a culture of commitment to all learners requires the ability to investigate, plan, and implement a rigorous curriculum. These tasks require significant capacity building. For example, in order to support the establishment and sustainability of culturally responsive pedagogy, educators need professional learning opportunities. Similarly, if school staff are expected to holistically assess and support learners' wellbeing, capacity building is essential. Leaders' understanding of effective, culturally responsive teaching and how to foster it, and their ability to inculcate of a sense of moral responsibility to value students' cultural backgrounds and to build and maintain culturally responsive, anti-racist learning environments are forms of instructional leadership that can and must be developed.

Developing Organizations to Support Desired Practices

The OLF highlights the importance of organizational development aimed at maintaining supportive infrastructures. Essential components include building teachers' collective efficacy, the likelihood of goal attainment given organizations' current capacity, relationships with school community members, and policies that support the school community's well-being. Leithwood (2012) explained the importance of including community stakeholders' perspectives in endeavors to strengthen schools' responsiveness. Reaching beyond leaders who hold formal administrative roles is considered essential to developing a well-rounded understanding of a school's organizational standing and health (Heller & Firestone, 1995; Ogawa & Bossert, 1995). Maintaining schools' infrastructure, and adjusting to contextualized changes, can be shared by community members, including staff, students, and parents.

Role of Seeing and Developing the System

As leaders engage with and share responsibilities with community members in the development of a culturally responsive environments, they build more inclusive ethos. These efforts involve institutional climate transformations to root out oppressive practices embedded throughout systems to create self-reflective and self-correcting spaces that include diverse perspectives and resist deficitized thinking (Kumashiro, 2002). Leaders must *see the system* and think strategically about how a particular problem of practice fits in the system, how it is supported or reinforced by the system, and what leverage there might be to make change. In such contexts, leaders resist inequitable and racist practices that have systemically informed and influenced students' access and resultant success and replace them with strategies that redefine the content and delivery within (Robinson, 2010). By understanding institutions' policies and instructional programs' inner workings, envisioning plans that positively reflect school community members' lived experiences, cultures, and contexts, and promoting and modeling culturally responsive approaches that embrace that milieu, leaders can establish systems that comprise comprehensive, culturally responsive pedagogy and effective instructional programs.

Improving Instructional Programs

Instructional programs include content, pedagogy, expectations and climate, and improving these factors is an essential and critical goal of anti-racist advocacy leadership. This requires leaders to develop instructional climates that transcend norms that have not served all children and to build teachers' commitment to pedagogical excellence rooted in students' experiences (Leithwood, 2012). Establishing a strategy with which all stakeholders can align, entails developing an instructional leadership model that "replaces a hierarchical and procedural notion with a model of *shared* instructional leadership" (Marks & Printy, 2003, p. 371). Concluding their study of 24 restructured public schools, Marks and Printy asserted that shared instructional leadership, when coupled with transformational leadership, resulted in considerable academic achievement and quality student schooling experiences. To create instruction that authentically includes students' cultures, leaders must strategically engage community members, including students, parents, and community stakeholders.

Role of Strategic Thinking

Promoting respectful partnerships with external communities and organizations offers many advantages, including accessing essential knowledge, skills, connections, and resources. Leaders must be able to read the community, think strategically about alliances and engagements, and have the capacity to develop mutually beneficial partnerships. In some cases, leaders may need to build coalitions that leverage resources for their students and in other cases they may choose to align with existing community led advocacy initiatives serving schools and communities writ large (Gooden, 2005; Green, 2015a; Yosso, 2005). This requires the ability to gather and analyze information, work collaboratively to set short- and long-term goals, and develop strategies that enable working in the present as partners build a foundation for a more equitable future. Leaders must develop a shared systemic theory of change—a road map of how they will bridge the gap between where they are and where they want to go. In this work, leaders are called to respect, validate, and model care for communities' cultural epistemologies and behaviors (Horsford et al., 2011) and students' social and cultural capital (Yosso, 2005) and to hold themselves accountable for decision making that advantages students and communities.

Securing Accountability

The educational policy requirements to which administrators and teachers have had to answer have influenced the slow but steady shift in schools' instructional climate from one in which educators were charged with providing a quality education to one in which educators are responsible for student learning outcomes (Young et al., 2017). While states have focused on establishing and maintaining learning standards and subsequent standardized test performance (Harris et al., 2014), anti-racist advocacy leaders reframe accountability as an imperfect tool within their leadership toolbox.

Role of Bricolage

To secure accountability for student learning, leaders need to understand accountability policies and how to use them to achieve outcomes that far surpass scores on a test to include goals for student learning, development, efficacy, and anti-racism. This work requires an entrepreneurial approach, which we refer to as bricolage or improvising with "whatever is at hand" (Levi-Strauss, 1966) to leverage tools of CRSL and improvement (Daly, 2009; Lee & Wong, 2004; Mintrop & Sunderman, 2009; Mintrop & Trujillo, 2007), among others, to design systems and practices that support teaching and learning and communicate progress to relevant stakeholders (Cosner, 2011). Here bricolage involves collecting an array of resources, repurposing the goals and processes of accountability, and engaging teachers, students, families, and communities to advocate and work for equity and excellence.

The Critical Capacities of Advocacy Leaders

Scholarship presented in the previous section helps identify capacities for advocacy leaders. First, advocacy leaders provide excellent and equitable education for all students; their notions of excellence are dependent upon equity. If you do not have equity, your school cannot be excellent. Second, advocacy leaders are human-centered; they care about and collaborate with the communities they serve. Third, advocacy leaders are anti-racist and culturally responsive. They promote an inclusive school climate and "create school contexts and curriculum that respond to the educational, social, political, and cultural needs of students," (Khalifa et al., p. 1278). Fourth, advocacy leaders have strong technical competence as instructional leaders. These four competencies are foundational to the work of advocacy leaders. In other words, one cannot practice advocacy leadership without an equity orientation, collaboration with school communities, culturally responsive leadership practices, and strong instructional leadership skills. However, these essential competencies, alone, will not support anti-racist advocacy leadership practice. That requires additional capacities.

First, advocacy leaders need to be able to identify and understand problems of practice: how to identify their root causes; how to think about, collect and use data; how to use multiple perspectives to critically reflect on and challenge their and others' thinking about problems, symptoms, contexts, conditions, contributing factors, and potential solutions; and how to engage in broad social analysis, while not being paralyzed by it. A good example of this can be pulled from Montgomery County Public Schools. Under the leadership of Jerry Weast, the district's equity audit revealed a link between the allocation of resources, race, and student performance. Based on these findings, they took steps, including the reallocation of district resources that had significant positive results for students of color (Childress et al., 2009).

Second, advocacy leaders need to understand how to find allies with essential skills, connections, and/or resources and be able to build and sustain alliances and coalitions with multiple groups to leverage resources and power. With these allies, they must build common understandings of essential problems of practice, shared visions of the future, and agreements for collaboration and communication. This bundle of competencies is essential to advocacy leadership: bringing people together around a common agenda, building collective capacity and responsibility, and ensuring everyone has the information, knowledge, and skills needed to make substantive contributions support success.

Third, advocacy leaders need to be able to work with their teams to set short- and long-term goals and develop strategies that enable them to work in the present as they build a foundation for a more equitable future (Welton et al., 2018). This includes a shared systemic theory of change—in other words, a road map of how they will bridge the gap between where they are and where they want to go.

Fourth, advocacy leaders need to be able to *see the system* and consider the systematic nature of challenges and potential solutions. Seeing the system is particularly essential to the work of anti-racism as institutional and societal forms of racism are often embedded in institutional and societal policies and practices. Seeing the system enables what Anderson (2009) describes as *policy appropriation*—wherein leaders use existing policies or processes in ways that are not necessarily intended, but enable the community to achieve short- and long-term equity goals.

Fifth, advocacy leaders need to understand and communicate about the non-existence of *silver bullets* and *one best* systems. In a world that promotes instant gratification and demands answers yesterday, this can be challenging. However, while there are no silver bullets, there are processes that can be followed. Equity audits, for example, help uncover patterns of inequity and provide focus for courageous conversations (Green, 2015b, 2017; Skrla et al., 2004). Systems thinking too can assist school communities in understanding the role that processes, conditions, prejudicial beliefs and practices operate system wide to exacerbate the problems they want to solve (Stroh, 2015). Finally, cycles of continuous improvement—including shared goals, strategies, measures, and making adjustments—can enable progressive movement toward greater equity.

Cultivating Anti-racist Advocacy Leaders

Evidence tilts in favor of advocacy leadership (Berkovich, 2014; Green, 2017; Hoffman, 2009; Ishimaru, 2013; Jordan & Wilson, 2015; Khalifa, 2012). As described above, anti-racist advocacy leadership encompasses aspects of social justice leadership, collaborative leadership, culturally responsive leadership, instructional leadership, critical reflection, critical consciousness, multiple perspectives taking, activism, systems thinking, and improvement leadership. However, while extensive, this articulation of competencies is by no means comprehensive. Rather, there are a variety of additional skill sets and strategies anti-racist advocacy leaders need in order to be successful, such as leading, managing, and delegating the development of action teams for specific purposes, developing communication campaigns, and organizing one-on-one house meetings, neighborhood walks, town halls and other forms of community assemblies. Other bolder tactics include vigils, banner hangs, sit-ins, direct action, guerrilla theater, flash mobs, and subvertizements (from: *Beautiful Trouble*; Anderson, 2009; Ishimaru, 2013).

It is important to keep in mind that building these capacities requires more than a focus on content (coalitions) and skills (building coalitions), it also requires what Young et al. (2017) refer to as *critical core propensities*: critical reflection, critical consciousness, and multiple perspective taking. First, critical reflection is a cognitive process that enables one to examine long-held, socially constructed ideas, beliefs, and assumptions about one's experiences (Mezirow, 1991), and scrutinize and analyze power relationships (Merriam et al., 2007). Mezirow (1991) argues that critically reflecting is related to transformative learning because it often begets change or transformation of perspective and an opportunity to self-define and self-value, replacing externally derived images with authentic images (Collins, 1986). Second, critical consciousness is a tool for thinking about education and society on multiple tracks simultaneously. It is the ability to engage in broad social analysis, take a macro-level perspective, which is essential to understanding education and its place in society, think about it strategically, and potentially change it. The third propensity, multiple perspective taking, is the ability and desire to consider issues from a variety of theoretical, experiential, and epistemological perspectives. One's perspective dictates to a large extent, the way one identifies problems, options or solutions one considers, and approaches one chooses to follow. Multiple perspective taking requires pausing and looking carefully through multiple lenses, both individually (e.g., anti-racism) and intersectionally. Doing so enables leaders to better understand problems, issues, and relationships, to check their understanding or tenets, which were formerly accepted as given (Young, 1999). Furthermore, multiple perspective taking enables understanding in new ways.

According to research on community organizing for education, when leaders are not prepared to support and lead advocacy work, they can be significant impediments to meaningful change (Schutz, 2006; Shirley, 1997). Paired with a commitment to anti-racism, appropriate content knowledge and skill building, these three propensities can help develop advocacy leaders who can, in turn, rethink, reimagine, and transcend current systems.

Conclusion

We need leaders who possess a powerful educational and social vision and who have the knowledge, skills, and will to act on these principles to make a significant difference.

(Meier, 2002)

The notion of leadership as apolitical and of principals and superintendents singularly responsible for the work of school leadership, until recently, has been reinforced in US education policy, in leadership evaluation practices, in state and national leadership standards, and in leadership preparation programs. However, this is changing.

Leadership preparation research and development has revealed a significant increase in focus on issues of shared, distributed, and collaborative leadership, on community engagement, and on advocacy, equity, social justice, and anti-racism (Garza & Merchant, 2015; Gooden & Dantley, 2012; Young & Laible, 2000; Young et al., 2017). It has also revealed the use of teaching strategies (e.g., case studies and equity audits) that explicitly focus on understanding the extent to which oppression and prejudice operate through education and society and what can be done to dismantle racism and other forms of oppression.

Even the best educators and principals cannot merely become anti-racist advocacy leaders because they *want* to make a difference; becoming an anti-racist advocacy leader requires engaging in learning and development that is explicitly designed for this purpose. Unfortunately, the skills, knowledge, and competencies that we have shared are not found in the majority of educational leadership development programs, which in some US states are limited by state laws concerning the number of classes and the key concepts covered. In other regions, leadership development programs appear to be engaged in a veritable race to the bottom in terms of requirements in an effort to attract tuition-generating students.

Many principals find themselves working in schools where inequities in opportunities and outcomes are fostered by district and state policies, the inequitable distribution of resources, and broader socioeconomic conditions. Such circumstances are the focus of those who advocate for the development of equity-oriented, socially just, culturally responsive, anti-racist advocacy leaders—leaders who determine challenges and respond with communities in equity-focused change (DeMatthews et al., 2019). Although not a silver bullet for achieving equity and not a guaranteed cure for the cynicism many educators experience today, advocacy leadership offers an opportunity to push through cynicism, to move beyond notions of superhero leaders working in isolation, and instead work collaboratively, critically, strategically, and systematically to dismantle racism and achieve greater equity and social justice.

9

Anti-racist Activist Leadership

Jason Salisbury and Meagan Richard

Introduction

Within this chapter we use data gathered from leaders in Chicago Public Schools (CPS) to illustrate how school leaders' out-of-school activist work can diminish the impacts of racialized community disinvestment by re-centering the school as a hub for the community. We take the focus on principal activism to demonstrate how outside-of-school activism presents as an undertheorized dimension of anti-racist leadership intended to disrupt the deleterious impacts of neoliberal policies on communities of color. For the purposes of this chapter, we understand school leader activism to be community-focused social justice work in which leaders work to address community needs in various ways (Green, 2015b). Chicago, an incubator for racist neoliberal policy, is an ideal setting within which to examine how school leaders respond to destructive neoliberal policies. And, while our data represents just one urban context, it yields understandings for other urban contexts that have experienced similar policies and processes.

Neoliberalism is "an ensemble of economic and social policies, forms of governance, and discourses and ideologies that promote individual self-interest, unrestricted flows of capital, deep reductions in the cost of labor, and sharp retrenchment of the public sphere" (Lipman, 2011, p. 7). In practice, neoliberal policies seek to weaken the public sphere by cutting public expenditures (i.e., public welfare), deregulating industry, and privatizing and marketizing public services (i.e., toll roads, hospitals, electricity, and schools) (Brewer, 2013; Martinez & Garcia, 1997). Scholars have noted that these processes are racialized and occur in the context of racial segregation and discrimination (Lipman, 2015). For example, while proponents claim that privatization should lead to better and more equitable provision of public services, critics of these policies note that privatization follows processes of disinvestment that provide a mechanism through which developers may claim a need to privatize (Harvey, 2005). In particular, disinvestment tends to occur in low-income neighborhoods of color, meaning that people of color are more likely to lose access to affordable housing, health services, public transit, education, and other public services (Harvey, 2005; Lipman, 2011).

However, research has shown that school leaders can address community disinvestment and injustice by integrating community activism into their practice (Anderson & Cohen, 2018; Dillard, 1995). Because schools are connected to their surrounding community and many root causes for challenges schools face are actually located at the community level, school leaders' work to address disinvestment within the community, such as by addressing food insecurity, may also help to promote student achievement and enrollment (Berkovich, 2014). This work allows the school to continue to serve as a hub that meets community and student needs. Within this chapter we contend that social justice leaders—and activist leaders, in particular—are one such group that can do this work.

Anti-racist Leadership

Since the Civil Rights movement, discussions of social justice and educational leadership have flourished; yet, scholars have not identified a singular definition of social justice leadership (Bogotch, 2002; DeMatthews, 2018b; Lewis, 2016). This fluid definition of social justice leadership creates space for scholars and practitioners to decenter anti-racism work in anti-oppressive leadership; in fact, scholars have argued that the broad focus of social justice leadership demonstrates the potential to water down anti-racist efforts to achieve racial equity (Holme et al., 2014). For this reason, we center our understandings of activist leadership that intentionally disrupts white supremacy embedded within neoliberal policies within conceptualizations of anti-racist leadership. Anti-racist leaders engage in three overlapping practices: (1) centering white supremacy in their work; (2) understanding how white supremacy functions in society, schools, and individuals; and (3) taking actions against white supremacy at the individual, school, and society level (Young & Laible, 2000). Scholarship related to anti-racist leadership clearly documents the ways that anti-racist leaders engage in activism outside of schools due to commitments to empathetic caring (Bass, 2012) and recognition of the connections between school and community (Dillard, 1995; Wilson & Johnson, 2015). In keeping with this tradition, we focus on leaders' anti-racist actions outside of the school that were working to disrupt racist policies that adversely impacted their communities.

Activism as a Dimension of Anti-racist Leadership

Activist leaders understand how policy outside of schools impacts what occurs within, and that schools cannot be separated from the contexts in which they are situated (Anderson, 2009; Green, 2015b; Khalifa, 2012; Marshall & Anderson, 2009; Rapp, 2002). Indeed, student achievement may be more reflective of community conditions than school conditions (Green, 2018). To address this, some research has extended justice-oriented forms of leadership to incorporate a two-pronged approach in which leaders attend to issues of justice within and outside of the school (Anderson, 2009; Berkovich, 2014; DeMatthews, 2018a; Hoffman, 2009). Some labels scholars have used to describe leaders who engage in community-focused social justice work include advocacy leadership (Anderson, 2009), activist leadership (Berkovich, 2014; Hoffman, 2009; Horsford, 2018), and community-engaged social justice leadership (DeMatthews, 2018a). Within this chapter we use the term "activist leadership." We center the term activist leadership because of its roots in anti-racist thought (i.e., Black feminist thought; Hill-Collins, 2002) and leadership as political activity (Bass, 2012; Dillard, 1995; Wilson & Johnson, 2015).

Activist leadership draws its roots from Black activist educators who made schools part of broader social justice movements—especially the Civil Rights movement (Anderson & Cohen, 2018; Dillard, 1995; Loder-Jackson, 2011). Historically, activist educators believed that they could not create change in schools without addressing oppressive structures such as racism that negatively impacted the communities in which their schools were located (Johnson, 2006; Marshall & Anderson, 2009; Murtadha & Watts, 2005; Wilson & Johnson, 2015). To do so, these leaders served as bridge-builders who connected schools and communities, and understood that the community could offer knowledge, power, and leadership to leaders' activist efforts (Welton & Freelon, 2018). More recent research has affirmed that school leaders can incorporate community activism to attend to community and student needs (Khalifa, 2012).

Of particular interest to this chapter is that activist leaders form authentic, collaborative relationships with the community that center racial justice and community needs rather than school needs (Blackmore, 2002; Khalifa, 2012; Sanders & Harvey, 2002). As part of these relationships, activist leaders encourage community groups to use school facilities and grounds (DeMatthews,

2018a; Gardiner & Enomoto, 2006); develop the community's capital, organizing capacity, and assets (Karpinski & Lugg, 2006; Riehl, 2000); and advocate for community causes (Green, 2015b; Khalifa, 2012). The second point is notable in that, by developing the community's capital and capacity, activist leaders seek to create sustainable change that will benefit future generations and fight the white supremacist goals of neoliberal policies (Berkovich, 2014). Additionally, while school officials may traditionally understand community members from a deficit lens, activist leaders recognize that communities that have faced racist disinvestment have many strengths (Welton & Freelon, 2018). Therefore, activist leaders can couple school and community capital to disrupt the white racist impacts of systematic disinvestments that occur through neoliberalism and attempt to establish more racially just community-oriented structures.

Methodology

The data that informs this chapter comes from semi-structured interviews we conducted with seven activist leaders in CPS. Participants were purposefully sampled (Patton, 2002) based on reputation within their communities as activist leaders that centered anti-racist practices in their activism. All seven individuals work in CPS and lead schools located within a diverse array of neighborhood contexts in Chicago. Given that activist leadership is a localized process, the diversity of contexts represented by our data is particularly helpful for understanding this phenomenon. For example, as we describe below, leaders who were working in schools with high populations of Latinx students and/or neighborhoods with high Latinx populations felt it was particularly important to respond to anti-immigrant policy. Leaders of schools in gentrifying neighborhoods, on the other hand, were particularly motivated to ensure rent levels remained affordable for local families.

Interviews lasted approximately ninety minutes with follow-up questions asked via email. Our interview protocol was informed through a pre-research focus group with ten CPS principals who self-identified as engaging in anti-racist activist leadership outside of their school. Focus groups supported developing nuanced open-ended questions to gain deeper understandings of leader activist actions that intended to disrupt racist neoliberal policies impacting communities in which schools were situated. Data were analyzed through a two-cycle analysis (Saldaña, 2013) with initial a priori codes stemming from researcher understandings of activist and anti-racist leadership. Second cycle coding focused on looking across leader actions to develop conceptual understandings of the anti-racist activism leaders engaged in.

Vignettes of Activist Leadership

To illustrate activist leadership in practice, we provide vignettes below of three CPS principals. The leaders highlighted in each vignette work at schools that are located in communities of color that continue to experience the racialized outcomes of neoliberal policies in Chicago. All three examples demonstrate different ways that activist leaders were able to (re)connect their school to their community to help combat racism embedded in neoliberal policy. The first example highlights how Carlos acted as a bridge builder through his activism around immigrant rights. The second example demonstrates how Mark leveraged his school as a tool in re-establishing community by renovating the school's playground and creating a community center at the playground. The final example reveals how Natalie redefined the border between school and community and established a medical and legal clinic in her school. There are a number of similarities across the three examples, and together the vignettes highlight how school leaders can engage in anti-racist activism that contests neoliberal policies.

Bridge Building: Supporting Immigrant Rights Education

Carlos, a principal in a gentrifying Latinx community, conducted a needs-assessment of his school and community. As a result, he realized many Latinx students were missing school because they and their families were terrified of racist Immigration Customs Enforcement (ICE) raids of the school. These fears were escalated because of ongoing gentrification and related racially hostile acts by newly arrived white residents toward Latinx community members. Carlos responded by scouring the communities around the school for meaningful supports related to immigration rights. As he noted, "It really was more about looking or scouting, you know, who's out there helping the community for a specific cause."

Carlos's activism was actualized in informational sessions for local community members run by local immigration experts. Through "scouting," Carlos found a local agency that specializes in immigration rights and asked them to lead a session to support Latinx families in navigating racist immigration policies.

Carlos recognized that community members in general—not just families with children at his school—were fearful of ICE, so he invited community members to attend informational sessions as well. At the event, the local agency shared vital information and agency contact information in case families needed direct assistance or support. According to Carlos, "It was more about, 'okay,' we have a need about legal assistance and about understanding laws … who's out there doing the work."

While Carlos's activist work did not dismantle racist immigration policy, it did support Latinx community members in developing knowledge of their rights and resources. Through his activist bridge-building work, Carlos leveraged his position as a principal to bring community members of color into contact with needed resources and agency, which supported Latinx students and families in feeling safer and allowed youth to attend school at increased rates. Additionally, his activist work (re)connected Latinx families with their neighborhood school and shifted views of the school as place of support for Latinx families.

Re-establishing a Sense of Community: Community Meeting Space and Playground

Mark is a principal on Chicago's Southwest side, a predominately Black community that has disproportionately felt the racist impacts of neoliberalism's disinvestment in public services. As a principal, he noticed this disinvestment in his community and school:

> When I got there at the school, apparently they had a playground years ago and they just kind of cut out the playground and kind of covered over some of the holes or metal rods sticking out, so there's tripping hazards galore, there's broken glass all over, there's some benches that were broken … You go there after school, you go there on the weekends, you'd see no kids in the neighborhood.

In talking with families and community members he was informed that families drove their children three miles east to the Hyde Park neighborhood when they wanted to access a playground with grass. Mark recognized this as a lack of community resources and understood that his school could help to address this.

After applying for and receiving a grant, Mark partnered with a neighborhood group to convert the old playground back into a green space and updated playground. By updating the playground, Mark sought to "recreate a community, you know—in order for a community to exist you need people just interacting in casual spaces." Also included in this work was the rehabilitation of an abandoned building located next to the playground. While the updated playground served as a play space for youth in the community, the rehabilitated building served as a meeting space for community members and organizations. According to Mark:

> I opened it up as a clubhouse to them (families and community organizations). I even gave some keys so they could come in after hours. And the notion was that, if you had a group of parents who are in this field house, even after hours, they could keep the park safe right, like this whole notion of positive loitering.

Important in Mark's activism work is the tension related to his comments about how the adult presence in the "clubhouse" would keep the "park safe at night." While this can feel like a deficit statement related to Black communities being unsafe, it can also read as a statement about creating opportunities for community care and reducing the need for the policing of Black bodies. This is especially true in light of Mark's reference to "positive loitering." By refreshing the dismantled school playground and giving the community keys—literally—to space on school grounds, Mark re-established a sense of community around the school and positioned the school as an instrument fighting against the marginalization and neglect embedded in racist neoliberal policies.

Establishing Permeability: Health and Legal Clinics

Natalie is a principal of a K-8 school on Chicago's Near West Side, less than two miles from million-dollar townhouses, corporate headquarters, and exclusive restaurants. Yet, due to privatization associated with neoliberal policies, the communities of color around her school lacked crucial supports. One key challenge was that, looking across her school and neighboring communities, Natalie realized there were no health clinics for expectant teen mothers or legal clinics for juveniles in contact with the justice system. According to Natalie, "we identified the fact that we had a large portion of pregnant teens and we needed help for them." This resulted in youth of color either forgoing these supports or having to traverse the city to find them, both of which resulted in students missing school.

To address this, Natalie reached out to community agencies to establish a legal and health clinic in her school. Natalie also opened the clinics to members of the community beyond the school walls: "[The clinics] housed their office in our building and they served our pregnant teens and any pregnant teens within a certain radius that didn't even come to our school ... And, the same thing with a legal aid clinic that supports juveniles that are in the criminal justice system." As the need for both resources fell within her school, Natalie supported the clinics in transitioning to spaces outside of the school and maintained a relationship with both resources:

> The caseload [pregnant students] fell to 4, 5 students that we had and so that wasn't a resource that we needed anymore. We maintained the relationship but they were no longer in the building. [We] have contact with those resources and you're able to create an intake through our social workers where they then connected them [students] with those [clinics]. So, what I did have to maintain was the resources for the social worker but they, like, maintained the relationships outside the building.

In the end, the health and legal clinics were able to begin their service to the community within the school and rely on some school resources, but both then transitioned out to permanent locations in the community.

Natalie's activist leadership generated a permeable boundary between the school and community where resources could flow between the two spaces. She leveraged the school as an incubator space for services that racist neoliberal policies have systematically removed from communities of color. By reconceptualizing the boundaries between school and community, Natalie's activism supported bringing vital resources into the community and shifted how the school was positioned within the community.

Lessons Learned

Looking across the activist work of Natalie, Mark, and Carlos, there are clear similarities in how they intentionally pushed against the racialized impacts of neoliberal policies. At the heart of this action was a desire to (re)connect their schools with the communities of color they served to disrupt racialized neoliberal policies. Natalie, Mark, and Carlos engaged in three similar practices: (a) recognizing the needs of their communities, (b) forming partnership with local agencies, and (c) understanding the school can meet the community needs. All of these actions (re)centered and (re)connected their schools with the local communities, which simultaneously met the needs of the community and students attending the school.

Recognizing Community Needs

Through their focus on meeting the needs of the communities of color surrounding their schools, all three leaders drew on the anti-racist history of activist leadership (Khalifa, 2012; Murtadha & Watts, 2005; Welton & Freelon, 2018) and social justice leadership's commitments to locally defined understandings of justice (Bogotch, 2002; DeMatthews, 2018a). For example, Carlos conducted a needs-assessment of the communities around his school that led him to learn that Latinx community members had a real and founded fear of ICE agents' terrorist acts, so he centered his activism in that area. Similarly, Natalie heard the voices of community members needing a medical and legal clinic since none existed and worked to make those a reality. Through centering the needs of the community, all three leaders helped ensure their activism was impactful and positioned the school as a hub of the local community.

It is important to note that without taking the time to identify community needs in thoughtful ways, Mark, Carlos, and Natalie would have been acting for their communities rather than with their communities. If activist leaders are serious about (re)connecting schools with the communities of color they serve, they need to approach communities as a learner and partner. By acting with, activist leaders can help erode the historical reality that schools have often served as an institution of whiteness and operated to marginalize and oppress communities of color (Spring, 2017). Furthermore, acting with positions schools as a valuable member of the community and supportive member in the fight against racism.

Forming Partnerships

Historically, activist leaders have recognized the importance of forming partnerships through bridge-building and other activities (Dillard, 1995; Welton & Freelon, 2018). Through centering community partnerships and bridge-building in their activism, Natalie, Mark, and Carlos all (re)connected their schools and communities, and multiplied the resources available to both. For example, Carlos connected Latinx community members with local immigration rights groups in order to increase awareness of rights and resources. Natalie connected with local community organizations to create a medical and legal clinic. Through these connections, all three leaders (re)connected their school with local families and community organizations, which strengthened the overall community and brought people together to counter the racialized effects of neoliberal policies.

All three leaders also brought creative understandings of partnerships. For example, in recognizing the permeability of the border between the school and community, Natalie formed a partnership that allowed the medical and legal clinic to incubate in the school and then shift to the community. Mark established a partnership with community groups that shifted the boundary between school and community when he shared a key to the "club house" with various community organizations. In both instances, by redrawing what the boundary between school and community looks like, leaders were able to (re)connect their school with the local community. In turn, this increases the ability of both the school and community to engage in anti-racist activism because the resource pool available has shifted.

These partnerships were possible because, as anti-racist activists, Mark, Natalie, and Carlos focused on developing understandings of the assets and needs of the communities their schools served. Understanding needs was not about deficit notions of local communities, but about understanding the racialized impacts of neoliberal policies. All three leaders then spent time getting to know community members and building the mutualistic trust with community members of color through genuine interactions and asset-mapping activities that allowed them to develop mutualistic trust between themselves and community members.

Rethinking Who Serves Who

A final commonality in the activist work of Mark, Carlos, and Natalie that enabled them to (re)connect their schools and surrounding communities to push against racist neoliberal policies was in their framing of who serves who. Activist leaders strive to disrupt deficit notions of the communities where their schools are located and the real-world implications of those deficit perspectives (Karpinski & Lugg, 2006; Riehl, 2000). The activist leaders we worked with undermined these deficit notions through particular understandings of who serves who; specifically, all three leaders took a mutualistic understanding of service by recognizing that they and their school served the community and that the community served the school. This was evidenced in Mark's comments about how having community members present in the "club house" after school hours would increase the safety of youth of color playing on the playground. By creating a mutualistic relationship between the community and school, Mark created a space where resource cuts could be offset by school and community partnerships. Natalie also demonstrated a nuanced understanding of the mutualistic relationship between school and community when she leveraged school resources to incubate a medical and legal clinic. Taking a mutualistic understanding of serving between the school and community creates a space where resources can flow between school and community, and positions schools and communities to take a unified stance against neoliberalism and racist outcomes.

This mutualistic understanding of service also demonstrated school leaders were invested in supporting the community and recognized the importance of community in the success of the school. Notions of mutualistic service disrupt the individualism present in the neoliberal agenda and open avenues for collaboration and partnership. In other words, leaders' activism pushed directly against the inherent competition for resources embedded in neoliberal policy mandates and ways of being. Through intentional activism that centered mutualistic service, all three leaders connected their schools and local communities to fight a common source of resource deprivation that provided needed resources for all involved, strengthened both schools and communities, and created potential avenues for future collaboration.

Engaging in Activism

We end our chapter by offering recommendations of ways leaders can engage in anti-racist activism that works to (re)connect schools and communities in fights against the racialized outcomes of neoliberal policies. This activist work was explicitly anti-racist through its recognition that there are racialized outcomes present in neoliberal policies, its intentional work to undermine those outcomes, and the centering of local communities of color voices in the direction of leader activism. Specifically anti-racist activist leaders need to:

- Assess the assets and needs of the communities they serve. This needs to include getting to know families, other stakeholders, and local community organizations. Through this relationship-building work, leaders can begin to identify potential areas of activism and avenues for collaboration. Leaders can also begin to develop understandings of the community assets present that racialized deficit narratives often hide in plain sight.
- See activism as a communal process as opposed to an individual endeavor. Taking a communal approach ensures that leaders are working with as opposed to for the community, which nurtures an authentic connection

between school and community. Additionally, a communal approach creates a system in which the resources and capacities of the school and communities come together to disrupt systems of oppression working to divest capital from communities of color.
- Recognize the resources under the control of their school that can be brought to bear in their activist work. Resources can include physical space, knowledge and expertise, time, and finances.

Activism demonstrates a powerful mechanism for (re)connecting schools and communities of color during a time when neoliberal policies are intentionally driving a wedge between communities and schools through systematic disinvestment and competition of limited resources. Through intentional activism, school leaders can work to disrupt this disinvestment and forge partnerships with their communities to support youth of color and local interests.

There is also a need to highlight that Natalie, Carlos, and Mark were engaged in anti-racist activism that helped their communities navigate the consequences of racist neoliberal policies through increasing access to resources in a time when policy is removing access. But, they were not intentionally engaged in activism that explicitly worked to eliminate or dismantle neoliberal policy (i.e., organizing political resistance). This could potentially result in burnout for leaders like Natalie, Carlos, and Mark because neoliberal policies will continue to operate and have disproportionate negative impacts on the communities of color they serve. In other words, without change at the policy level, these leaders and their work could burn out under the oppressive weight of neoliberalism. This highlights calls for ongoing both/and approaches where leaders like Natalie, Carlos, and Mark are engaging in anti-racist activism to work with communities to gain access to stripped resources while other anti-racist activists continue the fight to end neoliberalism.

10

Toward More Equitable Communities: Leadership Lessons for Systemic Social Change

Rhoda Freelon and Jeanette Taylor

Introduction

In many large urban cities, community organizers work tirelessly to preserve traditional public school options and foster the democratic engagement of parents in their neighborhood schools. At the center of these efforts is a desire for educational equity for a racially diverse and largely working-class group of educational stakeholders. Indeed, Communities of Color have a long and storied history engaging in struggles for educational justice and providing moral leadership to an educational system that purports to provide equal educational access and opportunity to all families (Mediratta et al., 2009; Oakes et al., 2006; Wilson, 2014). In Chicago, the focus of this chapter, families, and communities have actively engaged the school district and local government to help ensure educational opportunities for their communities (Rury, 1999; Stovall, 2016; Todd-Breland, 2018; Welton & Freelon, 2018).

Education organizing has a particular and important role in bringing about racial justice in the field of education. Within the current politics of the education landscape, there is no shortage of programs and solutions for improving the educational outcomes in schools with large populations of low-income and racially diverse families (Payne, 2008). These communities targeted by a host of educational reforms often lack the traditional power structures that are made available to more affluent and often white residents in a community. As a result, the collective engagement of Communities of Color often manifests as mirroring the skills and tactics of community organizers where power is built through contested and protracted struggles for racial equity in schools and communities (Mediratta et al., 2009; Oakes et al., 2006; Warren, 1998; Warren & Mapp, 2011). The principles of traditional community organizing are often deemed necessary in Communities of Color as they help consolidate the existing social capital that is found in neighborhoods (Warren, 2005). While some research and policy discourses frame low-income, racially segregated communities as being depleted and chaotic, when community members coalesce around justice issues such as housing, education, or access to jobs, it provides a counternarrative to this deficit thinking.

Although there is a growing body of scholarship making the case for more expansive notions of educational leadership (Bertrand & Rodela, 2018), the field continues to benefit from an evidentiary base that shares concrete lessons, capacities, and key qualities of how community-based educational leadership functions that contributes to educational equity rooted in racial justice. A wealth of scholarship has made a compelling case for why we should consider parents, students, and community members as leaders (Bertrand & Rodela, 2018; Fernández & Paredes Scribner, 2018; Ishimaru et al., 2019; Lac & Cumings Mansfield, 2018; Welton & Freelon, 2018). Moreover, the acknowledgment of these key stakeholders as leaders does not take away from the professional leadership skills that are needed to be an educator, school leader, or district administrator. Rather, this scholarship has argued that acknowledging and embracing community-based educational leadership are an asset for formal professional school- and district-based educators and leaders (Ishimaru, 2013). An attempt to better understand the ways that parents can contribute as educational leaders not only reminds traditional leaders of their role in advancing educational equity, it also provides them with an essential ally when this work inevitably becomes tenuous and political (Welton & Freelon, 2019). This is especially true for traditional educational leaders who seek to advance anti-racist policies and practices within their schools and districts.

In this chapter, we combine our individual knowledge and expertise about education into a research-practice-oriented collaboration to share insights on how parent and community-based leadership can help schools, districts, and communities advance more anti-racist practices and policies. We both identify as Black women with a particular set of lived experiences that help shape the narrative of this life history. One author's experiences as a family and community-based researcher coupled with that of a mother, parent leader, community organizer, and elected official to share a portrait of community-based leadership. This case study has the potential to not only advance educational equity, but also create the basis for broader movements that connect to city-wide racial justice and equity concerns in critical domains outside of education. Using the life history of the second author as a case study, we share lessons about how her parent leadership as a young mother positioned her for consequential educational leadership and broader justice concerns that catalyzed her nascent political career. In doing so, we also offer implications for leadership preparation programs that help prepare students and make the case that formal educational leaders and community organizers have a lot to learn from one another about anti-racist leadership.

To ground our discussion and analysis, we share five lessons from the second author's life that help illustrate the ways in which parent leadership has the potential to represent community-based educational leadership and promote racial equity in justice-related concerns that are connected to education. The lessons prove instructive because they provide concrete ideas about the skills and capacities that are necessary to better articulate the myriad ways grassroots leadership can support educational equity specifically and racial justice broadly. Through the lived experiences of the second author's engagement in struggles for educational justice and her motivation to pursue a political office, we demonstrate the potential role that community organizing and activism might play in the quest for schools and communities free of racial injustice. In the sections that follow, we share insights on Jeanette's life and demonstrate how her leadership qualities in education may be an example of moral and sacrificial leadership (Dantley & Tillman, 2006; Welton & Freelon, 2018). Further, her accomplishments in this arena served as a critical prerequisite to pursuing broader civic ideals through her campaign for and subsequent victory as an Alderwoman in the historically Black and largely low-income community she represents on Chicago's South Side.

Critical Leadership Lessons

Leadership Expertise Rooted in Lived Experiences

The first lesson we share confirms what scholars have documented elsewhere (Bertrand & Rodela, 2018; Welton & Freelon, 2018). Community-based educational leaders possess a wealth of expertise about the local conditions of schooling largely because they are closest to these educational challenges. Historically marginalized community members and education organizers are attuned to disparities and inequities in the school system. They are often faced with these issues because they are more likely to confront these challenges as they navigate schooling options in their neighborhoods. Experiencing inequities first hand does not always ensure that you might be moved to address the disparities, but the development of a critical consciousness around these issues is an important factor to consider working with the community to advance anti-racist practices and policies within a school or district. Due to levels of racial segregation in many American cities, it is often not initially obvious that a given community lacks essential resources.

As an example from Jeanette's own experience, she recalls first knowing that her children's school was operating with less than what they deserved when she begins to get involved in the Local School Council (LSC). In Chicago, LSCs are school governance bodies with democratically elected members consisting of parents, community members, teachers, and students. Each school in the district has regular LSC meetings that are fully open to the public. The council's responsibilities range from evaluating the school principal to monitoring the school budget each year. Jeanette's mother, a school clerk with Chicago Public Schools, strongly encouraged her to join the LSC and this prompted Jeanette's initial involvement. While Jeanette was reluctant to join the council, once she got involved, she quickly learned that the conditions of schooling were unjust. She states,

> *When I found out that the books that I was using, my kids were using, I knew it was a problem. I knew that when I was looking at these budgets, like we have the money, then all of a sudden it went somewhere, but we don't know where it went. And then, it was so bad, that I asked a local pastor to get on the LSC, because I got tired of fighting with them about kicking out young people, about mistreating teachers, about not having parent involvement unless you're on the LSC or part of the Parent Advisory Committee.*

In this excerpt, Jeanette recalls her early days on the LSC at her children's elementary school when she first discovered the array of challenges at her children's campus. The problems stemmed from inadequate resources to support teaching and learning as well as questionable leadership that did not treat teachers well and created tensions between parents in the school. It shows how she was made aware of systemic inequalities related to these school level resources and uncovers the way in which school leadership operated to limit parent engagement at the school. These opportunities impacted her greatly and put her in a position to advocate for school improvement. This type of engagement with the school fueled her commitment as a young mother and brought her in contact with important allies along the way.

Parent engagement that takes the form of site-level leadership linked to shared decision making among families and school leaders was a significant first step in Jeanette's anti-racist leadership development. This type of engagement from parents has the potential to make critical contributions to school improvement efforts (Bertrand & Rodela, 2018). Unfortunately, Jeanette's experience fell short of the promise of democratic engagement of school stakeholders as she was constantly pitted against school leadership and other parents for raising awareness about problems in the school. When critical educational stakeholders who may not hold typical positional authority within schools attempt to challenge fundamentally racialized institutional structures and their disparate outcomes, they are often deemed as troublemakers and agitators (Mediratta & Frutcher, 2001). However, Jeanette was particularly attuned to engaging in advocacy on behalf of teachers, parents, and students who were being marginalized in the school.

Leveraging Resistant Capital as a Tool for Change

Jeanette's lived experiences suggest that organizing and resistance are important for calling out racist school policies and initiating steps to dismantle such policies and practices. As an example, Jeanette and colleagues were part of a hunger strike in Chicago for a local high school, an action that received considerable national attention by the press (Ewing, 2015; Strauss, 2015). Scholars have characterized this as a form of community-based educational leadership rooted in personal sacrifice toward racial justice (Welton & Freelon, 2018). This effort to save one of the remaining neighborhood high schools on Chicago's South Side was based on their use of resistant capital (Yosso, 2005) as a lever for change. Resistant capital is defined as "those knowledges and skills fostered through oppositional behavior that challenges inequality" (Yosso, 2005, p. 80). Indeed, the hunger strike represented an attempt to challenge powerful decision makers in Chicago. However, the process to engage in this form of resistant capital was not easy for Jeanette or her colleagues. Here she recalls:

> *Realizing that Dyett was the only neighborhood high school left in the ward it was like we gotta fight. And so, what people don't know is, initially when they were talking about a hunger strike, I was like hell no. ... All I want to do is eat. It's my comfort, it's the way that I escape from this world. So it was a no for me. But then after seeing babies cry and beg for them not to close their school, "don't close my school, like what am I going to do". "Like this is the only family I know, school is my escape". After hearing mothers crying and saying, "I put all of my life into this school to be on this LSC to help it and now they want to close it"—it was just injustice to me. And so injustice anywhere is injustice everywhere. And so I was*

> like, "I'm in". And my decision was against my husband, it was against my mother, my oldest two kids were against it. And so I had a real internal battle with myself and my family, but I did it and I was really in.

Jeanette's reflection above belies a struggle she experienced in engaging in the sacrificial leadership of the hunger strike. Indeed, she and her family were worried about her health and wellbeing which were real concerns as she later faced a health scare during the strike.

> Sue Garza, the Alderman of the 10th ward gave me her space to speak at the CPS [Chicago Public Schools] Board meeting. And I was speaking and I hadn't eaten in so many days so I passed out. And [the district] didn't want it to be on the news, they didn't want people to see it, but all it did was make it even worse for them. And it made it harder for me a little bit because my oldest living aunt at the time said to me, "Baby, those people will let you die and I can't let them do that, I need you to get off the hunger strike." And we kind of went back and forth on why I had to get back on it and I let her know what was at stake. ... And after that conversation she was just like, "I didn't realize that you all had it this bad or the schools were not what they should have been." And she was like, I want you to get off, but I know you're strong-willed, so fight on.

Again, out of deep concern for her health and wellbeing, family members pushed Jeanette to reconsider her activism, but her engagement in the hunger strike was informed by her critique of the social conditions in her community that created the racialized disparities that she and others were experiencing. Indeed, as Yosso (2005) reminds us, "recognition of the structural nature of oppression and the motivation to work toward social and racial justice, resistance takes on a transformative form" (p. 81). Jeanette and her colleagues' transformational resistance (Solorzano & Bernal, 2001) was rooted in a quest for justice for a local community and this desire was wholly outside of her and her family's personal needs. It became more about the struggle to advance racial equity in this local community. The resistance to oppressive policies in itself is not sufficient, but coupling these actions with plans and recommendations for improving educational futures for their community was essential to her resistance efforts.

Using Local Knowledge to Develop More Equitable Solutions

As the previous section highlights, Communities of Color possess resistance capital, but they are also uniquely positioned to use the local knowledge of their community's strengths to advance an anti-racist, social justice educational agenda. Additionally, through principles of self-determination, they can also use that local knowledge to build toward viable solutions for their community. Jeannette and her colleagues were able to do this when they chose to advance a proposal for a new school. Their partnership with local education scholars and curricular experts is important to note as families and communities often do not get to weigh in on school design in such a consequential manner.

In addition to participating in the hunger strike, Jeanette was also part of the Coalition to Revitalize Dyett. This group of community members, local educators, and education researchers made a specific contribution to the development of a comprehensive school plan for Dyett to remain open with a renewed curriculum. Analysis of the Coalition's plan reveals that it not only articulated a clear vision of academic content aligned with national- and state-level educational standards, it was designed to meet the social-emotional needs of students as well as the material needs of local families. The mission and vision statements from the plan stated:

> *Mission:* Our mission is to have a student-centered community school with a culture of high expectations that, through its partnership among teachers, administrators, parents, and community residents, provides every student an exceptional education with an emphasis on leadership development and green technology.
>
> *Vision:* Dyett Global Leadership and Green Technology Community High School will develop our students into "community centered scholars," with the confidence, competence and compassion to positively develop themselves, their school, their community, and society overall. (Coalition to Revitalize Walter H. Dyett High School, 2015, p. 1)

With its focus on partnerships between educators, families, and communities, their plans reflected a pivot from the traditional public school relationship with educational stakeholders. Auerbach (2011) defines authentic partnerships as "respectful alliances among educators, families, and community groups that value relationship building, dialogue across difference, and sharing power in pursuit of a common purpose in socially just, democratic schools" (p. 29). At the outset, the Coalition had this vision. Further, the Coalition's plan represented an integral part of Jeanette's orientation to parent and community organizing since her early days as a new Mother and LSC member. Auerbach (2011) describes respectful alliances as ones that welcome and honor family and community contributions, respect and affirm families' cultures, and operate from an understanding that schools are part of the seamless fabric of a local community. However, it is important to note that getting to more authentic partnerships or respectful alliances does require time as building relational trust is an important ingredient to developing this type of aspirational goal for equitable partnerships and collaborations. Conversations about resources and disrupting hegemonic decision making in place of more racially just and equity-minded reforms and practices are inherently contested terrain. As a result, initial attempts by community members and parents asserting their power in spaces with formal educators and school leaders could be challenged. However, striving for respectful alliances would allow formal school leaders an opportunity to view parents and community members as experts on their own experience and ultimately lead to collaboration and power-sharing. Members of the Coalition were made up of community members, parents, educators, administrators, education researchers, and curriculum experts. It took this fusion of knowledge across critical domains to create a thoughtful educational plan to revamp Dyett High School. In this way, families and community members' knowledge and expertise were brought to bear to advance a well-reasoned agenda for families on the South Side of Chicago.

Building Power: The Role of Justice-focused Community-based Organizations (CBOs)

Community-based organizations also play a critically important role in advancing the political education of community members and centering their issues and concerns in struggles for social justice (Evans, 2019; Ferman, 2017; Warren, 1998; Welton & Freelon, 2018). They can represent a natural extension of residents' existing social capital and provide resources and opportunities for robust civic engagement. In community-based advocacy organizations that focus on education and other connected social systems, members and the organizations' leaders leverage collective engagement of local residents to address systemic inequities in racially and economically marginalized contexts.

Throughout Jeanette's life, she was pushed and encouraged by her Mother, Aunts, and former teachers to become a parent leader for her children's schools. However, it wasn't until she met key leaders in a local community-based organization that her existing critical consciousness related to equity and justice was made clear. As a member of her school's LSC, she availed herself of various district-sponsored trainings as they regularly provide trainings for LSC members. However, local community groups also provide training sessions for LSC members. On a fateful day, Jeanette received a flyer from the Kenwood Oakland Community Organization (KOCO). She decided to attend this training and her connection with this organization contributed to her development as a parent leader and organizer. She essentially received a political awakening during her time working with KOCO. Here Jeanette reflects on her initial meeting:

> So I got this flyer and it was left in the mailbox at the school and I read it and it says, "do you know your real role as an LSC member and do you want this training?" And so I convinced myself, the principal, and another person to go to this training and the first thing that came out of Brother Jitu's [KOCO's Education Organizer at the time] mouth after introductions was, "Do you know you have the power to hire and fire the principal?" And I was like, where does it say that. Nobody ever told me that. He was like, "Do you know that you all have a say about the budget at your school?" And I was confused, I was like what book is he reading because I had five or six training books and none said anything like that. And so, when I figured out what he was saying was true and that he was reading from state law, I was like, oh—wow! And I kept saying to myself, what does it benefit him to tell us the truth and so, I figured out it was KOCO.

Jeanette's introduction to KOCO led to sustained engagement with the organization that was initiated around education advocacy, but also included issues such as housing and resident displacement; youth engagement and development; and local ordinances for businesses to help keep communities safe (Kenwood Oakland Community Organization, n.d.).

Beyond Schools: Transforming Public Systems

The final lesson we share is based on the reflection of Jeanette's life as a working-class Black woman, mother, community organizer, education advocate, and elected official. While the struggles that families and community members go through with public education are important, Jeanette's understanding of how this work is connected to broader themes of social justice and equity in families' daily lives was essential to her transition from community organizer to elected official. That families like her would face a new set of challenges that could end up pushing them out of their local neighborhood was of great concern. Issues such as job opportunities, criminal justice reform, and quality schooling are all connected issues in her mind.

When Jeanette speaks of why she chose to run for office, it generally starts with sharing her experience about being priced out of the neighborhood she grew up in because of gentrification. Experiencing rapidly rising rents forced her to seek housing further outside of the Bronzeville community, a neighborhood in South

Side Chicago. As a result, she moved to a different South Side neighborhood, Woodlawn, and quickly realized local changes there could easily push her out as well. This neighborhood displacement became more of a possibility when President Obama announced the location of the new Presidential Center in Jackson Park, a neighborhood adjacent to Woodlawn. The Center is being touted as an economic engine that will powerfully transform the local surrounding neighborhoods. Many proponents of the Library's location argue that it represents a historic opportunity and potential tool to lift the economic profile of the South Side. However, community organizers wanted commitments and reassurances from the City that there would be equitable growth and development that stemmed from the Library's presence. A Community Benefits Agreement Coalition was formed to organize and raise questions about the role of the community voice in the development process.

At this point, Jeanette was no longer formerly employed with KOCO and was contemplating her next career move. The Obama Community Benefits Agreement Coalition, which was led by residents with the support of several justice-focused community groups, began to take shape requesting that the City and the Obama Foundation enter into a formal agreement with the community about how to make sure that any ancillary development from the new Center would be equitably distributed. Their agreement was to provide job opportunities and housing protections for residents in the three surrounding communities—South Shore, Washington Park, and Woodlawn. As a Woodlawn resident, Jeanette believed she needed to use her voice to speak out on this issue. Reflecting on her new role in City Council, she stated:

> *It's hard—it's extremely hard in this space, but I'm up for the challenge. I think working with community organizations has prepared me to kind of deal with it all, so I'm up for the challenge. I have my days, but I decided a long time ago that the truth is important. I didn't have these lived experiences and go through all that I've gone through not to use my voice or not to make sure that I'm speaking up for everybody. Not just people who can't afford it, but also the middle class. I'm speaking up for people who never get a seat at the table and I want to bring them to the table.*

Jeanette's ultimate efforts to advance the goals of the community on critical social issues stemmed from her earlier organizing roots and her deep compassion for those whose voices are often marginalized. While the Obama Center plans were the catalyst to this type of broad-based leadership for her, broadly speaking it is also what motivated her to run for office and it is also what is sustaining her in this new role. Jeanette's decision to run for office was linked to a desire to ensure a more racially and economically just set of outcomes for working families and seniors who many were afraid would be left behind, especially as the neighborhood changes. It certainly would have been easier for her to not run for office, but her success in the political arena represents a renewal and restoration of faith in public systems for many of her constituents. During summer 2020, in conjunction with residents, community groups, and the Mayor's office, Jeanette helped establish a community benefits agreement that would provide housing with housing protections for low-income residents due to the impending Obama Presidential Center (Cherone, 2020). While Jeanette did not characterize this as a total victory, she states, the ordinance was "a step in the right direction." In her current role she has been able to do important work to represent and advance justice-oriented causes; yet, she often feels like system actors and bureaucratic constraints make it harder to do her job. Still, she is most encouraged when she's able to meet the needs of local constituents and live up to her goals of providing a voice for the most vulnerable members of her community.

Conclusion and Implications

The everyday leadership of families and community members has the potential to not only shed light on critical issues in education, but also help traditional systems leaders address these concerns for educational justice. In this chapter we share glimpses from key moments of Jeanette's life as a community organizer and social justice advocate in order to illuminate important insights for advancing anti-racist leadership principles. Five essential lessons were documented toward a vision of creating and sustaining more equitable and just futures. First, demonstrated leadership rooted in the lived experiences of marginalized community members has the potential to confront systemic educational disparities. Second, while resistance may sometimes be viewed negatively by some, resistance capital can be harnessed as a tool for social change. Third, centering and honoring local knowledge can lead to innovative solutions to educational challenges that are born out of the needs and concerns of local residents. Fourth, sharing and building power is often a result of learning and collaborating with experienced advocacy groups. And the final lesson speaks to the transformative potential of justice-minded leadership where a focus on the interconnected nature of social issues can help spark and renew faith in public systems.

These lessons can be shared with educational leadership preparation programs, especially ones that have an expressed goal of preparing anti-racist leaders. Leaders who recognize and acknowledge the strength, knowledge, and equity commitments of local communities are better positioned to challenge the status quo and advance racial equity in schools (Bertrand & Rodela, 2018; Ryan, 2010). Further, it is critical that anti-racist leaders consider the ways that education is connected to larger structures and patterns of inequality across a range of social issues in marginalized communities. Jeanette's early school-based leadership as a concerned parent on the LSC as well as her subsequent work as an education and community organizer helped catalyze her career in municipal government. It allowed her to readily see the ways that systems of oppression are not relegated to one social domain. School and systems leaders who recognize this interconnectedness can work in authentic collaboration with parents, community members, and students to ensure a more just and equitable educational system. Further, beyond collaboration with parents, school and district leaders should embrace the boundless potential that comes when they recognize the critical role that families and community members of color can play in the quest for racial equity in schools.

11

(Re)Imagining "Successful" University–District–Community Partnerships

Decoteau J. Irby, Bradley W. Carpenter, and Erica Young

Introduction

This chapter aims to disrupt the race-neutral conversation about university–district partnerships and to point out the racist structures that constrain how we imagine anti-racist university–district–community partnerships. University–district partnerships refer to the broad range of activities that bring together university (faculty, staff, and students) and school district-affiliated (leaders, teachers, and students) people into working relationships that aim to improve or solve problems in each partner's respective contexts. University–district partnerships also involve non-district and non-university entities that have stakes in the school community in which universities partner (e.g., Kronick et al., 2013). The partners are often non-profit organizations, municipal agencies, religious institutions, parents, or other groups that constitute the "community," and its contested meanings referenced in university–district–community partnerships (LeChasseur, 2014). Within this broad definition, the types, nature, and extent of district–university partnerships vary widely and can involve college-level partnerships, department- and program-level partnerships, and even faculty-initiated partnerships (McConn, 2019; Stephens & Boldt, 2004; Walsh & Backe, 2013).

Scholars agree that to achieve and sustain successful partnerships requires active participation from all partners who gain mutual benefits of shared knowledge and resources, strengthening of curriculum, potential for organizational growth, and better communication (Thorkildsen & Stein, 1996). In theory, successful partnerships lead to the continued renewal of both colleges of education and of K-12 schools (Stephens & Boldt, 2004). University–district partnerships provide students enrolled in teacher and leader preparation programs with field-based and clinical learning opportunities in school settings that are required for degree attainment and credentialing. They provide faculty and graduate students opportunities to gain knowledge through conducting research. Local districts, regions, and the field at-large benefit from a steady stream of teacher and leader candidates to meet the continued demand for teachers and leaders. Practitioners gain access to skilled personnel who support program evaluation, curriculum development, and professional development. Stevenson and Shetley (2015) note that in theory the partners "participate in these collaborations, and do a better job together than either could accomplish alone, and hence both become better" (p. 172).

The mutual benefits of such an arrangement seem apparent. Yet, the benefits of partnerships—in terms of shared knowledge and resources, strengthening of curriculum, potential for organizational growth, and better communication—are not well documented. Where impactful benefits are apparent they fall disproportionately to universities' benefit rather than to districts and schools (Stevenson & Shetley, 2015). To be fair, the majority of university–district partnerships featured in the educational research focus on teacher education (Walsh & Backe, 2013) and school leader preparation (Browne-Ferrigno, 2011; Goldring & Sims, 2005; Gooden et al., 2011). Such university–district partnerships are common because they satisfy a mutual interest in supporting the development of the field. These two configurations notwithstanding, the mutually beneficial "win-win" theory of university–district partnerships working together on common goals remains suspect.

While the empirical literature on university–district partnerships still lags in the field of educational leadership (Coleman & Reames, 2018), the partnerships that have been documented are frequently constructed as temporary fixes to complex issues; developed with deficit ideals or worldviews about the community itself; and are enacted without a collaborative, consensual, and equity-minded focus on development, implementation, and sustainability (Aleman et al., 2017). Many studies are misguided because the metrics for determining what constitutes a successful partnership are often race-neutral and do not account for the substantial power differentials between university and districts, the wants and needs of districts, and especially the aspirations, wants, and needs of "community" stakeholders. Partnerships are often constructed in a superficial way that exacerbates the cultural and aspirational differences between universities and the communities with whom they seek to collaborate (Moultrie et al., 2017). There are almost no accounts of research partnerships gone wrong to learn from. Partnership cases of any type that convey deleterious outcomes or negative experiences are not a part of the university–district–community collaboration literature in education (for an exception, see Irby & Drame, 2016)—instances where researchers and community members report on experiences of exploitation, pillaging of local knowledge, and relational harm are rare exceptions (Bolling, 2016; Mawhinney & Irby, 2016). Authors willing to name racism and racial subjugation as part of their partnership experiences are still rarer (Mawhinney & Irby, 2016). Despite the vast research literature covering the university–district partnership, not enough researchers confront how racism and racial oppression shape university–district partnerships.

Building Our Anti-racist Imaginations

This chapter presents two university-based researchers' conversation and thinking about the role university leaders, broadly conceived, can play in cultivating anti-racist district–university partnerships. Throughout, we name racist structural and ideological underpinnings of district–university–community partnerships. "Let's build" is a common colloquialism hip-hop cultural insiders use to denote the importance of making time to reflect, imagine, and work toward achieving a broad range of ends, as an explicitly anti-racist endeavor to disrupt traditional models of university–district partnerships and reimagine a more collaborative, empowered way forward. By anti-racist, we mean a way of doing and thinking that disrupts patterns that reify white supremacy. All three of us used the development of the chapter to rethink our past partnership experiences, from the vantage points of graduate students, school-based administrators, and faculty members at universities and as a Black man, white man, and white woman. We each experienced multiple sides of partnerships, as convener, school-based, community-based, and university-based. In developing this chapter, we sought to disrupt our own white-centric metrics of what counts as effective university–district partnerships and to imagine what racially affirming partnerships that privilege the wants, needs, and desires of local communities must necessarily entail. The following questions guided our self-inquiry:

1. What's been your overall approach to district–university–community partnerships?
2. What is a project you've been a part of that most closely exemplifies a "successful" partnership?
3. How have such partnerships been "measured" for success?

4. What did the partnership "build" that stemmed from the project?
5. What about the partnership design or planning enabled it to build toward alternate outcomes in the interest of students, families, and communities?
6. What are the challenges of such partnerships and how might researchers navigate these challenges?
7. Why do (should) universities, districts, and communities partner?
8. How does racism shape partnerships?

Building on Theory

We use Hinton's (2015) conceptualization of resistance, trust, spirituality, and love to serve as a provocative and aspirational framework to interrogate our previous experiences, as well as (re)imagine the ways we might engage in anti-racist district–university–community partnerships. Hinton (2015), while appreciative of community cultural wealth (Yosso, 2005), calls into question research shaped by theories of capital, as he questions the premise that by centering capital, such theories may, in fact, "reproduce" the very discourses that privilege capitalistic discourse. Subsequently, such frameworks may not serve as the most appropriate metaphor to describe the cultures of communities of color, in particular in regard to morality and justice (p. 329). After providing critiques of metaphorical capital (social, human, cultural), and Yosso's (2005) "community cultural wealth," Hinton (2015) proposes four metaphorical frameworks of "possibility"—resistance, trust, spirituality, and love—that he suggests may "illuminate social and cultural interaction" (p. 310). These frameworks provide a unique lens through which we examine university–district–community partnerships centering the strengths of the community rather than privileging the educational expertise or financial means of the university. Resistance, trust, spirituality, and love also reflect the abundance of resources and reframe our thinking beyond the constraints of time and money. Hinton's frameworks of "possibility" help us to build context for how we envision anti-racist leadership within university–district–community partnerships to deeply value and humanize the connections and outcomes.

Building on Our Experiences

Based upon our collective experiences with university–district–community partnerships, we collaboratively developed an interview protocol. Dr. Young used the protocol to conduct an informal but structured audio-recorded conversation. We viewed this as an opportunity for personal reflection about our commitments as researchers, the kind of research projects we want most to participate in carrying out, as well as what we hope to personally and professionally gain and contribute in the process. Second, in part, we decided to use this format because the three of us collectively desire to strengthen our relationships through the process of working together. We asked questions, listened, and probed. We learned from one another in real time and fostered deeper relational connections. Third, we viewed this opportunity to surface a data set for this chapter. Finally, we were able to use Hinton's (2015) conceptualizations of resistance, trust, spirituality, and love to evaluate our past work as well as (re)imagine our future work in this arena.

After we identified conversational exchanges from our building session, we analyzed problems inherent in university–district–school partnerships, giving specific attention to our own tendency to acquiesce to normative racial structures. We also engaged in future-looking imaginings of what it would look like to put universities, districts, and communities in a position where partnership would be mutually beneficial such that they would generate more bountiful wealth—broadly conceived—for all involved. We noticed in our own conversation that we did not talk about the endemic racism of university–district–community partnerships as much as we could have. With this consideration in mind, we further built on our conversation by re-imagining it from a race-conscious lens. That conversation is presented below.

Building

Erica: Let's start by you sharing your earliest partnership experiences.

Decoteau: My earliest university–district partnership experience was when I was a graduate student working as a research assistant. I was a Black evaluator for a federal grant that required university, district, and community partners. As part of the grant, the district established a parent center to serve its largely Black and African immigrant student populations. The parent center the district created was just a building that was empty most of the time. It was in a weird location.

We would write these reports "We recommend that you put the parent center in the school." The district would respond with, "The school cannot stay open after these hours." It was just an uncoordinated mess, which is how districts often treat Black students and families. When the grant ended, the parent center closed.

Bradley: Yeah, that tracks my first experiences with district–community partnerships. I was on the school side though as a young assistant principal.

While our goal was to engage the community, looking back, I would say we did not have authentic and engaged relationships with stakeholders.

Our partnerships followed the old school model … that measured successful [parent/community] involvement by whether or not stakeholders were coming up to school during the school day and helping teachers laminate, make copies, put together bulletin boards … the token model of parent involvement.

The most authentic partnerships I witnessed were facilitated by Communities-In-Schools (CIS), which approached partnerships with parents and the community from a social work perspective of offering wrap-around services. The problem is that many programs like CIS were being, and continue to be, de-funded.

Decoteau: Right, an important consideration is who has what resources to bring to the collaboration. And if those resources are valued or not. Money and access to space drives the partnerships. White people have disproportionate access to those resources. Students and families in particular have experiential knowledge, which is a resource, but which is undervalued. What I see as the benefits of a partnership and what I can learn from a partnership is that I genuinely believe that Black people's knowledge is an invaluable resource. To understand where Black people are coming from requires me, even as a Black person myself, to kind of sit with and seek to understand people's point of view.

Bradley: That investment of time is so important. The people in higher education I most admire are those that speak with a seeming sense of freedom, in that they find the time to devote to these types of partnerships. So, I have to ask myself some tough questions, such as: Are my boundaries defined by selfishness as opposed to being caught in a system? Why am I not the embedded scholar I wanted to be at this point in my career? How can I become that scholar while trying to be a tenure-track professor, dad, and a complimentary partner in my own marriage, right?

Decoteau: What it sounds to me like you're saying is that you need time to develop deeper relationships. Racism complicates that process. So does class and the different priorities partners bring to the project. Things like the pace of the publication demands come to mind. The tenure clock runs too fast. But that's not any district or community person's problem. I don't know everyday folks who understand the process at all. Yet, the sense of urgency that tenure demands shapes relationships. We can't spend enough time in the field building strong relationships.

The tenure clock is fast. It does not incentivize or reward people for taking the time to develop the deep relationships where even people inside the district are mutually invested in the research. So in hindsight, it's important to name the constraints as a first priority of laying a partnership foundation.

Bradley: Agreed. I fought against that clock when I started at the University of Louisville. I do feel as if I built momentum and developed a few authentic and embedded relationships with community members in Louisville, as is evidenced by the fact that I still work with a number of people from that community.

That type of community embeddedness was completely derailed when I moved to a new university ... and I was only in Houston for three years. It is going to take me three or four more years at Baylor [Waco, TX] to even get back to that space where I was in Louisville, so while it may be attractive to move ... I think we have to ask ourselves, "What are we moving for?"

Like, I feel like many people in my Ph.D. program were socialized in a way that we needed to keep climbing [moving institutions], you know, keep climbing for something "better." It took several of us like five or six years to shed that socialization. We had agency obviously, but I think we accepted a specific narrative from several of our mentors.

Decoteau: For sure. I came to my current university in 2015 and I am only now, this year, getting ready to start doing Chicago-based research. It took five years for people to decide for themselves "yeah, he's a good person to work with." You've got to earn approval. That's because universities disrespect the very communities in which they exist. Universities uproot people. And yet my goal is to achieve rootedness. I think that is one of the reasons why it makes it difficult for me to imagine moving universities too often. My aspiration is not to climb, but to dig in, to be planted and firm. I like to call it resisting middle class maneuvering.

Bradley: Yeah, what is funny is like a lot of my peers from my Ph.D. program are now in a space where they want to go somewhere where they can simply be happy while also doing work that allows them to be involved in the community ... they are no longer "climbing."

So, when we look at our [tenure-track professors] space within higher education ... people are getting tenure, getting grants, making a living, yet there is often no authentic ... and I mean, I hate to say, but I think that is a qualifier that is coming to my mind right now ... no authentic connection [to the community and collaborative work]. No respect for the community, right?

And so, when we talk about re-imagining partnerships between universities and districts, they, through their policies and incentive structures, [higher education institutions] are often like, "We cannot change." Well, we [higher education] can [change] but it is difficult and takes time. We can change the people that are provided access to academia. We can recruit more diverse student populations. We can put different leaders in power, like department chairs, deans; and, we can develop different policies that change what is valued when seeking to procure tenure.

Erica: When you are doing more innovative work and getting deeper in the community, how do your colleagues see that? Is there any push back you get from colleagues or challenges among other people in your field?

Decoteau: I haven't experienced push back, per se. But it's also not rewarded and held in high regard. And what's held in high regard has everything to do with race and racism. We have to break free of the white supremacist psychology of scarcity. At the same time, scarcity is very real. I try to operate from a place of abundance, prioritize cooperativism, and reciprocity as relational principles. I try to resist being transactional. And extractive. That's what universities teach us to do—extract knowledge and present it as "findings."

Bradley: Agreed. Looking back on my experiences in higher education, I think this scarcity mindset pushed some colleagues to focus more on themselves than on building programs that actually benefit local communities. They were incentivized to close their doors and to be productive as a solo researcher. Subsequently, I think many early career professors operationalize their work in communities in more of a transactional fashion.

Decoteau: So, in this vein, if we are speaking about transforming a transactional framework of university–district–community partnerships, what if funders and agencies gave the money to the community to dole out for partnerships they see as beneficial? What if community stakeholders were actually the people who granted the funds to a university, a school, or a district? Better yet, why do they not do that?

What if a dean or provost determined ways to evaluate community-engaged scholarship? "Hey, research should not exploit communities. Reciprocity is part of your tenure requirements." That type of change is actually very easy. Now how can you demonstrate that outcome? Letters or testimonials from district or community partners. The publication should be accompanied by a cover letter outlining what led to the publication. That would change the game.

Now, that does put labor on people to draft letters, but again, the solution is simple: compensate people, minimally, for the letters they write. If not a letter, host a tenure panel where community members can speak to your contribution. Or a phone reference. If you can't get folks to show up that's telling. The panel would ask "did professors extract everything from your community and your knowledge, or did they not? What did you and your community gain from working with this person"? It is actually pretty easy to do. That literally would give power to people and create more balance.

Bradley: Yeah, I like this type of community-based accountability. If researchers and universities were having to compete to get money allotted by communities, right? This would allow the community to set the agenda and to evaluate partnerships for effectiveness. It [change] has to be about distribution of money and also the rewriting of tenure and evaluation policies to reflect a different value orientation toward relationship and mutual benefit and gain. Imagine that.

Erica: Even within schools, the people that have relationships with the community are often classified staff like the security guards, the cafeteria staff and the front office staff. They have deep community connections. Finding ways to connect with them is key. So, maybe not going to the higher levels within the district from the university perspective.

Discussion

In our conversation, we talked aloud about what ideal partnerships might look like if they were not constrained by racist priorities of hurriedness, career climbing, outcomes-orientation, and extraction. Watson and Fullan (1992) noted these tensions early on naming them as problems with organizational cultures that operate with different conceptions of work tempo and nature of time, professional focus—theoretical and practical, reward structure, and sense of personal power. These are differences that have racial consequences. With few exceptions, universities are primarily white organizations (Ray, 2019); however, the districts and communities with which university faculty and staff partner are often much more racially and ethnically diverse. It is precisely the racial knowledge held within the community that leadership in higher education readily ignore.

To ensure anti-racist partnerships, university leaders must fully acknowledge what is and is not valued within each partner's domain. Partners have interests. Interests shape how partnerships are formed and enacted. These interests are too often not openly acknowledge. Cultural assumptions and frames that go unacknowledged lay the groundwork for eventual harm. Take, for example, the white supremacist conception of treating everything in terms of scarcity, which leads to rapid exploitation of resources, including research relationships, time, publication outlets, and conference acceptances, which academia constructs as hyper-scarce. A perspective of abundance honors the value and strengths within the communities, appreciates communities, and slows scholars down enough to engage in the foundational work of conversing that creates more authentic partnerships. University leaders and faculty would benefit district and community partners if they built in time for relational development, as an expected aspect of research commitments.

Hinton's (2015) frameworks of possibility emphasize the values we want to change. We want to build outside of the existing oppressive structures of tenure and publication timelines to create new systems that allow for time to develop deep, meaningful relationships and community embeddedness within the contexts of resistance, trust, spirituality, and love. In our relationships, we want to acknowledge spirituality and honor the unique soul of each individual involved in research. We want to take the time to dig in and develop trust with individuals in the communities we connect with in a way that amplifies our shared work and possibilities for the future. Connections that endure beyond the timeframe of a single research project root us in the love that sustains us. We want the strength to resist the narrative emphasizing our own careers over community wellbeing. Trust and love strengthen our ability to collaborate, build foundations for future work, and resist inequity and oppression together. The frameworks of resistance, trust, spirituality, and love are abundant and help us to reframe the focus of our work.

As we re-imagine institutional practices and how we can demand and support redistribution of power and resources, we critique the racist systems in which we have participated with a move toward transformational resistance. In the interest of social justice and anti-racist efforts, we need to build new policies and practices, for example, the tenure process, that challenge the existing notions of power—who has power and who does not. We resist the oppressive nature of the tenure system and seek to transform it through prioritizing trust in community relationships which take time to develop and deepen. While existing literature on community engaged and public scholarship demonstrates movement in the direction of anti-racism, we push further. What we seek to build differs from the few university researchers and policies that value community engagement with a focus on collaboration and equality, incremental change, and the superhuman change-agent mentality (Changfoot et al., 2020). We assert that university researchers should be reporting to the community to rectify this imbalance of power. Systems must change so that researchers do not have to sacrifice their personal lives, feel they are working two jobs, or wait until they are tenured to do the work they believe in (Changfoot et al., 2020).

We can create shifts by moving away from systems that rely on perceived scarcity of material resources to promote selfishness (one's own career goals) and immorality (exploitation of communities). We resist the capitalist frameworks of scarcity and the notion that relationships are transactional to focus on engaging with communities and districts authentically and with reciprocity in mind. We can refocus reciprocity and ensure that communities gain health and happiness from partnerships with universities and are not held as sites of excavation. The purpose of research and partnerships is not to merely move forward a career or secure funding, but to promote community wellbeing and create just and equitable schools.

The good news is that an increasing number of researchers share the concern for mutual benefit. Warren, Park, and Tieken (2016) outline processes for beginning to train doctoral students in models of community-engaged research. DeLugan, Roussos, and Skram's (2014) research reports on their more than seven-year process of working to integrate a commitment to community-engaged research into the cultural milieu of their university. But we would be naïve to conflate community engagement with anti-racism engagement and partnership. We imagine that anti-racist partnerships go beyond mutual benefit. Anti-racist educational leaders who seek to promote these practices and policies within our institutions must: (1) define and incorporate community-engaged scholarship within the university; (2) change tenure policies to not only allow or accommodate community-engagement, but expect it and require evidence from community voices; (3) prioritize the voices of community members and build contexts in which they have the power and control of setting research agendas, positioning the researcher as a listener and learner rather than expert; and (4) create coalitions across universities to enact broad anti-racist systemic change within academia in which community agendas are sought out and centered. By valuing and emphasizing the unlimited resources of resistance, trust, spirituality, and love within the communities we serve, we can further our work for infinite influence in a way that is anti-racist, ethical, meaningful, and transformative.

Part IV

Recognizing and Accounting for the Work of Anti-racist Leadership

12

The Invisible Labor of PK-20 BIPOC Leaders

Zelideh R. Martinez Hoy, Dennis J. Perkins Jr., and
David Hoa Khoa Nguyen

Introduction: "You Can't Be What You Can't See"

We want to highlight that the term educator is used to define individuals who utilize formal and informal ways of knowing to educate students in PK-20 settings. Further, this chapter does not do justice to the needed recognition of Black, Indigenous, and People of Color (BIPOC) educators who practice pedagogies of survival and emancipation to protect the students and communities they work with, nor does it assume that one individual, campus, or district will dismantle 400 years of oppression. But rather, this chapter reintroduces and challenges coined terms, such as compassion fatigue (Koenig et al., 2018; Raimondi, 2019), racial battle fatigue (Pizarro & Kohli, 2018), moral distress (Santoro, 2018), etc., all terms used in attempts to name the emotional cost of working with students, families, and educators but fall short in acknowledging the invisible labor of those who present as, and many times come from, the marginalized and disenfranchised communities they serve. Because the terminology has primarily called on change to reside at the individual level in the form of resilience and self-care (Beltman et al., 2011; Mansfield et al., 2012), we call upon the re-examination of terminology that denies inclusion, protection, and recognition of the labor of BIPOC leaders and present action amongst all levels of preparation programs and educational administration in both PK-12 and higher education to manifest in their leadership practice.

Institutions of learning, from pre-kindergarten to graduate schools in efforts to diversify the workforce and keep up with the demographic shifts and growth of BIPOC students, have attempted to recruit from historically underrepresented groups (Carver-Thomas, 2018). Unfortunately, those efforts have not taken into account the structural racism upheld in these spaces—those that are dominated and operating with white, patriarchal, Christian, heteronormative, ableist, English dominant, xenophobic, and capitalistic structures—much less the hiring units' supports and resources that acknowledge working directly with marginalized populations within these structures, which many times further converges as a disconnect between educators' identity and lived experiences (Nguyen & Ward, 2019).

This chapter is a call to action that extends the responsibility beyond the individual and self-care and demands that organizations and leaders take decisive action in recognizing the invisible labor and emotional toll of BIPOC educators. By framing Critical Race Consciousness as a foundation, we identify challenges and possibilities, and structure narratives that limit the recruitment, retention, and promotion of BIPOC educational leaders. We propose that Critical Race Theory and consciousness must be used as a seminal and dynamic approach for authentic institutional efforts to demonstrate sustained investment toward anti-racist leadership practices, as well as support and advance BIPOC educators at all levels. We end the chapter with recommendations for leaders to examine their anti-racist leadership practice to provide professional space in recognition and understanding of this invisible labor and how leaders can design organizational cultures to foster space for anti-racism and inclusivity.

The Emotional Cost and Critical Race Consciousness

Very few studies have examined the emotional cost and invisible labor among educators and organizational leadership in PK-12 and higher education. Some have termed this invisible labor and its emotional costs as emotional labor (Humphrey, 2012), compassion fatigue (Martinez Hoy & Nguyen, 2019), secondary trauma (Lynch, 2017), racial battle fatigue (Smith, 2008), and burnout (Haberman, 2005). Either way, each of these concepts addresses the individual negative outcomes from professional work that BIPOC leaders face, and most studies discuss the implications for self-care (Quaye et al., 2019).

Literature in higher education has been generally sparse and has focused on the experiences of student affairs administrators (Long, 2012). Student affairs practitioners hold multiple roles and multifaceted job responsibilities to support their students while not being properly supported by their institutions nor their graduate preparation programs (Martinez Hoy & Gilbert, 2011), which can lead toward practitioners' attrition, job satisfaction, and burnout (Howard-Hamilton et al., 1998). Among PK-12 teachers and leaders, researchers examined how leadership can respond to the invisible labor, coined as emotional labor (Brown et al., 2014) or emotional toll (Cranston & Kusanovich, 2015). These studies have examined the intersections of the educational environment, workplace, and teachers' goals when working with students and their families. These demands may pose a variety of challenges that manifest in feelings of hopelessness, defeat, lacking efficacy in their role, and even complicity in supporting racist structures.

The Emotional Cost: Compassion Fatigue, Secondary Traumatic Stress, and Racial Battle Fatigue

Compassion fatigue is a result of "helping or wanting to help a traumatized ... person" (Figley, 2002, p. 1435). Since education is a helping profession, practitioners build empathetic relationships and can be emotionally affected by students' problems and trauma. This can include emotional exhaustion, disconnection, and callousness that leads to burnout (Stoves, 2014). Most studies that have addressed compassion fatigue were among the professions of psychotherapy, medicine, nursing, and the judicial system (Figley, 2002; Osofsky et al., 2008; Sabo, 2006). Only a few scholars have examined this phenomenon in student affairs (Bernstein Chernoff, 2016; Martinez Hoy & Nguyen, 2019; Raimondi, 2019) and identified that similar to other helping professions, student affairs educators experience similar symptoms and interventions due to the ongoing exposure to secondary trauma. In PK-12, there is limited research on the experience of compassion fatigue (Hoffman et al., 2007). Studies that have applied the compassion fatigue framework focus on those working in special education. Their findings are similar to studies in higher education, but none of them have examined issues that intersect with race and ethnicity or any other marginalized identity. Secondary traumatic stress can be synonymous with compassion fatigue. With the marked increase in the number of college students experiencing trauma, varying from sexual assault, alcohol and drug dependency, mental health issues, racialized trauma, violence, and suicide ideation, these have also had a secondary impact on practitioners (Silverman & Glick, 2010) who serve and support these students. Limited research on secondary or vicarious trauma (Parker & Henfield, 2012) in PK-12 has focused on school shootings and other school crises (Brock et al., 2002; Fein et al., 2008).

Racial battle fatigue is the physical and psychological toll on a person due to the constant discrimination, microaggressions, and stereotype threat (Smith,

2008). Racial battle fatigue has been studied among various racial groups, such as African-American/Blacks (Smith et al., 2007), Latinos (Call-Cummings & Martinez, 2017), and people of color, generally, and professional populations in higher education, such as graduate students (Harris et al., 2015), faculty (Smith, 2014), student affairs professionals (Hubain et al., 2016), and scholar activists (Gorski & Erakat, 2019). BIPOC practitioners that work in traditionally white spaces can experience a variety of issues, such as social withdrawal from colleagues, hypervigilance, hyper-visibility and hyper-invisibility, self-censorship, loss of self-confidence, adopting dominant paradigms and practices, among others. These can lead to anxiety, frustration, anger, helplessness, and depression. As a result, scholars have examined how to practice self-care from racial battle fatigue (Quaye et al., 2019).

Pizarro and Kohli (2018) have applied the racial battle fatigue framework to illuminate counterstories of BIPOC teachers working in a predominately white profession. Their research found that the policies, beliefs, and practices of the predominately white profession have created emotional and psychological trauma for BIPOC teachers and have led to attrition and burnout. Pizarro and Kohli (2018) suggest that it is critical that beyond teacher preparation programs, districts, and schools aim to diversify the teaching force and must center the work and expertise of BIPOC teachers. Tantamount is the need for leaders to move from recognizing the labor and implications to action. Policy and curriculum development must be led by and made up of BIPOC educators and communities.

Critical Race Consciousness

To examine how invisible labor has an impact on BIPOC educators, we frame our thinking through Critical Race Consciousness from Critical Race Theory (CRT). Ladson-Billings (1994a) used CRT to further analyze and critique educational research and practice and assess inequities in education. She argues that in order to move the racial justice needle forward, one must understand that the treatment amongst marginalized racial groups is inequitable to their white counterparts. Hiraldo (2010) contends that racism is seen as an inherent part of American civilization, privileging white individuals over BIPOC in most areas of life, including education.

As a result, DeCuir and Dixson (2004) stated that counter-stories are a resource that both expose and critique the dominant (male, white, heterosexual) ideology, which perpetuates racial stereotypes. Bell (1992) wrote that "the United States is known for its 'equality for all' image, but how far does this image go?" (p. 61). Although laws are put in place to promote and establish equality and justice for all, does society view its members as equals? Bell (1992) argued then and those who use CRT as part of their research also contend that without a true understanding of the tenets of CRT we cannot begin to understand the exploitation of BIPOC's bodies within the United States' education system.

Seminal Actions to Recognize Invisible Labor

Responding to the emotional toll and invisible labor of BIPOC educators must move beyond concepts of individual resilience and self-care. Pearlman and Saakvitne (1995) first called upon a multilayered approach to prevent vicarious trauma, including at and within the personal, professional, and organizational contexts. While Pearlman and Saakvitne (1995) were one of the first to move beyond resilience and self-care, their model did not consider the impact of racial trauma. As a result, educational leaders must self-evaluate their own leadership practice while also transforming their own organizational cultures with a clear understanding of anti-racist practices. The following recommendations invite leaders at various levels to approach and engage in the work with openness and curiosity; question, dissect, adapt, and above all recognize that sustainable change takes work and will be encountered with challenges.

Leaders Must See and Act

As an educational leader, seeking to see invisible labor and mitigate conditions is of utmost importance to first understand what Amado Padilla (1994) coined as *cultural taxation*. Cultural taxation describes the burden placed on underrepresented and BIPOC educators because of their identity or perceived identity as an ethnic or marginalized person. Padilla (1994) defined it as the obligation to demonstrate social responsibility toward the organization by serving as the ethnic representative on committees and provide expertise on an affinity group to support organizational diversity goals. This labor many times is unseen and unknown to leaders and supervisors since it is not directly assigned nor compensated. However, given the social responsibility and lack of diversity, BIPOC undertake these additional duties.

As a leader, it is critical to acknowledge the labor involved and the value to the organization. Leaders should ask and reflect upon the following prompts:

1. In reexamining the mission and vision of my unit, BIPOC staff are acknowledged and recognized within the outcomes and goals.
2. What implicit and explicit expectations do I recognize the organization has for BIPOC educators?
3. Knowing BIPOC students and their families often seek support from educators of the same background, how am I supporting my staff members in their explicit (or implicit) roles as advocates, counselors, or mentors for students?
4. How do I use my leadership to mitigate cultural taxation amongst my colleagues or staff?

Recognizing that most school systems and institutions are ill-equipped to deal with racial trauma, nor positioned to address the impact of historically disadvantaged communities, and where protocols dealing with families and students from such trauma are deficited (detention, suspension, dismissing of parent voices, etc.), we are calling on leaders to reimagine the role they play in highlighting community, family, and students' strengths and contributions. Leaders must ask and reflect upon the following points:

1. *Do I understand or recognize that systemic racism impacts BIPOC families and the students I serve and in turn my workplace and community?*
2. *How does minimizing the voices of BIPOC students and communities impact the work of educators advocating for those voices? What role do I play in minimizing these voices? How can I support these voices?*
3. *Do I recognize that the disproportionate silencing of parents and disciplining of BIPOC students' impacts BIPOC educators working with these students and families? Do I recognize that the trust and cultural brokering work of the BIPOC staff/educator are challenged by systemic disproportionality?*
4. *I seek to understand and meet students and caretakers where they are at without judgment and deficit commentary amongst colleagues.*

Leaders, regardless of identity, must recognize that most of their educational and professional experiences have been informed by the same systems of which we currently work. As recipients and representatives, we have witnessed the changing demographics but with limited response—what Welton, Diem, and Holme (2015) call being color-conscious, but colorblind. Colorblindness is what makes the labor invisible—there is no room to center dialogue around race. Further, training programs have lacked in curricula to address issues of social justice (Diem & Carpenter, 2012). We argue that culturally responsive pedagogy serves as a conduit for centering issues of race at various levels (Singleton & Linton, 2005). As leaders, we are called upon to identify our own positionalities and complicitness in supporting systems of oppression.

1. *Do I recognize or understand the need for culturally responsive pedagogy and programming?*
2. *Where and how do I call for the investment of culturally responsive pedagogy and programming?*
3. *How do I support or show up for culturally responsive pedagogy and programming?*

Building on the work of McIntosh's (1988), we recognize privilege as a series of interrelated hierarchies and power dynamics that impact all facets of life and include but are not limited to race, class, gender identity, sexual orientation, religion, education, age, physical ability, and expand to include ability to speak standard English and have a legal status or citizenship. Because these social constructs operate within hierarchies of power, it is important to recognize that having privilege in one way does not mean not being underprivileged in another, even within a group. Understanding the critical importance of access to power, we call upon leaders to be a conduit of access to those who may never otherwise have it. Leaders should reflect upon the following prompts:

1. Do I recognize my privilege?
2. In recognizing areas of disadvantaged or oppression, how do I avoid partaking in the oppression olympics, in other words, trying to "one up" the other?
3. In understanding my privilege, how do I listen, show up, and cede power?
4. Do I insist on diversity on leadership teams?
5. Do I seek to understand implicit bias in the workplace?
6. Do I seek to mentor, support, and connect staff at all levels and encourage other leaders to do the same?

Leaders must work intentionally to create environments that reflect genuine and intentional inclusion. These actions, while at the individual level, support an anti-racist work culture:

1. I am in the habit of sitting and interacting with someone I don't know well during meetings or communal gatherings.
2. I create opportunities to discuss issues of inequities in a non-judgmental setting.

Organizations Must Move beyond Symbolism

In order for there to be sustained improvement and lasting change for BIPOC educators, leaders must work at shifting their organizational cultures to acknowledge and understand their whiteness (Patton & Haynes, 2020), their anti-Blackness (Welton, 2020), and begin the collective effort at addressing these systemic and institutionalized oppressive practices.

After the murders of George Floyd, Breonna Taylor, among many more, and with the increased visibility of the Black Lives Matter movement and calls for anti-racist change, institutions and leaders in many industries and sectors, including educational institutions, published statements denouncing anti-Blackness and called to action for both internal and external work to dismantle systemic racism. Many educational institutions are also reexamining their campus monuments and the names of their physical structures as evidence of systemic racism. While this is a start, these actions are merely symbolic.

The work to address policies and practices that impact BIPOC educators' emotional toll from the work must be a commitment from the broader organizational collective. This work cannot be placed on BIPOC. This practice would further culturally tax BIPOC educators. For example, while many institutions have chief diversity officers, current practices place the burden on these equity, diversity, and inclusion (EDI) officers and educators to plan and implement programming, educate members of the community, respond to bias incidents, and become the institutions' spokesperson for all things "diversity." This cannot and must no longer be an institutional practice. While it is critical to leverage the expertise of our EDI leaders and educators to be a consultant, and a catalyst for cultural brokering, the work of transformation cannot rest on these individuals but with the collective, and leaders must become examples for this change.

While institutions engage in intentional hire and promotion practices to advance diversity, many do not have sustainable and tangible support systems to navigate these spaces. Below are some organizational practices that can help address the emotional toll felt by BIPOC educators in the organizational context:

1. The wearing of "multiple hats" in the resource scarce educational environment cannot be used to ignore the additional work BIPOC take on to support underserved and underrepresented communities.
2. Organizations and administrators must review and change institutional/organizational policies and practices that place invisible labor on BIPOC educators.

3. In order for sustained dismantling of institutionalized racism, the organizational culture must allow and encourage open dialogue, and support vulnerability among its staff for critical transformation.
4. Organizations and leaders must assign tasks that challenge white staff and equitably share the labor with BIPOC educators.
5. Organizations must provide space for physical and emotional sustainability through an environment where BIPOC educators can "tap out" for a break.
6. Lastly, but most importantly, institutions must address pay gaps, and compensate BIPOC educators equitably with a direct recognition of their invisible labor.

Conclusion

The field of education has been examining how best to address issues impacting students and their communities through trauma-informed practices, but very limited work has focused on the role and emotional labor of BIPOC educators. More than considering who is at the table, BIPOC educators are called to push themselves to re-conceptualize their own workplaces and personal lives. At the expense of reconceptualizing their lives in order to operate in predominately white spaces, BIPOC educators have taken on the burden to sacrifice their bodies and minds to serve their communities. Unfortunately, this work has seldom been recognized, nor compensated, thus highlighting the continued exploitation of BIPOC bodies. More importantly, their working environments have played a role in experiencing a variety of negative symptoms. While we are able to theoretically understand these symptoms and practically find ways to relieve these symptoms, we call upon a sustainable approach to dismantle the institutionalized racism and systemic oppression that play a role. Advancing this work is critical to address not only systemic racial justice but provide a just work environment for BIPOC educators and the communities they serve.

13

On the Backs of Black Women: Examining How the Supporting Administrative Role Is Entrenched in Racism

Asia Fuller Hamilton and Mykah Jackson

The lassitude spurred by the ongoing racial injustices that have happened toward Black people in the United States compels us as authors to bring to the forefront the experiences of Black children and Black educators in PK-12 schools. It is impossible for us to disconnect what is occurring in cities and states across America from what occurs behind the schoolhouse walls. In direct parallelism with what is happening in communities, the policing, surveillance, and villainization of the character of our Black youth is happening with an all-too-high frequency (Crenshaw et al., 2015; Morris, 2019). The undergirding question of how to create better outcomes for our Black children so that they have greater opportunities continues to persist. One way to begin to mitigate these disparities is by employing Black teachers of excellence as educators and administrators. Literature demonstrates the benefits of Black students having Black educators during the span of their K-12 education, including a firmer rooting in being more culturally competent in understanding the needs and talents of Black students (Ladson-Billings, 1995). Additionally, Black educators are more likely to create atmospheres that cultivate trust and belief of Black students (Rudd, 2014). However, we continue to see a dearth of Black teachers in the teaching force, with only 7 percent of the teaching force being Black compared to 80 percent being white (NCES, 2020). Similarly, we continue to witness stagnation in the percentage of Black educators who are principals, with the percentage holding steady at 11 percent since 1999 (NCES, 2020). While both teachers and principals are situated prominently in the literature, what is more obscure is other positions that fall between teacher and principal in the leadership realm, such as dean of students, assistant principal, vice principal, and associate principal. As we assume an anti-racist stance to our work in schools it is critical for us to amplify the voices of Black women in leadership, highlighting supporting leadership roles (associate principals, assistant principals, deans of students). In this chapter, we work to identify the racial hindrances that exist in those leadership roles based on our collective experiences. We also work to demonstrate how we used these experiences to break the cycle of oppression for ourselves and other Black women who aspire to become education administrators in the future.

CRT Lens and Black Feminism

Our leadership journey draws upon both Critical Race Theory (CRT) tenets and Black Feminism as the undergirding for explaining how race is embedded in all aspects of society and how it carries out in educational institutions for Black women. CRT allows us to look closely at the daily interactions of persons and find the racial components in them (Byrd, 2007), as well as bring out the position of race and racism in education as a means to also eliminate "subordination based on gender, class, sexual orientation, language, and national origin" (Solorzano & Yosso, 2002, p. 25). Our journeys embody CRT's five tenets: recognition that racism is normalized and is ingrained in US society; challenging of dominant ideology; recognition of the experiential knowledge of persons of color through counter-storytelling; commitment to social justice in efforts to rid racial subordination of all minoritized groups; and the challenging of ahistoricism by centering our experiences with racism in an educational context (Delgado, 1989; Parker & Lynn, 2002; Solorzano & Yosso, 2002). Additionally, using Tate's (1997) comprehensive review, the historical and theoretical foundations of CRT within education reveal two key components of CRT furthered by Derrick Bell. The first concept is that of the interest convergence principle which "is built on political history as legal precedent and emphasizes that significant progress for African Americans is achieved only when the goals of Blacks are consistent with the needs of whites"; and the second is the price of racial remedies which illustrates that "whites will not support civil rights policies that appear to threaten their superior social status" (Tate, 1997, pp. 214–15). CRT disrupts majoritarian stories that seek to silence the voices of racially minoritized groups by bringing to light the extent to which society inherently maintains the status quo of white people.

In this chapter, we will relate the interest-convergence principle to the experience of Black women in supportive administrative roles in the field of education. Like scholars who have come before us, "we are attempting to sing a new scholarly song—even if to some listeners our style is strange, our lyrics unseemly" (Bell, 1992b, p. 144). Our stories and narratives as Black women educators and leaders share the truths that are too often hidden. Through our experiences, we demonstrate how white leaders, under the guise of having diverse administrative teams, have used our talent, bodies, and skills for their own interests, including protecting themselves, profiting from our work and skills as they see fit.

Furthering the foundation of CRT, our chapter also centers Black feminism foundational principles. As Black women, our experiences of racism, sexism, and classism are intertwined and inseparable and because they exist intersectionally and must be addressed simultaneously (Collins, 2015). Additionally, there is a distinction from our needs and views as Black women from those of Black men and white women (Peterson, 2019), and in our connection and relationship to each other, we as Black women hold the capacity to help each other thrive and survive (Cooper, 2018).

We use the CRT methodological tool counter-storytelling to counter any belief that once a Black woman enters into a leadership position that they have somehow transcended racial strife. Instead we use our collective autobiographical stories to demonstrate that within supportive administrative positions, we have experienced racism by telling our stories; we seek to help other Black women in administration to resist racism in this form. Using counter-storytelling we describe, when navigating through the ranks, how we began to experience racism as leaders held three distinctions: suppression, grooming toward policing, and mammification. The first distinction can be described as an overt attempt to keep opportunities, examples of Black excellence, and access from our immediate reach. We assert that these were both blatant and subtle attempts to keep us "in our place." We define grooming toward policing as an attempt to hold Black administrators responsible for the oversight of maintaining the disciplinary and academic status quo. Lastly, the mammification distinction discusses how our bodies as Black women leaders are often used as shields that serve the interests of our white leaders that we served under.

Black Women in Educational Leadership

Our pathways in leadership are both similar and non-monolithic. Both of us began as teachers within a force that held an overrepresentation of women in teaching positions, with the vast majority of those teachers being white. We both began in the same diverse district that was recruiting minority teachers during which time the district had recently entered a formal consent decree—a federally mandated agreement of resolve between parties with the absence of liability. This consent decree detailed the district's neglect of Black students academically within both general education and accelerated courses and an over-identification of Black students with regard to recorded disciplinary infractions and out-of-school suspensions. The consent decree outlined necessary action steps needed in order for the district to be relieved from the federal and community oversight. As new Black educators coming into the district during the beginning of the consent decree, our ascension into leadership positions held us in positions as inextricably both pawn and queen—positions of vulnerability and of power. The melanin in our skin would, at times, be used as an access pass to demonstrating that the goals of the decree were headed in the right direction—a modern-day Blackface. It would not be until later that we would recognize how much power we held and begin to utilize it.

On the Back of Black Women: Asia's Narrative

I was young when I assumed my first leadership role as dean of students in a middle school—just twenty-six years old. The school was located in a district that had been held in contempt by the Black community for not fulfilling its obligation to fully and properly educate Black students. Black students at all levels throughout the district held disproportionately higher numbers of suspension than their white counterparts and they held the highest numbers of failing grades. The district had also failed to ensure that Black students had access to and were enrolled in rigorous academic courses. The school district was under a legal mandate to improve the learning conditions for Black students. When I became dean, the district was in its sixth year under this mandate.

The position I held was considered to be an entry-level position for new administrators within the district and it entailed primarily dealing with discipline issues that arose across three grade levels. When I reflect on the role of being a dean of students, it was a gatekeeping position, which, in my mind, I have no doubt contributed to the historical lack of Black woman principals in our district. Having been mired in emotionally stress-filled duties with little immediate rewards, many Black women in the district either wanted nothing to do with the dean position, served in the position and moved on to other ventures unrelated to the principal track, or became relegated to the position, unable to move because they were not promoted.

Nonetheless, at the time I was so happy that I had been hired to be in an administrative role that I did not realize the weight of what I would carry. Neither did I realize how I would become the administrator who would deal with students and parents who would be found undesirable or difficult for my principal—a white woman, or the assistant principal—a Black male, to interact with. Although I knew that I had to work in a position that was considered to be grunt work, I was intentional and optimistic about seeing the role as an opportunity to build relationships with students and their families.

For the first couple of years, I entered the position with rose-colored glasses. I worked hard to do well at my job and even held the mindset of "My job is to make my boss look good." In my third year, the glasses began to crack which yielded the fallacy of that mindset. I was eight months pregnant and had endured an exceptionally hard week with girl fights. On this particular day, the mothers of two of the girls wanted to come in for a discussion with each other. They were tired of the back-and-forth arguing. The parents had asked to speak to the principal and were very clear about not wanting to see the assistant principal because they did not trust him. My principal agreed to meet with them but had asked me to help facilitate the conversation with the two women, who were also Black. When we entered the conversation with the women, they began telling their sides of the story, each in defense of their daughter. The conversation was intense with many expletives and the volume at which each mother was speaking was very high. In the middle of this conversation, my principal excused herself for lunch duty. I continued to try to de-escalate the conversation with mounting frustration at the fact that the conversation seemed circular. Still, I remained calm and continued to try to mediate the conversation. After about forty minutes, the conversation continued to escalate with threats of violence between the two mothers.

At eight months pregnant, I knew that I would need some support, but needed to figure out an opportune time to retrieve it since my pregnancy placed me in a compromising position if any fighting occurred. It was at this heightened moment that the office door opened and my colleague, another Black woman who was many years my senior who had mentored me throughout my tenure at the school, burst through the door and inquired if I was okay. I said yes, but was relieved to see her. She dispersed the parents telling them that they needed to solve this problem outside of school and that she wouldn't allow them to put me in harm's way. After the parents left, she came over to me and said, "That's a doggone shame! That woman left you in here alone knowing you were eight months pregnant while she stood outside the door listening!" The gravity of what she said didn't fall upon me until much later. The entire time my principal was outside the door when she could have intervened at any time. In reflecting on this moment, I realized she was too afraid to come in, but she allowed me to stay in there.

In that moment, I recognized that I was a pawn that was able to be sacrificed. I had considered my principal to be a mentor, but I saw instead that she was more interested in self-preservation and saw me as expendable to that moment. Even though she would say that I was invaluable to her and that my work was excellent work, and my evaluations would also substantiate this, I would find out two years later that when she was approached by the superintendent of schools and asked if I was ready to become a principal, she told him that I was not. Finding out that my boss that I worked so diligently under had told the assistant superintendent that I was not ready for a principal position cut me to my core. It was rooted in selfishness. Every evaluation, every positive word spoken was all about acceleration and moving me to the next level of administration. She wanted me to continue helping her in the capacity in which I was serving, that she decided to clip my wings. If it had not been for another Black woman's advocacy, I am not sure I would be in my leadership journey. It made me wonder what other acts of violence had been committed against me.

Make You Look Good—I Am Invisible: Mykah's Narrative

I began my educational leadership career in my eighth year in education. I was thirty years old, had just celebrated my one-year wedding anniversary, and I was excited for the new opportunity ahead. I had hopes of having an even greater impact on student learning. I began as an assistant principal at an elementary school. This was the entry-level administrative position at the elementary level.

I was truly grateful for the opportunity to be an assistant principal. My experience up to this time was at the middle school but I experienced little success moving up at this level. I was told that it was not uncommon, especially seeing that all of the middle schools had at least one administrator of color.

I began administration in a district that was recently released from a legal mandate for its lack of accountability to the achievement of Black students. Black students were disproportionately suspended at higher rates than their white counterparts. Black students held the highest numbers of failing grades and less seats in rigorous academic courses. The district looked healthy on Report Card data. However, when disaggregated across race, disproportionalities across various categories were apparent.

I soon came to fully realize what racism looked like in leadership a week into my new position. My principal and I were sitting in the office after a long day at work. She (white female) shared something with me that would forever change my perspective. She shared that she was so glad that she reached out to my other references. My previous principal, a white female, had given me a bad reference. I was stunned, hurt, and confused all that same time.

Truly this was confidential but also odd to hear coming from another white female. My previous white female principal had served as my team leader for two years. This same white female then served as my assistant principal and evaluator for four years. She rated me as an "excellent" teacher. This same white female would go on to serve as my principal for one year prior to my transition into leadership. My classroom served as a "showcase" when visitors came and she was able to "count on me" to hold down my hallway even though the hall monitor was stationed outside my classroom.

After catching my breath, I realized that I should have not been surprised. After all, it was the Black female assistant principal who asked me, "What do you plan to do with your career in leadership"? It was the Black female assistant principal who asked if I had seen the job openings and she already had a letter of recommendation prepared. It was the Black female assistant principal who encouraged me to apply for a summer school admin substitute position to improve my resume.

It was the Latino male assistant principal who called for me to sub for him as summer school principal. It was the Latino male who encouraged me to apply for administrative openings because he "saw something in me."

My previous white female principal never encouraged me to move forward in leadership. She never shared any words of wisdom along my journey. While she acknowledged my work, obviously it was only from a positive lens as long as I stayed in her building. I came to understand that while I respected her for her work ethic and ability to lead, she did not respect my work ethic and ability to lead if she was not able to benefit from it.

My thinking was confirmed when a few years down the line, the Black female assistant principal shared that she was glad to have left from under our former white female principal. She shared that she was yelled at when our principal discovered that she wrote me a letter of recommendation. She was told that it was her job to find another teacher "that would hold down my area."

From this experience, I realized that to be an anti-racist leader is a conscious decision. It was another white female colleague who shed light on the malpractices too often inflicted upon Black women in their ascension to and within supportive administrative roles. I am grateful for the experience. It made me even more proud of my firm work ethic and high regard for integrity. Those essential traits showed in my curriculum vitae, letters of recommendation, my students' portfolios, *and within my personal testimony during my interviews. My personal narrative overcame the falsely constructed narrative of my oppressor.*

Analysis

When analyzing our experiences as administrators, we were situated in a male-dominated field. We expected to encounter the patriarchal oppression from our male colleagues. Collins (1989, 2000) concludes how women in leadership have not received as much attention primarily due to systems that value male-controlled leadership, which unfortunately suppresses and oppresses the contributions of women in leadership. This was especially true in our district where the values of patriarchy were strong with the school board, central office, and among school leaders. What was not as evident, at the time, was the number of racist encounters, micro-aggressions, and oppression we would receive at the hands of white women leaders. We were young and had not yet fully understood the gravity of how our intersectionality would affect our experiences.

Studies have revealed that Black women leaders and administrators had different experiences than white women (Hite, 2004; King & Ferguson, 2001; Kimball & Sirontnik, 2000). Researchers came to the realization that women of color experienced conditions affecting them differently. As a result, it became evident that Black women in leadership have different experiences that warrant their own area of research to capture their uniqueness expressed through multiple areas (King & Ferguson, 2001). Stressors experienced by Black women that affect them differently include:

> (1) the isolation black women experience in dominant culture organizations; (2) the high visibility black women experience due to their race and gender and their subsequent need to make choices about public association; (3) the need to invest in alliance-building with the power elite; (4) the personal overload stemming from participation in two or more cultures (e.g., racial/ethnic culture, dominant culture); (5) the conflicts stemming from pressures to fulfill race and gender-role expectations in contexts that have conflicting norms and values; (6) the ambiguity of being in a non-traditional profession, or of having a level of authority beyond that which is customarily expected for black women. (King & Ferguson, 2001, p. 128)

We observe three dominant themes that emerge as we recount our stories and interactions. These following themes help us to identify the racism we experienced so that we can work to dismantle it.

Suppression

Suppression is a theme that seems to emerge throughout our tenure as Black women leaders. Experiences with suppression include, but are not limited to, withheld information, delayed or withheld experiences, lack of accessibility to other Black leaders.

Mykah

The Black women role models were few and almost not accessible. I recall my first mentor in the aspect of educational leadership being a Black woman. I had the opportunity to see her entire tenure as a principal. This had a great impact on my career and sparked my interest in leadership. She was an assistant principal for eight years prior to acquiring the position as principal. She was sharp, informed, and always mindful of her surroundings. She often shared that we always have to work twice as hard and be twice as smart as our counterparts. I learned from her that despite obstacles, if you lead with passion you would succeed. It was her passion that kept her going when her school, staff, students, and families were continuously overlooked by the shadow of her white counterpart across town. Her counterpart appeared to have a way of getting her school highlighted more often by the local press. Her access within the community allowed her the ability to appear as though she was doing more. You always saw this white female leader's face while everyone knew the three Black women on her staff were doing the work but were never in the forefront, never mentioned in the press, left out of the discussions that led to higher positions.

Looking back, as Black women we were spread out across the district. Not enough opportunities were afforded us to dialogue about our experiences. If this were so, we would have realized that we were not alone. Too often, we operated as outsiders within our schools while others operated within the school community. They benefited as participants while we were working to create a space for ourselves and our students of color.

Mammification and Policing

Another theme that arose in our sharing of experiences is the depiction of Black woman as a mammy holds its historical roots during the time after slavery as a form of reimaging the Black woman from the previous branding of being "lascivious, wanton and sexual" to something that would be more palatable to the white women that would have them working in their homes (Harris-Perry, 2011). This long-standing exploitation of Black women has been a long-standing practice in post-slavery American society. The model is one that has been depicted in the media as unintelligent (*Gone With the Wind*), battered with limited options (*The Help*), and an overt pleaser with no regard for herself (*The Imitation of Life*). In many ways, these depictions have pervaded the educational leadership realm with respect to Black women. In our experiences, working under white women head leaders has been like being subjected to mammy roles. It can feel like a situation of being "told your place and staying there"—a conditional sub-servitude that remains intact unless you break that yoke. Especially in the position of dean of students, it felt as though it were at times a subservient role where we're also expected to police the very families we wanted to serve. We were held responsible for the oversight of maintaining the disciplinary and academic status quo.

Mykah

I like to think that the secretaries tell it all when it comes to the discussion of how our bodies as Black women leaders are used as shields to serve the interest of our white leaders that we served under. I recall the times, and this would occur often, when I would be called to the office by the secretaries for support with parents of color, many of whom were in a heightened state by the time of my arrival.

There was one occasion where a father came into express concerns about interactions with his son and another student. He was upset that he had to speak with me as he requested to speak with the principal who was not available at the time. The parent quickly escalated as he expressed his concerns and reached a level to where I had to shift the conversation. I shared that I want to hear your concerns and I will do my best to support but I need for you to bring it down just a little. We were in the conference room which was situated between the principal's office, my office, and was practically still in the main office.

The parent escalated even more to the point where I told him, this meeting is over. We can reconvene when you are in a more responsive position. However, at this time, I need for you to leave. At this moment, I think that we both were shocked that it had reached this point. He continued to share his concerns aloud as he exited the building.

The secretaries said, "Are you okay?" "We were wondering if we needed to call the police." I reassured them that I was okay. I was even more concerned for the student and his parents. I asked if they were able to reach our principal. I still remember the look on her face when one of the secretaries said, "I think he is in his office."

The thought that my principal was near and would not respond to support was disheartening. I was positioned as the heavy, disciplinarian, or someone to call on to save staff. Never from the position of instructional leader, never in the forefront or mentioned outside of discipline, left out of the discussions that led to higher positions. I remember being treated like I was a secretary to my white male principal—good enough to carry out assigned tasks that allowed me to assist others in particular ways that were rarely mentioned openly.

Asia

I would be the first one called for fights between Black students. I was the one called to speak to or sit in on conferences with "angry Black mommas" or to diffuse the arguments between Black girls. Even though I was the dean of students, I began to realize that when I made decisions about the consequences of behavior, I was being a modern-day patty roller. The day I realized this was the day that I decided my position was one where I could give voice and agency to students—to be able to offer restorative justice.

Conclusion: Dismantling Racism as Lead Administrators

We both currently serve as school principals. As we recount these experiences, we want to go further than just reliving these experiences. It is important for us to ensure that we illuminate the pathway for other Black women who have the goals and ambition to become education administrators. We offer insight into what we do now as principals to make this a reality. First, we offer mentorship to people who seem reluctant to ask and oblige those who do. This mentorship is transparent and can include lessons learned, but really focuses on the needs and insights of the person asking. We also attempt to tear down the barrier by allowing aspiring Black women leaders to see what the offerings in leadership may be. Our goal is to provide them with the mentorship that is brokered by the curiosity they may have.

Next, we expand the learning field. Being a lead administrator means we have to broaden the spectrum of experiences that young, interested Black women in leadership positions have exposure to. We invite them to meetings, ask them to serve on or visit school-level and district-level meetings, or allow them to lead a particular venture of their choosing—and then we discuss after. The discussion portion is one that can lead to new requests and new shared insights. We feel that it is incumbent upon us to not become the gatekeepers that serve to hinder us.

Lastly, we share our stories. Our stories are at times a reassurance to aspiring Black women educational leaders that are not alone in their journey. Our stories can also service as conduits for change and inspiration. They are a culmination of warning signs and a bridge that helps make the chasms that exist in the world of educational leadership easier to cross. Allowing other Black women leaders in supporting roles who aspire to escalate into higher positions to find their successes to stand on our shoulders is the only allowances we are willing to make.

14

Anti-racism for White People: From Inactivism to Activism

Jeffrey S. Brooks

The high-profile murders of George Floyd, Breonna Taylor, and Ahmaud Arbrey in quick succession were collectively a catalyst for huge and vigorous anti-racism protests around the world, many of which united people across color lines and prompted previously silent citizens to speak out against violence, oppression, and hatred. Certainly, this is commendable—the trouble is, we have been here before. While the names listed above are now widely known, we can add many others to a list of people killed in the United States just for being Black: Trayvon Martin, Eric Garner, Michael Brown, Philando Castile, Tamir Rice, Renisha McBride, Laquan McDonald, Freddie Gray, Addie Mae Collins, Emmett Till, Cynthia Wesley, Carole Robertson, Carol Denise McNair, and thousands of others through the country's troubled history. You may recall some of these names with great clarity, but why are some forgotten or unfamiliar? Because many white people in the United States lose interest in the struggle for racial equality soon after the news fades to commercial. Because white people fail to educate themselves about the history, contemporary context, and possible futures of racism and anti-racism in their community and country. Because white people with "good intentions" fail to speak out and stand up when they see micro-aggressions in their family, city, school, and workplace (Keels et al., 2017; Stovall, 2006; Sue, 2010). Because white people are afraid to jeopardize or problematize their cultural capital, economic position, or formal and informal privilege in institutions that are consistently hostile or violent toward people of color. Because white people don't know what to do, and so many of them do nothing—perpetuating silent obedience and consent to white supremacy and contributing to the pervasive existential threat and actual violence that people of color deal with as a daily matter of routine (Bell, 2004).

The question is—what are white people like me going to do about it? It is up to us to play a leading, active, and visible role in the difficult and dangerous work of unlearning the racism we have been taught—and that we are perpetuating through our silence and inaction. It is the responsibility of white people to recognize and dismantle the racist institutions we benefit from and we strengthen through omission and commission. It is up to white people, as individuals and through collective political will and action, to learn, teach, inspire, act, and create an abolitionist future through small and grand anti-racist strategies across all sectors (Bell, 2004; Delpit, 1995; Leonardo, 2009; Stovall, 2013; West, 2017; Wilson & Johnson, 2015). Are you in? In for the work long-term, or just here to wave a flag and post a selfie at a rally wearing a Black Lives Matter t-shirt? Are you in? In to learn new ideas from old teachers and to challenge and unlearn false "knowledge" that forms the foundation of your worldview? If you *are* in, I invite you to keep reading and consider what moving from inactivism to activism in relation to racism will look like for you—as you have been taught racism, so too can you unlearn it—by actively changing what is in your head, heart, conversations, community, and country you can play an important role in dismantling racism (Hacker, 1992; Welton & Freelon, 2018).

White People, Racism, and Anti-racism

Anyone who studies racism will find most of what I wrote in the preceding introduction familiar. I am not saying anything here that great scholars, politicians, and activists haven't said before, many of it said much better by scholars of color (Bonilla-Silva, 2006; DuBois, 1903; Fordham, 1996; Jackson, 1988; Tatum, 2003). It is important to explain that I am not pretending to put forth a new way of conceptualizing or engaging with racism—the purpose of this chapter is rather to (a) make an appeal to white people for action, (b) provide a systematic way for developing a deeper understanding of racism and anti-racism, (c) help identify what racism and anti-racism look like historically and in your own context, (d) form intention around the various strategies that might be used to act against racism, and (e) encourage action that will facilitate change in people, institutions, and society. Change is not only possible, it is inevitable—the question we must all answer individually is whether our own actions will contribute to a positive change toward a just or anti-racist society, or to a negative change that strengthens hatred, division, and violence. At this point, it is important to define a few key terms. We need to know what we are up against if we have any hope of developing effective strategies for working against it.

Defining Racism

Race is a cultural construct used by one group of people to oppress another group of people based on nothing more than the color of their skin. Racism, then, is the psychological, emotional, ideological, social, political, physical, legal, and economic manifestation and expression of this oppressive cultural construct—that is to say that racism is a ubiquitous malevolent force that shapes the way we think and act, what is considered "normal" and "abnormal" in community and country, and the ways that certain people are included in (or excluded from) certain opportunities (Brooks, 2012; Brooks & Watson, 2018; Fluehr-Lobban, 2006). If you are a white person who has grown up in the United States, your life has been significantly shaped by racism and you have benefited from privilege, whether or not you are aware of this. By and large, white people experience a community and school life where their culture is considered normal, their skin is beautiful, and their opportunities for achievement are constrained only by the limits of their ability and the circumstances of their birth. Conversely, people of color in the United States are born criminalized, their bodies predisposing them to greater disadvantage, violence, and marginalization across all sectors of society (Yancy, 2016). People of color are born into a culture that devalues them, debases them, and stereotypes them into roles and expectations that put physical, cultural, educational, and economic barriers in the way and limit (or prevent) opportunity. On top of cultural bias and institutionalized racism is the constant threat of psychological and physical violence that could come from anyone at any time across any sector—from friends and colleagues, police officers and real-estate agents, baristas, politicians, teachers, and priests (Bonilla-Silva, 2006). Being a person of color in the United States is to live in a different country from white Americans—it is having your identity and relationship with people and institutions shaped by an intricate network of invisible and visible barriers and an arsenal of weapons of hatred constantly trained on you, and to walk among people and systems that see you at best as an inferior "other" at best, and at worst an enemy (Hacker, 1992). That is not to say that every white person has a great life and that every person of color does not. Indeed, nearly everyone can point to examples contrary to that perspective, but it is certainly the case that people of color *must* navigate dangers at every turn and overcome additional and daunting obstacles that white people have never considered as an issue. As racism has persisted for hundreds of years, it is cumulative, meaning that injustices compound over time as more and more white people benefit from privilege and people of color are victims of oppression and violence (West, 2017).

Yet, racism does not just naturally exist; it is taught (Tatum, 1994). Paradoxically, one of the most terrible and encouraging aspects of racism is that it is learned—which means that it can be unlearned. That said, unlearning your miseducation about race is a daunting and lifelong prospect, as the lessons come from every sector of society and from nearly everyone around you. Racism is taught informally in homes across the country where parents make disparaging comments in front of their children that establishes a superior "we" and an inferior "they." In many households, this transmission of attitude and message is even more direct, as family members who are vocally racist indoctrinate children into a racist worldview purposefully and at a young and impressionable age (Bonilla-Silva, 2001). Home life is not the only teacher of racism, however. Lessons are taught across sectors and through every medium. The nightly news often reinforces stereotypes and sensationalizes or amplifies crime in communities of color, as much reporting is shaped by inaccurate cultural assumptions and a lack of depth in coverage of historical conditions that established and perpetuated racism in the country. As mass media news has become increasingly fractured and partisan and social media has increased the flow of erroneous or heavily slanted messages, the potential for racism to be taught informally has increased dramatically. Bigoted messages are freely accessible across many platforms and institutions, from social media to houses of worship, and are active as well as passive, aggressively targeted to mislead people interested in learning more about issues related to racism (Leonardo, 2004). The fact that racist messages come small and large, and via every possible means of communication, demands that we all raise our critical consciousness, develop critical media literacy skills, and seek to discern the source, biases, and motives behind information, reporting, and messaging (Bliuc et al., 2018).

Identifying racist messages is made all the more difficult because racism manifests in both overt and covert ways (Coates, 2011). It is "in your face" in the form of obviously spiteful rhetoric, racist policies, prejudicial practices, offensive art, bigoted music, and obvious misinformation. Such expressions of racism are rightly characterized as hate speech, and are often grounded in unsubstantiated claims or narratives that present an incomplete and slanted perspective on a complex social phenomenon. Covert racism takes many forms: hostile glances or tones of voice; inequitable policies that seem to give everyone a fair chance but that in practice punish, devalue, or exclude people of color; historical legacies in the form of unwelcoming spaces or monuments to racist institutions or "heroes." People and institutions can be racist even if they don't shout it from the rooftops—it is an unspoken menace. People who do not see themselves as racist, or who have intentions to be anti-racist, perpetuate or practice covert racism if they are not actively working to unlearn racism by (a) reflecting on their assumptions and unlearning oppressive assumptions; (b) learning about racism in general and educating themselves about what it looks like in their immediate contexts; and (c) interrogating their behavior in work, school, home, and community contexts. Even by "working on the work," as Watson (personal communication, 2020) often says, it is important to note that one does not *become* anti-racist as it is not a state to achieve or place to arrive, but rather anti-racism is an *ongoing lifelong process* of critical reflection, unlearning, discovery, and creation of a new personal and institutional reality.

The "definition" I offer above is complicated. There are personal, relational, and institutional elements to it, and these are rooted in historical precedent. Racism is everywhere, while at the same time, constantly changing. This underscores the dynamic nature of racism and anti-racism, and reinforces the point that it is important to be always working on the work in your own space, actively unlearning your miseducation. Silence is not neutrality; silence is racism (Singleton, 2014). But what does speaking out and standing up look like? And what are you up against?

From Inactivism to Activism: A Typology of Modes for Racist and Anti-racist Behavior

White racism in the United States has a much longer history than white anti-racism—400 years of oppression versus 50 years of inconsistent and random acts of symbolic resistance. This means there are a lot of deeply entrenched practices and powerful institutions that need dismantling and reimagining. It will not be achieved by bursts of activity alternating with moments of silence (Fredrickson, 2015). White people have created institutions that don't allow people of color to "rest" as they are beset by racism across all sectors, by many of the people in their communities and via a non-stop media, news, and policy campaign. Choosing the path of anti-racism is making a choice that will exhaust and challenge you in ways you have never considered. Nonetheless the time has come to act. But what actions are most effective, and how do we answer one of the most important questions that white people have in relation to racism—what can I do about it?

There are a range of ways people and institutions engage with racism and anti-racism (Diem & Welton, 2017). Racism is a fluid phenomenon, and so are the responses to it, and actions against it (Brooks et al., 2013). In this section of the chapter, I discuss a typology of action, beginning with racist activism, moving into forms of inactivism and then finally discussing activist modes of addressing racism. Importantly, I describe these as "modes" in keeping with my assumption that we will address issues in different modes for various reasons. You don't *arrive* in a mode, you *act* in a mode.

Racist Modes of Activism

Racism operates in different spaces and functions under privileged rules, relative to anti-racism.[1] In many instances, mechanisms for changing racist policies are controlled by racist procedures that exclude minoritized voices or dissent from the majority. That said, it is useful to identify some of the more common forms of racist activism in order to understand what actions and reactions might be most effective against them.

Architectural Mode

People who operate in architectural mode create, sustain, and strengthen institutional racisms. These are the people, groups, and organizations who put policies, laws, and rules into place that are either overtly or covertly racist. They operate in three basic phases: policy development, policy implementation, and policy revision. Often, the formal documents used to strengthen such institutions in the policy development phase are "colorblind" or written and spoken about in the language of equity and social justice (Larson & Murtadha, 2002). At the policy implementation phase, incentives and sanctions are used to shape the real-world meaning of the policy into a force for or against racism, and often they can be a combination of the two. The policy revision phase is routinely slow, excludes the concerns of people of color, and is crafted by white people who stand to benefit from the status quo.

Antagonist Mode

People who act in the antagonist mode are overtly and belligerently racist. This can take the form of an aggressive and loud angry mob (or individual) or the impassive countenance of a person steadfastly committed to a racist process or outcome who refuses to act in a just manner. Antagonist mode takes the form of micro-aggressions, which are subtle slights, exclusions, or passive-aggressive expressions that help create a hostile environment for people of color

(Sue, 2010). Another common strategy for people in antagonist mode is silence or bystanderism when racial compassion and anti-racist intervention are needed (Brooks & Jean-Marie, 2007). People and organizations acting in antagonist mode will often act violently and openly use offensive and abusive language. They will also issue statements reinforcing and defending a racist practice, support and share racist media and social media, and paradoxically accuse victims of racism of being racist themselves. Significantly, antagonist mode is what many people think of as the *only* kind of racism. They believe that if they refrain from acting in this manner they are anti-racist, when in fact there are several other modes of racist behavior, including no behavior at all.

Absolvist Mode

People and organizations in absolvist mode believe that race is not their problem. They may believe that because they live in a racially homogeneous community, they are somehow enlightened by physical proximity, they may "have Black friends," they may leave the work to others because it is too difficult, confusing, or dangerous, they may be ignorant of racial dynamics, or they may believe that because they have good intentions in their heart they are not part of the problem. But, as we are part of a fluid global community and racial issues permeate all levels of society, the idea that engaging racial issues "is someone else's job" is misguided.

Alchemist Mode

Alchemists' attitudes toward issues of race are based on the false assumption that what they have always done is tantamount to social justice and anti-racism. This is because Alchemists behave in anti-racist ways in one aspect of life or work, only to practice racism in another. This essentializing way of looking at anti-racism is hugely problematic and akin to white saviorism where a white person is anti-racist in their rhetoric or symbolic behavior, but either perpetuating or passive in relation to institutional racism. It is possible that white saviors deliver diversity workshops and do some good, but it is done by centering and privileging their own experience rather than the identities and work of people of color. This is often based on the "irrefutable proof" that they once had a student of color who graduated against the odds or that they "advocate for all students, regardless of race," allowing them to wear a few incidents as social justice badges of honor while neglecting to continue learning and unlearning how they might be practicing racism in other aspects of their life.

Apathetic Mode

People operating in apathetic mode have some awareness and knowledge of racial issues, but they do not speak out or act on this awareness. A great many people default to this mode due to fear—fear of saying or doing the wrong thing. But as with so many things in life, education is the key to developing the confidence to act. Learning more about concepts, histories, issues, and forms of action will embolden and help would-be anti-racists' move from inaction to action. The key is to be proactive and responsible about learning without placing a burden on people of color to teach you, and to be observant of conversations around the world and in your context that shape the way you experience and understand racism and anti-racism.

Neutral Modes of Activism

There are no neutral modes of activism—you either support racism through your work or silence, or you actively work against it.

Anti-racist Modes of Activism

While I have suggested some issues already, one of many questions that remains is "should white people be doing anti-racist activism?" The short answer is yes—and that work should be visible and occur in all the spaces you live and work—not just in safe spaces or among like-minded peers. The longer answer is that there are many situational, contextual, and cultural considerations to take into account (Horsford, 2011). Equally important is not to center the white experience or privilege white "solutions" to Black problems. You cannot be silent, but equally you are not a savior—you cannot do activism *at* or *for* people, it must be done *with* people—and the work must be guided and shaped by the people and communities it intends to benefit.

It is difficult to unlearn your racism in public, but anti-racist activism must be done in public for it to be effective. The manner in which this happens will be distinct for every person and in every context, but the maxim guiding the work is "stand up and speak out," not "be nice and stay quiet." Don't give up. When you have a setback, learn from it, reflect, have the humility to acknowledge you were wrong, and then get back in and start fighting again—there is no other way.

Activism is also about using your privilege to dismantle institutions that have benefited you your whole life. This is one of the principal reasons the work is so difficult and seldom goes beyond good intentions—you must actually work against an injustice from which you benefit. This is where too many white people stop. That said, if we accept that you are working either for or against racism and that a neutral stance is impossible, it is incumbent on white people to redistribute power and privilege—through both soft and hard revolutions (Postman & Weingartner, 1971).

Soft revolutions are strategies that seek to change a system from within, using the system's own protocols, procedures, and policies to shift the institution from one of oppression to one of social justice. These strategies include things like supporting an anti-racist candidate for an elected position, working through an approval process to see equity-focused books included in a curriculum, petitioning for a new law, or creating a new policy that undoes an unjust one. A hard revolution is when strategies seek to force change on an institution through external pressure. This need not be violent. Indeed, the likes of Martin Luther King, Jr. (2011) and Mahatma Gandhi (1951) showed the world that non-violent resistance and Satyagraha could change society. Hard revolutions might also take the form of sit-ins, demonstrations, picket lines, strikes, teach-outs, social media campaigns, boycotts, and mass movements, among others. The important point is that there are a wide range of activist strategies that can be effective (Wilson & Johnson, 2015).

Ally Mode

An ally is a vocal anti-racist who also works with others for racial equity behind the scenes. Being an ally can be tricky, as there is both a public and private aspect to this form of activism. Importantly, an ally is not just someone who encourages others to act while they sit on the sidelines. Instead, allies listen, learn, and work to change racist practices, policies, and behaviors in service of others, often in silent but effective ways that make a substantive and positive difference in racist dynamics. These are the people who learn about an injustice, follow up to learn the various options for changing it, and then instigate action. This is often in the workplace, community, or in professional organizations as they use their privilege and persistence to make such institutions more just, caring and welcoming to victims (and potential victims) of racism (Blumer & Tatum, 1999).

Advocate Mode

Advocates urge people and institutions to change their behavior on behalf of other people or groups of people. Their work is highly visible and they position themselves as active supporters in an effort to be a role model who demonstrates what just action should look like in a given situation. Advocates often have specialized skills, and may be lawyers, researchers, teachers, social workers, or other highly informed community members who put these skills to use in promoting anti-racism in various institutions (Cochran-Smith, 2000). Advocates are working against formal and informal precedents, and as their work is visible it can be dangerous, personally and professionally. Advocates can work from within or from the outside of institutions, and their work is crucial in order for substantive and structural change to take place.

Abolitionist Mode

Abolitionist mode is working toward the eradication of racism rather than just against it. This is an important distinction and in some ways a philosophical one—the question is whether the activist believes it is possible to overcome racism entirely and move into a "post-racial" era, or whether they see anti-racism as an ongoing conflict that requires constant diligence, struggle, and effort. Personally, while I find the concept of abolitionism laudable, we are working against hundreds of years of personal and institutional violence. Like Dr. King, I dream of a day when all will be regarded as equal, but I also agree with him that it is a goal unlikely to be achieved in my lifetime. As such, I will continue to unlearn my racism and develop my understanding of anti-racism while growing into activist modes without the expectation of reaching a promised land of racial social justice (Leonardo, 2009).

Importantly, this section has identified modes of activity—my main contention is that given the context and a particular situation, most of us will behave in one of these ways. These are modes one acts in, not destinations or badges someone can earn. For example, a teacher may feel confident about acting in an advocate mode to make change in their school curriculum, but be timid when it comes to doing anything about the over-suspension of Black students in their school and may instead act in an "Almost-antiracist" mode on that issue. It will be rare that anyone acts in anti-racist modes at all times, and I would suggest that what is most important is to always be learning and growing across issues rather than absolving responsibility for issues that are "not your concern," because again, it is all your concern—you are either racist or anti-racist, either moving toward or away from practicing social justice. It is up to you whether you will play your part in the arc of the moral universe bending toward justice (King & Washington, 1986).

Inactivism or Activism—Which Will You Choose?

Becoming anti-racist is in many ways three processes happening at once: (1) *Unlearning* the miseducation you have co-constructed that teaches you to think and behave in a racist manner; (2) *Learning* anti-racist history, strategies, and contexts by reading, studying your community, and engaging in deep reflection; and (3) *Moving from inaction to action* in your contexts and acting substantively and structurally rather than symbolically. This entails both individual and collective work, and will be accompanied by setbacks, failure, fatigue, and accepting the consequences of acting against powerful institutions (Gorski & Erakat, 2019). These processes are also not linear. They require steadfast attention, a willingness to make and learn from mistakes, and the need to be adaptable to new situations and new information. Importantly, there is a wealth of great thinkers and activists who will teach you about enacting anti-racist activism.

Learning about racism and anti-racism demands that you know yourself (Larson & Murtadha, 2002). This means it is important to investigate your personal history and generational relationship to racism and anti-racism. You should have an understanding of where you came from in order to conceptualize where you might be going. In doing so, you should identify critical incidents that shape how you think about and engage with racism—why do you think what you think? What has happened in (and before) your life to put you in a place of social, cultural, political, and economic privilege? What does your current context look like both to you and others? Do people of color see your town, neighborhood, workplace, government, schools, universities, restaurants, or friends the same way as you? What are the possible pasts and potential futures that shape the way racism is manifest in your community and around the world?

We are all ignorant about certain aspects of racism—what defines us is not our lack of knowledge but our commitment to becoming better informed. Whom do we read, watch, and listen to understand these issues and actions? Where do we ask questions with the intent to inform action, and with whom do you share what you learn? The aim is ultimately to move from ignorance to information; from information to intention; from intention to speaking out; from speaking out to standing up; and from standing up to activism and then to leadership. The benefits of the work are a more ethical and just society, institutions that avail opportunity and access to all (or at least more) and justice to people who have suffered existential and actual violence in personal, community, and national contexts for generations. You are choosing a position every day through your actions and inactions. It is up to you.[2]

15

Sameness and Conformity in Predominately White School Districts

Sharon I. Radd

In 2017, of the 50.7 million students enrolled in public elementary and secondary schools, 48 percent of them were white, 27 percent Latino/a/x, and 15 percent were Black (National Center for Education Statistics, 2020). Among those students, white students are overwhelmingly more likely to attend school with their racial peers, where they are racially segregated and in the racial majority in that setting, as shown in Table 15.1.

While much attention has been devoted to inequities associated with segregated schooling and their impacts on students who are racially minoritized (see, e.g., Khalil & Brown, 2020; Leonard et al., 2020; McCardle, 2020; Weathers et al., 2019), far less attention has been paid to the fact that white students make up the racial group most likely to be in a racially homogenous setting with their racial peers. Still, this is an important area for exploration: though certainly every district has its own unique qualities, the milieu of a predominantly white school district (PWSD) is distinct (see, e.g., Demerath, 2009; Kahlenberg et al., 2019). Exacerbated by an all-encompassing preponderance of racism and white supremacy in the broader society, a PWSD creates a context of racial homogeneity that, when combined with white racial dominance, significantly complicates educational equity efforts. These complications are qualitatively different than the challenges found in more racially diverse settings, or in settings that are racially homogenous with students of one or two racially minoritized identity/ies.

In this chapter, I introduce and describe a discursive phenomenon found in PWSDs that I've termed the *Homogenous Whole*.[1] In doing so, I summarize qualities, factors, and dynamics found in this context, detailing how a focus on similarity thwarts anti-racist efforts. I close with recommendations for anti-racist leadership practice.

Table 15.1 Percentage of students who attend schools with racial peers by race in 2017.

	≥75% of students are racial peers[1]	50% of students are racial peers[2]	<25% of students are racial peers[3]
White	48%	86.1%	6%
Black	25%	44.1%	32%
Latino/a/x	32%	56.7%	21%
Two or more races	<1%	Data not available	>50%
Pacific Islander	2%	Data not available	>50%
Asian	3%	Data not available	>50%
American Indian/ Alaskan Native	17%	23.3%	>50%

[1]Data in this column from https://nces.ed.gov/programs/coe/indicator_cge.asp

[2]Data in this column from https://www.pewresearch.org/fact-tank/2017/10/25/many-minority-students-go-to-schools-where-at-least-half-of-their-peers-are-their-race-or-ethnicity/ft_17-10-24_raceeducation_nearlytwothirds/

[3]Data in this column from https://nces.ed.gov/programs/coe/indicator_cge.asp

The *Homogenous Whole* as a PWSD Phenomenon

The *Homogenous Whole* is used to describe one particular aspect of predominantly white settings. The *Homogenous Whole* phenomenon exists when white people recognize a lack of racial diversity in the setting where they spend a significant amount of time, and proceed to proclaim, "we are all the same, we don't really have any difference." This statement becomes and serves as a mantra among white people and represents a belief that everyone in the group is the same, and simultaneously, that this sameness is what defines and binds the group in community. Sometimes the mantra is used as a proclamation of pride, and sometimes—especially when anti-racist diversity, inclusion, and equity work are proposed—it is used as a concession. In all cases, it becomes a collective identity and has deleterious effects, particularly for anti-racist equity efforts.

In this way, *the Homogenous Whole* is a discursive phenomenon that shapes the context, experience, and culture of the district. Discourses operate in a "relentless and all-encompassing" manner:

> They involve ways of knowing, acting, judging, and thinking [and] they function to direct how power and resources are distributed. In addition to serving as the tools of social construction and, thus, the undergirdment of social systems, they inhabit the minds, emotions, and bodies of individuals within those systems.
>
> (Radd & Grosland, 2019, p. 660)

As a discursive phenomenon, the Homogenous Whole is a social construction that influences and directs how individuals think of, value, and make meaning of similarity and differences among, within, and between people and groups. Further, it dictates where power and resources are directed, available, and used; for whose benefit; and at whose expense. It does so in a seemingly transparent (rather than apparent) way, as the mantra, *we are all the same, we don't really have any difference*, may initially appear innocuous, particularly for those in the racial majority. However, the idea represented in this mantra is not a benign factor nor is the mantra itself an innocent description of a community. Instead it supports the development and maintenance of the Homogenous Whole as a discursive phenomenon.

The Self-replicating Cycle of the Homogenous Whole

The discursive phenomenon of the Homogenous Whole begins with an overwhelmingly white population in a bounded community and cycles through several stations in a cyclical, iterative, and self-sustaining way (see Figure 15.1). In this section, I detail each of these steps of the cycle, then follow with

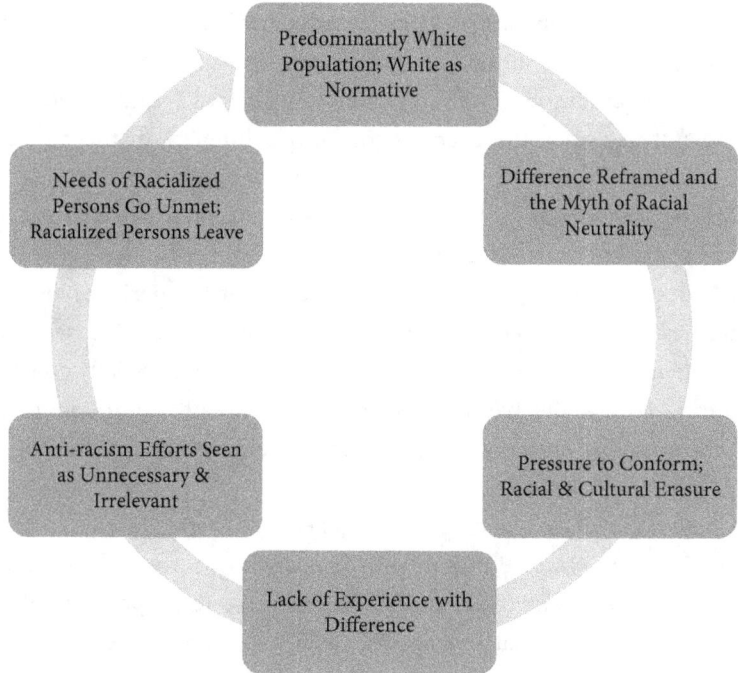

Figure 15.1 The self-replicating cycle of the Homogenous Whole.

an explanation of how this focus on sameness undermines anti-racist efforts, closing with recommendations for anti-racist leaders.

Predominantly White Population: White as Normative

In order for the Homogenous Whole phenomenon to set in, the community in question must be overwhelmingly made up of people who identify as white. Further, in the local context of a majority white population, and because white supremacy and racism are both ordinary and omnipresent in the larger context (Delgado & Stefancic, 2001), white is seen as the "normal" or defining race, and any other race is seen as "different." Specifically,

> Whites do not see themselves as having a race, but being, simply, people. They do not believe that they think and reason from a white viewpoint, but from a universally valid one—'the truth'—what everyone knows. By the same token, many Whites will strenuously deny that they have benefited from white privilege.
> (Delgado & Stefancic, 2001, p. 80)

In this context where whiteness is "perspectiveless and transparent" (p. 80), few students see their racial community, culture, and history represented in the curriculum. For students who are Black, Indigenous, and People of Color (BIPOC), the curriculum simply does not adequately or appropriately include such representations. Simultaneously, white students tend to see a white-male-dominated curriculum as simply the curriculum, with "regular people" in it; they tend not to notice the preponderance of whiteness in the curriculum, nor the absence of a diversity of races, cultures, languages, abilities, genders, religions, and perspectives. Further, white students may see anti-racist and multicultural curriculum as a threat, and thus claim that their identity is a specific European heritage (rather than white or Euro-American), even when their families have lived in the United States for centuries. In all cases, students are not instructed in the complexity of race and culture as socially constructed phenomena, nor as the basis upon which those with dominant identities target, exclude, discriminate, and/or perpetuate physical violence on those with marginalized identities.

The perception and reality of homogeneity bolsters the strength of this normative identity (NAACP, in Kahlenberg et al., 2019), creating the perception that there is *one right way* to act and be. This can create a type of certainty and even cognitive rigidity that becomes a default position when encountering racial, cultural, or even personal style differences. The presence of this dynamic creates a pressure to conform, as well as the conditions for marginalization. In other words, when there is just *one right way* to act and be, or even just a few "right" ways, then there are multiple *wrong* ways to act and be. For example, if the Homogenous Whole dictates that the proper way to address a problem is in a neutral tone and pitch of voice, without emotional expression, then tears, an elevated volume, and expressive hand gestures are all seen as wrong, immature, unprofessional, or even aggressive, and can lead to unfair consequences for the person using these forms of expression.

Difference Redefined and the Myth of Racial Neutrality

As anti-racist leadership seeks to prioritize anti-racism and educational equity, other non-racial types of differences precipitously surface as socially valid and important. While those in the Homogenous Whole see value in "not noticing" the racial identity of students with BIPOC identities, the Homogenous Whole takes on a patriarchal and benevolent tone in talking about students living in poverty, LGBTQI+ students, and those with disabilities, even as a great deal of exclusion and aggression continues for students across those groups.

Concurrently, the *myth of racial neutrality* (Radd et al., 2021), i.e., the idea that race doesn't matter or isn't noticeable, takes hold, denying the presence and impact of race and many other forms of meaningful differences along with it. White staff, students, and community members paradoxically employ the mantra (i.e., we are all the same), comment on racial differences, *and* state that BIPOC people are "just the same" and "treated just the same." These statements compare the existence and experience of BIPOC individuals to those of white people. This is further exemplified when school staff describe students who struggle with their academics, or families who left the district, and proclaim these outcomes unrelated to racial differences or exclusion. At the same time, BIPOC students and families describe poor treatment, backed by ample evidence, confirming that racial differences do in fact play a significant role in their experiences. The phenomenon that white people believe they are acting with benevolence and racial neutrality while, in fact, noticing racial differences and acting differently toward BIPOCs is common (see, e.g., Bonilla-Silva, 2012) but even more pronounced in PWSDs.

Pressure to Conform Leads to Racial and Cultural Erasure

In denying the existence and value of difference, the Homogenous Whole reifies the value of sameness and creates pressure to conform: if there is one right way to act and be, then that way becomes the standard by which to judge other ways of acting and being. Other ways of acting and being are deemed "less than" and in need of remediation. In this context, the implied message is "come on in, but leave your differences behind." All are pressured to conform to the fictional standard, regardless of identity; yet, it is easier for those who represent the "right" way: i.e., those who embody whiteness in its light-skinned, male-centric, cisgender, straight, English-speaking, Christian, non-disabled, and middle- or upper-class forms.

Importantly, as a cluster of dominant and dominating identities, conformity to the Homogenous Whole offers substantial material, social, and personal advantages (Radd & Grosland, 2018) in the form of employment, high grades, reduced discipline, social belonging, social networks, assistance, enhancements, and "the benefit of the doubt." Those who bring "difference" to the Homogenous Whole—for example, BIPOC students; students who live in poverty; individuals who identify as, or are perceived to be, gay, bisexual, or gender non-conforming; and students with disabilities—fear ostracism, disenfranchisement, and exclusion if they do not conform.

The overall impact of this dynamic is racial and difference erasure (McKenzie & Scheurich, 2004; Radd et al., 2021), i.e., the increasing absence, hiding, and exclusion of differences. This can occur in at least three ways in a PWSD. First, individuals with marginalized identities may strive to hide the ways they differ from the Homogenous Whole. Second, for those unwilling or unable to hide the ways they differ from the Homogenous Whole, they are excluded in various ways, including under-representation in prized curricular and co-curricular activities, and over-representation in special education, alternative, and other pull-out programs. Finally, multi-racial, multicultural, and multi-identity perspectives are absent from the curriculum and overall program of the school and district.

Lack of Experience with Difference

With the active and persistent erasure of difference, the community lacks meaningful experience with difference in all forms. Those who see themselves as part of the Homogenous Whole spend both their personal and their professional time with people who look like them and who come from similar backgrounds. They believe it is valuable and right to not notice or see difference, even when its presence is visible, and further, that an important way to prevent discrimination and inequity is to see similarity, and overlook difference.

While those in the Homogenous Whole repeat the *"we are all the same"* mantra to specifically refer to a lack of racial diversity, the mantra also serves to circumvent and preclude other meaningful expressions and experiences of diversity and bolsters the strength of whiteness as a constellation of normative identities. This strong focus on and valuing of sameness denies the reality that there are multiple, equally valid perspectives on any given situation. Accordingly, certainty and even cognitive rigidity become the default approach when encountering racial, cultural, or even personal style differences, rendering the community unmotivated and without skills to create difference-inclusive spaces in which various forms of diversity are welcomed, embraced, and valued.

Anti-racism Efforts Seen as Unnecessary and Irrelevant

Finally, when the Homogenous Whole regards the community as all the same, and functionally denies the value of difference, cultural responsiveness and anti-racism are seen as morally worthy but functionally and personally irrelevant. In other words, if racial and cultural differences are not present then one does not need skills to accommodate or adapt to differences, nor does one need a critique of systems of power in order to create more inclusion and racial justice, both in the classroom and, more broadly, in the world at large. While it is common for PWSDs to include diversity, cultural responsiveness, or global citizenship in their overall strategic plan, this work is depersonalized and becomes qualitatively distanced from classrooms, meeting rooms, and informal conversations. Even among a clear set of pro-social values, such as respect, kindness, fairness, cooperation, hard work, caring, and a priority to meet individual student's needs, the notion that one should "not see color" or not see BIPOC students "as any different" is common.

This is a self-perpetuating cycle in which the Homogenous Whole does not see meaningful difference, so meaningful differences that are present are sequestered, minimized, and marginalized, the perception and weight of homogeneity are maintained, and the perceived need to accommodate and adapt to difference remains negligible. Across time, the overall context of the PWSD does not see racial and cultural diversity as important, nor does it appear to value racial differences in any way.

Needs of Racialized Persons Go Unmet and They Leave

In this context, the experience of marginalization is pronounced and painful for those who experience it, and is marked by unmet needs for racially minoritized students, staff, and families. Specifically, racially minoritized individuals are consistently unable to trust their experience will be physically, emotionally, and psychically safe, and free from aggression; that they will be able to endure across settings (or anywhere) as their authentic self; nor that the curriculum, pedagogy, and community will be culturally sensitive, responsive, and supportive.

In turn, most students—including a majority of white students—hear or see racist or prejudiced words or actions while at school. Adults in the school may or may not notice racist or prejudiced acts as they happen, but in either case they lack the skill, motivation, and/or confidence to take constructive action in those situations. Those who don't fit the Homogenous Whole experience both interactional and material impacts as a result. This shows up in achievement disparities across all subgroups (Stanford Center for Education Policy Analysis, 2020), as well as in experiences of teasing and bullying (Peguero, 2019), placement in special settings (US Department of Education, in Sullivan & Proctor, 2016), and disproportionate discipline (Nguyen et al., 2019), eventually choosing to flee. In other words, families, students, and even staff leave the district, having effectively been "pushed out" by the weight of homogeneity. Others take "internal flight," the act of withdrawing from the Homogenous Whole by keeping to oneself or again, hiding differences. In the end, this cycle maintains the persistence, pressure, and weight of the Homogenous Whole.

Recommendations for Anti-racist Leadership

Again, the Homogenous Whole is a discursive phenomenon that shapes the context, experience, and culture of the district in a relentless, all-encompassing manner. Anti-racist leaders seeking to disrupt this phenomenon and create more racially inclusive systems contend with a series of complex dynamics. For example, the educational system has structural qualities that perpetuate inequity, such as the substantive and structural dilemmas at the intersection of race and disability, or the intersection of race and class (Radd et al., 2021). Further, school-based inequities not only replicate the historical and institutionalized inequities that have marginalized and disenfranchised BIPOC communities for centuries in the broader society, but actually exacerbate and magnify existing inequality (Burkam & Lee, 2002). Most organizational change efforts fail to manifest the vision of transformation they intend, regardless of their goal (Tasler, 2017) and whiteness continues to manifest through equity efforts in PWSDs, reinforcing white supremacy and white institutionalized and systemic racism (Radd & Grosland, 2018). As discourses of inequity inhabit people's minds and emotions, and dictate the use and beneficiaries of power and resources, whiteness predictability shows up in forms ranging from white fragility (DiAngelo, 2011) to organized anti-change efforts and hostile actions (see, e.g., Berlatsky, 2019; Garcia Cano & Rankin, 2020; Radd et al., 2020) when pursuing anti-racism in PWSDs. To be effective in this context, three priorities are clear: anti-racist leaders should start with the self (Gooden & Dantley, 2012); disrupt the perception of homogeneity; and champion the relevance of anti-racism and equity work.

Start with the Self

The work to disrupt the problem of the Homogenous Whole is everyone's work and begins with individual leaders, whether they are positional or informal in their leadership. Anti-racist equity requires never-ending learning and never-ending work; it's vital for anti-racist leaders to begin *now* and accelerate their own learning in order to provide leadership for those in their sphere of influence. Leaders can focus on two aspects of their development: intercultural sensitivity (Bennett, 1986; Hammer, 2020) and the use of race language (Glaude, in Gooden & Dantley, 2012).

In terms of intercultural competency, the Developmental Model of Intercultural Sensitivity (Bennett, 1986) offers a powerful and validated framework for how individuals think about and react to difference and similarity. The accompanying tool, the Intercultural Development Inventory (Hammer, 2020), offers a means to measure an individual and/or group's competency related to intercultural sensitivity. Effective use of this framework and tool offers a means of measuring and personalizing one's own competence and areas for growth.

In addition, white leaders in PWSDs are often uncomfortable and limited in their race talk (DiAngelo, 2011; Irby & Clark, 2018; Sue, 2015; Yoon, 2012). Developing this competency is vital:

> [This] has to be without apology, forthright and incisive … As long as there is a vanilla, benign language used to describe the inequality that takes place in schools and the issue of race is obfuscated through homogenized language, then an agenda to deal with the actual root of much of the discrepancies in schools will never take place.
>
> (Gooden & Dantley, 2012, p. 243)

In PWSDs, race talk is often underdeveloped and used problematically (Sue, 2015; Yoon, 2012), and as noted earlier, adults in the system lack the capacity to effectively intervene, teach, and lead with greater competence and commitment. Books such as *The Power of Talk* (Briscoe et al., 2009), *Race Talk and the Conspiracy of Silence* (Wing, 2015), and *So You Want to Talk About Race* (Oluo, 2018) are useful guides for developing one's race talk competence. In addition, online resources such as ADL's *Race Talk* (https://www.adl.org/education/resources/tools-and-strategies/race-talk-engaging-young-people-in-conversations-about) or the podcast *Counter Stories* (https://www.npr.org/podcasts/414686898/counter-stories) offer valuable guidance and exposure to strategies for and use of race talk. Finally, a simple internet search for "race talk glossary" or "diversity, equity and inclusion glossary" will yield useful resources (such as the one found at https://www.racialequitytools.org/glossary) that define and explain terms.

Disrupt the Perception of Homogeneity and Work toward Difference Competence

Once an anti-racist leader has begun their own individual development related to intercultural competence and race talk, they can proceed to work on disrupting the perception of homogeneity and developing difference competence within themselves and others. Anti-racist leaders should note that when groups and organizations are overly focused on similarity, their analysis often begins with an identity category (i.e., we are all white or Norwegian or Catholic, etc.). The impact of this, however, translates into a much deeper and more constricting definition of similarity. Specifically, it begins to dictate the appear-to-be-agreed-upon norms, which then become both unquestioned and powerful. These norms manifest in micro-interactions and micro-moments that often go unnoticed by those who consider themselves part of the Whole. For example, a history teacher's decision to teach "Westward Expansion" and "Manifest Destiny" rather than "Invasion from the East" and "American Genocide" reflects a dominant (and dominating) perspective that centers white American actors and history, rather than a more complete, complex, and accurate recounting of history. When an administrator refers to people of "other races" or people who speak "a different language" and does not indicate *other than* or *different from what*, she continues to center and normalize the dominant and dominating identity. When a school counselor asks a cisgender female student, "do you have a boyfriend?" as a means to build connection, she/he/they is perpetuating heteronormativity rather than gender and sexual inclusion.

Disrupting the perception of homogeneity and working toward difference competence is perhaps the most important strategy in unseating the Homogenous Whole and can be done in many ways. First, anti-racist school leaders should pay attention to both difference and similarity, noticing differences within groups that are thought of as similar, and similarity between individuals who are in different groups. For example, what are some differences among individuals who identify as white? What are some similarities between those who identify as white and those who identify as BIPOC? The key purpose here is to begin to see and think of both similarity and difference as normal, complex, and occurring across identity categories.

Anti-racist leaders can check their own reaction to difference: does it seem exotic? Something to be minimized? A deterrence to connection? Especially interesting? It is important that anti-racist leaders guard against expectations of assimilation, and instead, develop the skills to meaningfully surface, consider, and engage different perspectives. Anti-racist leaders should work to normalize difference, and frame it as equally valid and valuable as similarity. Using language, mantras, protocols, and techniques that authentically seek and engage difference can send a powerful message about the value of difference.

To build community, anti-racist leaders must contend with the tension that difference is what makes people unique and distinct while similarity is often what binds them together in groups. Too much focus on similarity often results in exclusion. For example, consider who is excluded from a father–daughter dance or a Christmas party. Who is over-represented in alternative and special education settings, as well as in discipline referrals, suspensions, expulsions, absenteeism, and drop-out rates? These exclusions represent a more deep-seated lack of inclusion in the regular, everyday operation of the school and district. Anti-racist leaders need to address both the markers and the causes of these exclusions.

Further, it is important to construct a group identity that values differences within the group and includes the entire community, inclusive of various differences in identity. In practice, this means fostering the development and valuing of a multicultural community at all levels. To be successful, leaders and other adults in the system should work to become familiar with the unwritten, unspoken, and unconscious aspects of culture, and develop and lead with more flexibility and creativity in response to potentially conflicting norms. This also requires the decentering of whiteness and other normative identities, perspectives, and approaches in all aspects of the school/district, including the curriculum, in favor of delivering a truly multi-racial, multicultural, and authentically diverse educational experience.

Make the Case and Make It Relevant

Again, while racial sensitivity and cultural proficiency may be seen as admirable goals in PWSDs, they are often not viewed as relevant or necessary. This is particularly true when posed alongside other important needs for professional learning and organizational development, particularly in a time of scarce resources and overly taxing work demands. Thus, anti-racist leaders need to "make the case" and highlight the relevance, for the district, as well as individuals, teams, and sites within it, to engage in this work.

In doing so, anti-racist leaders can highlight the moral and human relations rationale for engaging in this work, a statement to "do the right thing." In other words, there is a moral imperative to be inclusive and respectful of all, and it is the role of the school district to educate all students in a culturally responsive and safe environment. While the Homogenous Whole frames this work as morally virtuous but functionally irrelevant, anti-racist leaders can share data to demonstrate that this morally virtuous work is in reality, also functionally relevant. Such sharing of data must be done skillfully so as not to undermine the purpose of doing so.

Next, Gooden and Dantley (2012) note the importance of integrating attention to race and racism with attention to "other political, economic, and cultural concerns" (p. 243). Recognizing that racism is integrally connected to other forms of exclusion, anti-racist leaders can take an anti-racist/anti-oppressive approach that offers opportunities for more community members to "see" themselves and their experiences in their new learning. When a family with a gender non-conforming child sees similarities with the experiences of a Black teacher, a high school student with a disability, and a family living in poverty, they increase their capacity to see, respect, and value the differences among them as well. Further, they become more open to the ways that structures and systems perpetuate marginalization, and can be revised to become more inclusive.

Finally, everyone in the school community can benefit when the system becomes more adaptable to and inclusive of racial diversity and other types of differences. For example, students need to be prepared to live and work in a diverse world, and a monoracial experience and monocultural perspective fail to provide the necessary skills and mindset for personal and professional success. At a functional and financial level, particularly in wealthy PWSDs, the district needs to ensure that it is a safe and welcoming place for all students and employees, noting that there is a financial cost to the district when students and staff leave as a result of feeling or experiencing marginalization and exclusion.

Conclusion

As a discursive phenomenon, the Homogenous Whole stems from, creates, and perpetuates a value of sameness that precludes the type of anti-racist and anti-oppressive equity work that is long overdue in school districts and needed far into the future. The purpose of this chapter is to fully describe this phenomenon in order that school leaders learn to recognize it in action, and act skillfully to unseat its impact in their striving to create anti-racist environments. Such an approach is admittedly insufficient when enacted in isolation. Still, without addressing and dismantling the Homogenous Whole phenomenon in PWSDs, school leaders will battle exclusionary and inhumane conceptions of who belongs in community and who is not worthy of learning, achievement, belonging, safety in all its forms, and a promising future.

16

Developing Anti-racist Leaders through Equity-expansive Technical Assistance

Kathleen A. King Thorius and Tiffany S. Kyser

Formerly known as Desegregation Assistance Centers, four regional Equity Assistance Centers (EACs) are funded by the US Department of Education to "address special educational problems as a result of the racial desegregation of public schools" as part of a larger network of federally funded technical assistance (TA) centers. Since their origin under Title IV of the Civil Rights Act of 1964, EACs have worked with local and state educational agencies to remediate inequities in student access, participation, and outcomes, and the conditions that create inequities through the preparation, adoption, and implementation of plans to desegregate public schools.

Ten years earlier, the US Supreme Court in *Brown v. Board of Education of Topeka* (1954) ruled that racial segregation in public schools violated the Fourteenth Amendment of the US Constitution. As much as *Brown* ignited and reinforced the hope that racial inequities in education would be eliminated, Black, Latinx, Indigenous students, and other people of color (BIPOC) continue to experience racist educational policies and practices along with corresponding negative outcomes. Public schools and the educators and administrators within them continue to suspend, expel, track, exclude, discourage, silence, restrain, retain, seclude, segregate, harm, and even kill youth of color and other intersectional identities (e.g., disabled, LGBTQIA+) through systems of formal and informal surveillance and policing (Government Accountability Office, 2009; Katsiyannis et al., 2020; Southern Poverty Law Center & The Center for Civil Rights Remedies, 2019).

The authors acknowledge funding support from the US Department of Education's Office of Elementary and Secondary Education under grant S004D110021. However, these contents do not necessarily represent endorsement by the federal government.

Many historians and educational scholars have asserted that the primary reason that racial inequities continue to exist despite *Brown* and its influence on the modern Civil Rights Movement is that the same system of white supremacy that undergirded public school segregation remains intact. Dominant white beliefs in the intellectual inferiority of Black people (Campbell, 2020), along with widespread systemic advantage for white people (Roithmayr, 2014) dependent on the systemic oppression of People of Color (i.e., racism), galvanized powerful resistance to the *Brown* decision, and to subsequent desegregation rulings by the Supreme Court such as *Green v. County School Board of New Kent County* (1968) and *Alexander v. Holmes County Bd. of Ed.* (1969), which required school districts to develop more viable and extensive desegregation plans. The time of highest school integration occurred in the late 1980s, and through a series of Court decisions releasing districts from desegregation orders and eliminating the consideration of race in student assignment, schools began resegregating throughout the 1990s. According to a study by the Harvard Civil Rights Project, schools were more segregated in 2000 than they were in 1970 at the beginning of busing for desegregation as a result of the Court's ruling in *Swann v. Charlotte-Mecklenberg Board of Education*. As Boddie (2020) reminds us,

> School segregation lies at the epicenter of racial inequity in this country. Students in schools that are segregated by race and poverty have a much harder time graduating from high school and going to college, which makes it harder to get a job and to earn an income that allows them to support themselves and their family. School segregation also feeds into housing segregation, which is a major source of the racial wealth gap. So, in order to deal with racial inequity, we have to address segregation (n.p.).

The same holds true in our schools.

The continued manifestations of racism in schools reflect a US sociopolitical context of state-sponsored killing of Black people (Hill, 2018), and a president (Trump) who retweets racist symbols, slogans, and videos, including one of his supporters driving a golf cart and yelling "white power" (NPR, 2020). Such examples are powerful reminders that much of the work of remediating racist policies and practices that have pervaded US schools and schooling requires explicit and focused work to dismantle the white supremacy at their core and in all facets of US society. The recent groundswell of anti-racist social movements throughout the United States and around the world reignites our hope and provides momentum for these same anti-racist movements to take hold in schools and move us closer to realizing the promise of racially just and equitable schooling. Anti-racist leaders believe and express anti-racist consciousness: "The idea that racial groups are equals and none needs developing," and support "policy that reduces racial inequity" (Kendi, 2019, p. 24). But doing so requires that we explicitly name racist practice and policy in our educational systems, and develop processes and tools for direct remediation. The TA provided by EACs is a resource for educational systems engaged in this work, particularly due to EACs' unique focus on civil rights in public education.

At the Midwest and Plains Equity Assistance Center (MAP Center), our TA includes facilitation of processes with school, district, and state department of education leaders to examine the conditions that have existed locally and globally to create and sustain racial and other intersectional inequities. Over the past nine years, including five years as the Region V EAC and four as the Region III EAC, we have engaged with hundreds of public education agencies in our most intensive form of TA, *systemic equity partnerships*, in response to requests for assistance (RFA) from those in agency leadership roles (e.g., superintendents, cabinet members, board members, and principals). In the remainder of this chapter, we describe features of MAP Center TA specific to supporting the development of anti-racist leadership in K-12 public schools given the urgency and momentum of our current US sociopolitical landscape. Specifically, we detail MAP Center TA that aims to build the capacity of anti-racist educational leaders who galvanize and facilitate:

1. Processes by which those within educational organizations develop a comprehensive understanding of how racism manifests and operates within its policies, practices, and relationships (Thorius, 2019) including leadership practices that serve to maintain systems of advantage for white educators and students such as individualism and autonomy, racial neutrality, and enactments of superiority and authoritarianism (Brooks & Miles, 2010) and
2. The cultivation of dispositions, behaviors, tools and resources, policies, cultures, and communities to realize racial equity and social justice (Brooks & Miles, 2010; Brooks & Witherspoon Arnold, 2013; Marshall & Oliva, 2006) by disrupting and countering the manifestations of racism within their organization and beyond.

The Origins of Technical Assistance in Education

On the surface, TA began as an approach to foreign aid by international agencies such as the United Nations, as well as economically robust nations such as the United States to build developing countries' capitalist economic infrastructure and stave off communism following the Second World War. As part of a larger geo-political development strategy, US President Truman's 1949 Point Four Program aimed to create economic markets for the United States by reducing poverty and increasing production in developing countries, and diminish support for communism by supporting countries to prosper under capitalism, which remained goals for US foreign aid through the 1970s. Under the Point Four Program, the United States provided TA largely through sending experts abroad to teach skills and to help solve problems in their areas of expertise, with an emphasis on the fields of agriculture, education, and public health. At the same time, these and similar approaches to foreign aid have been critiqued through the lens of post-colonial theory on the basis that they maintain the hegemony of dominant nations (e.g., Kim & Garland, 2019) and do not sufficiently account for root causes of global inequality between nations grounded in complex social systems of domination and oppression in relation to race, ethnicity, and a world order founded on European colonialism (Saull, 2010).

Domestically, the US Department of Education developed a network of TA Centers in the early 1980s as a widespread approach for supporting state and local education agencies to enact federal policy mandates, although the EACs had been around since their origin in 1964 to support enactment of *Brown v. Board* and the Civil Rights Act. Over time, domestic approaches to TA, like their foreign policy forebearers, continued to rely on a public health prevention model (Schalock et al., 1994; Senge, 1990; Trohanis, 1982) of universal prevention, targeted, and intensive intervention (Datnow & Stringfield, 2000; Fixsen et al., 2005).

Accordingly, McInerney and Hamilton (2007) summarized two common definitions of TA in educational research: a top-down approach for shepherding policy from federal to local systems, and a bottom-up approach for developing local interventions and scaling them up into standardized policies across larger systems. Both rely on an expert/novice paradigm (Sawyer, 2005) characterized by providers' consultation on programs, policies, or practices to build organizational capacity (Fixsen & Blase, 2009; Katz & Wandersman, 2016; Trohanis, 1982). Critiquing this research and reflective of critiques to foreign aid approaches to TA, Kozleski and Artiles (2012) asserted that TA must stimulate complex solutions to historical issues undergirded by systemic oppressions, and should remediate how systems facilitate equity rather than simply consult on equity-neutral technical improvements to existing operations, since TA has largely failed to redress educational inequities across and between student groups. Kozleski and Artiles led national and regional TA centers to support public education agencies' enactment of federal mandates to measure, report, and remediate racial disproportionality in special education, and first posed the ways in which cultural historical activity theory could be leveraged as a powerful tool in doing so (Kozleski & Artiles, 2012, 2015). More recently, Thorius (2016, 2019) and colleagues (González & Artiles, 2020) expanded on theory and methods for equity-focused TA.

A Theory of Equity-expansive Technical Assistance

TA that aims to remediate education inequities must explicitly examine and transform underlying socio-historical and political contexts that have contributed to these inequities. For EACs, this requires TA that accounts for longstanding and systemic issues of racism and related classification and sorting of youth by race along a continuum of opportunities for educational access, participation, and outcomes directly related to student racial identity. There are overlapping personal, policy, and practical applications of this work, and our approach to TA is grounded in a theory of equity-expansive learning (Tan & Thorius, 2019; Thorius, 2016, 2019) which facilitates educators' development as anti-racist leaders. At the heart of our partnerships is the intentional design of processes by which TA providers facilitate educators' tension-provoking encounters with manifestations of systemic and individual racism that contribute to racial and intersecting forms of injustice (e.g., disability, gender) locally, and subsequent and cyclical adaptation and development of tools in order to counter these injustices (Thorius, 2019).

More specifically, our theoretical and conceptual framework for equity-focused TA is characterized by three key elements that reflect a departure from historical approaches to TA:

1. Explicit concerns with systemic equity as an overarching goal (Kozleski & Artiles, 2012), informed by and in response to local context and history, including the experiences of those who have experienced marginalization

within these systems (Fraser, 2008), and in particular BIPOC at other identity intersections.
2. Shift from top-down/expert novice knowledge transfer to a relational partnership in which the TA provider is a critical friend, thought partner, and bearer of expertise—but not an expert—who supports partners in examining and disrupting inequities in the status quo.
3. Shifts from primary concerns with technical improvements in isolated policies and practices, to a process-based conceptualization of systemic transformation informed by expansive learning (Engeström, 2001): a concept from cultural-historical activity theory (Cole, 1996) and drawing from Vygotsky's principle of double stimulation (1978). Expansive learning occurs when people working together in collective activity engage in transforming an activity system through reconceptualization of the object and motive of their activity, "embracing a radically wider horizon of possibilities than in the previous mode of activity" (Engeström 2001, p. 137). Double-stimulation (Vgotsky, 1978) refers to people's capacity to purposefully transform dissonant circumstances with assistance (here, tools introduced by TA providers).

Taken together, these elements for equity-focused TA stimulate participants' encountering "a problematic and contradictory object," embedded in their daily practice. Over time, TA responds to partners' development of agency, with the goal of "generate(ing) new concepts … enacted via participants' agency in other settings as frames for the design of locally appropriate new solutions" (Engeström, 2011, p. 606). The role of the TA provider is to sustain a focus on systemic equity throughout this process, and to introduce tools that support partners' location of and tensions in response to the equity contradictions they unearth and examine in their own systems. Such tools are informed by critical sociocultural theories including but not limited to critical race theory in education (Delgado & Stefancic, 2000), critical whiteness studies (Dyer, 1997; Nayak, 2007), disability studies in education (Gabel, 2005; Linton, 1998), and disability critical race theory (Annamma et al., 2018), and provide educators with tools for understanding and countering these contradictions. Elsewhere, Thorius (2016, 2019) has discussed the power of artifacts drawn from such theories (e.g., history of eugenics and traces in modern special education policies and practices) that support cultural-historical analyses of social and political forces contributing to inequities and bring educators in contact with contradictions between their expressed goals of eliminating inequities and their pathologization of children's differences at the intersection of race, disability, and other social memberships.

From Theory to Anti-racist Leadership Praxis: The Relationship between Equity-expansive TA and Anti-racist Leadership Development

To move from a theory of equity-expansive TA to anti-racist leadership praxis, our center engages education leaders in a rigorous partner onboarding process, consisting of a series of phone and video calls to co-generate partnership goals and objectives, along with the scope and sequence of TA activities. Although they vary in length of time and intensity, partnerships are framed with explicit expectations for gradual release of support as leaders grow their capacity to support and sustain anti-racist work in their school communities. Next, we highlight three key areas of development and action for anti-racist leaders, providing details of partnership activities that facilitate this work and align with the three theoretical features of equity-expansive TA.

Anti-racist Communication and Governance Structures to Drive Systemic Improvement Planning and Action

Twenty plus collective years of leading equity-focused TA Centers have confirmed for us in practice what educational leadership scholars have repeatedly documented through research: that systemic transformation requires strong leaders who seek a balance between centralized decision making and decentralized governance that engages a diverse group of systemic stakeholders (Fullan, 2003). In doing so, school leaders must be effective and inclusive communicators (Kowalski, 2005) given that cultural shifts are necessary for enacting and sustaining systemic change (Björk et al., 2018).

Yet, anti-racist leaders must go beyond efforts aimed at creating more "inclusive" or "democratic" communication and governance opportunities for all system stakeholders. Even with shifts from top-down directives to multi-directional communication patterns and governance structures that engage all stakeholders-community members, families, students, teachers, staff, and those in building and district leadership positions across demographic groups, such efforts do not go far enough to actively address the impacts of systemic racism and intersecting marginalization. Anti-racist leaders are anti-neutral in their actions to remedy the impacts of racism in their systems, reflective of Welton and colleagues' (2018) assertion that "in reality, for anti-racist education to work, there must be an action-oriented commitment from the individual as well as the larger institution" (p. 6).

Given that our center praxis shifts from a historical focus on technical and equity-neutral fixes to equity-expansive, contextually-informed, systemic transformation, our TA supports anti-racist leaders to create and refine communication and governance structures that value and take direction from the experiences and expertise of those within the system who have been historically marginalized, particularly in relation to race. In turn, leaders are supported to expand the object of TA from a technical solution for a discrete issue (e.g., a racist incident between two students) to a complex systemic anti-racist response (e.g., policy and practice review and capacity building to foster white racial literacy (DiAngelo, 2012) and to create racially just teaching, learning, and social climates). In turn, these structures can be leveraged to facilitate the development of systemic improvement plans that intentionally address the negative racial impact of past and current policies and practices.

TA that supports this work engages partners in professional development wherein they examine how status quo approaches to strategic planning are complicit in racial oppression. This process is then coupled with guiding our partners through explicitly anti-racist strategic planning where we introduce tools that make racial inequities more perceivable, and then co-develop policy and practice responses to these inequities. For example, over the past three years our center has partnered with a suburban school district outside of a large Midwestern city. The superintendent's original request for assistance was in response to mounting racial tensions as the once small, majority white suburb began to grow dramatically and experience a significant increase in racial diversity. Prompted by increased critique of the inequitable experience of Black and Latinx students from various community stakeholders, our partnership has supported district leadership in forming a diverse stakeholder team to research and write a history of racial tension and inequities in the district, as well as to develop priorities for systemic change. This work has been supported through a combination of regular consultation calls with leadership focused on approaches for earning the trust of community members (Johnson, 2014)—particularly those who have been historically disenfranchised, decentering their own power, redistributing power to community members such as non-dominant youth, parents/caregivers, families (González et al., 2017), in ways that afford authority in decision-making, leveraging school community resources to advance collective goals of the entire school community, as well as seeking out opportunities to leverage community assets to advance their own learning (Kyser et al., 2015).

Other TA activities that support this partnership include center staff participation in the team's efforts along with the introduction of and guidance for engaging with several center-developed resources for the team to accomplish this work. One center resource that has guided this work is a year-long data collection and analysis process that results in a comprehensive strategic equity plan generated by a diverse cross section of students, community members, board members, staff, and teachers (i.e., Equity Context Analysis Process, 2017), and another is our Policy Equity Analysis Toolkit (Kyser et al., 2016). The latter includes a suggested protocol for composing and facilitating a team to review district and school policy for racial and other negative impact, along with a number of additional resources such as a research-to-practice brief entitled *Engaging School Communities in Critical Reflection* (Macey et al., 2012). Outcomes from such partnerships include identification of a lack of educator racial representation and cultural responsiveness among district staff and corresponding planning and action to recruit and sustain racially diverse school personnel which reflect the racial identities of the students, and professional development to build white educators' capacities as culturally responsive anti-racist educators. Plans include actions that push back against traditional conflations of workforce "diversity" with "race" (Hanover Research, 2014), and move toward fostering dispositions toward racial justice in the recruitment, retention, and ongoing support of racially diverse, culturally responsive, and anti-racist school educators (Jackson et al., 2016).

Anticipation, Preparation, and Anti-racist Response to Resistance and Pressure to Maintain the Status Quo

Anti-racist leaders recognize and respond to ways in which status quo versions of educational leadership favor white dominant norms of individualism, racial neutrality, and sanctioned beliefs of superiority and authoritarianism (Brooks & Miles, 2010). Specifically, our TA approaches support the understanding of educational leadership as inherently about equity (Brooks & Miles, 2010; Brooks & Witherspoon, 2013; Marshall & Oliva, 2006) as a racial and intersectional justice endeavor which requires leaders work alongside stakeholders to examine how their systems benefit some and disadvantage others, most often in relation to race and other intersectional identities. Our processes support leaders to acknowledge and disrupt this status quo in order to bring concerns with remediating the pernicious impacts of racism and intersecting oppressions to the center of systemic improvement efforts. Anti-racist leaders persist—not only to dismantle "historical legacies of normative assumptions, beliefs, and practices about individual characteristics and cultural identities that marginalize and disenfranchise people and groups of people" (Warren et al., 2016, p. 2), but also to realize educational equity, no matter the push-back. Welton et al. (2018) discuss the anti-racist leader's ability to persist through uncomfortable and challenging perspectives noting, "For real, substantial anti-racist change to occur the institutional leaders must first be able to withstand the resistance and pushback that comes when members try to avoid engaging in discussions about race, let alone changes that push them to alter institutional policies and practices" (p. 11).

Accordingly, in many of our TA partnerships leaders are supported in anticipating and responding to dominant white norms about schooling and beliefs about children and families of color that manifest as lowered expectations, racial erasure and neutrality, defensiveness and avoidance in relation to examination of racism and negative racial impact, along with internalized racism and impacts for BIPOC educators. A specific example of TA that supports anti-racist leadership development in this area is a four-day face-to-face professional learning series developed by the MAP Center, entitled *Leading Equity Focused Initiatives*, scheduled over one academic semester. Diverse stakeholder teams from five or so districts come together to build community and create alliances in order to galvanize themselves for persistence in leading anti-racist systemic change in the context of systems grounded in white supremacy and white-dominant norms. Activities and discussions include examination of specific barriers to racial justice and other equity work in school systems, including white supremacy and white saviorism (Aronson, 2017), internalized racism (Kohli, 2014), white fragility (DiAngelo, 2011), and the compounded impact of multiple forms of marginalization at the intersection of race (i.e., intersectionality, Crenshaw, 1991), including disability (Waitoller & Thorius, 2016) and sexual orientation (Bracho & Hayes, 2020). As our partners discuss and reflect on the deeply personal ways these barriers have manifested in their own lives and educational settings and offer guidance and support to each other, the TA content also offers opportunities for developing communications and leadership actions that respond to common scenarios within which these barriers emerge (MAP Center, 2019).

Facilitate Racial Healing, White Accountability, and Community Care

Anti-racist leaders know that systemic racism is fueled by the complex relationship between racial power and oppression, and those who experience these phenomena. Therefore, they ensure ongoing opportunities to discuss race and racism in order to strengthen cross-racial interpersonal relationships between educators (Welton et al., 2018). They also provide specific support systems for BIPOC that include opportunities for healing and rejuvenation (Cross et al., 2019), and create and support accountability structures for white educators to grow in their anti-racist identity development and actions through examination of their own benefit from, participation in, and opportunities to redress racist beliefs and actions.

Examples of TA activities that support anti-racist leaders in this key area of practice include those that build their capacity to develop caring and authentic relationships between multi-racial teams of educators and between educators, students, and families. Our TA in this area includes facilitated examination of the importance of and approaches for community care and building trust in inter-racial professional and personal relationships. For example, in the midst of a TA partnership with a Midwestern school district initially focused on equity-driven strategic planning, our center staff members came to recognize emerging and unresolved racial tensions between school board members and the superintendent and cabinet. Accordingly, the focus of our partnership shifted toward examining differential impacts of racism and racial positionality amongst school board members and between the board and cabinet members over a series of all-day Saturday professional learning dialogues in which individuals aired experiences of racial harm, took responsibility, and developed ideas for remediation.

In other instances, our TA to develop this area of anti-racist leadership practice includes coaching to develop leaders' understanding of and communication about the potential of racial affinity groups within their educational systems. Within many of our center-provided leadership academies, our staff facilitate and model such groups with leaders and system stakeholder participants. For BIPOC, these groups focus on "cultivating sacred spaces" (Pour-Korshid, 2018) to construct and share racial identity in the absence of white people, share experiences of racial harm, and resistance, while galvanizing and appreciating the strength and accomplishments of peers within inherently racist educational and societal systems. For white people, affinity groups are spaces to learn about race and racism in the absence of BIPOC, identify and critically reflect on one's own socialization into whiteness, benefit from and participation in white privilege and white racism, and develop plans for accountability for racial harm (Michael & Conger, 2009).

Anti-racism as an Un-fixed Identity: The Importance of Partnerships for Persistence

As Kendi (2019) reminds us, "racist and anti-racist are not fixed identities ... What we say about race, what we do about race, in each moment, determines what—not who—we are" (p. 10). As we describe in theory and praxis, the development and support of anti-racist leaders through TA that facilitates the examination of systemic and personal histories along with current actions in relation to race and racism also prepares leaders to provide space and resources for those within their educational systems to do the same. At the same time, such TA supports leaders in responding to powerful resistance from those who seek to preserve the racial status quo. Although brief, it is our hope that the descriptions of the equity-expansive TA processes and resources we engage with our partners and as an EAC are useful for your own professional and personal growth as anti-racist leaders in your own contexts.

Notes

Chapter 3

1. We would like to thank Walter Stern and Larry Brown for careful and insightful feedback on this work. Errors, if any, remain our own.

Chapter 14

1. I originally explored this idea in Brooks, J. S. (2007, Summer). Race and educational leadership: Conversation catalysts to prompt reflection, discussion, and action for individuals and organizations. *UCEA Review, XLVII,* (2), 1–3 and then expanded it in Brooks, J. S. (2012). *Black school, white school: Racism and educational (mis)leadership.* Teachers College Press. The version presented in this chapter represents a significant re-working and expansion of the original idea.
2. In this chapter I have (almost) exclusively cited authors and co-authors of color. I do this as both an intentional political act working in a field that has marginalized their work and centered the research of white scholars, and also as an acknowledgment of the quality and insights of this research. I have in a few places cited white scholars and have also included a few of my own works in order to illustrate the way my own thinking as a white scholar has progressed over time.

Chapter 15

1. The content for this chapter is based on my practice in the field, and was developed by using the scholarly literature to guide my theorization and analysis of that practice, both as a school administrator and subsequently as an organizational equity consultant. That said, my colleagues in the field and in the academy have added invaluably to my understanding and framing of these dynamics, and to those many with whom I've discussed these ideas, I express my gratitude.

References

Acker, J. (2006). Inequality regimes gender, class, and race in organizations. *Gender and Society, 20*(4), 441–464.

Advancement Project. (2010). *Test, punish, and push out: How "zero tolerance" and high stakes testing funnel youth into the school-to-prison pipeline*. Washington, DC. http://www.advancementproject.org/sites/default/files/publications/rev_fin.pdf

Advancement Project and Alliance for Educational Justice. (2018). *We came to learn: A call to action for police-free schools*. Washington, DC. https://advancementproject.org/wecametolearn/.

Alemán, E., Freire, J. A., McKinney, A., & Bernal, D. D. (2017). School–university–community pathways to higher education: Teacher perceptions, school culture and partnership building. *The Urban Review, 49*(5), 852–873.

Alexander, M. (2010). *The new Jim Crow: Mass incarceration in the age of colorblindness*. The New Press.

Alvarez, A., & Milner, I. V., H. R. (2018). Exploring teachers' beliefs and feelings about race and police violence. *Teaching Education, 29*(4), 383–394.

Amiot, M. N., Mayer-Glenn, J., & Parker, L. (2020). Applied critical race theory: Educational leadership actions for student equity. *Race Ethnicity and Education, 23*(2), 200–220.

Anderman, E. M. (1991). *Teacher commitment and job satisfaction: The role of school culture and principal leadership*. National Center for School Leadership.

Anderson, B. (1983). *Imagined communities: Reflections on the origin and spread of nationalism*. Verso.

Anderson, C. (2016). *White rage: The unspoken truth of our racial divide*. Bloomsbury.

Anderson, G., & Cohen, M. (2018). *The new democratic professional in education*. Teachers College Press.

Anderson, G. L. (2009). *Advocacy leadership: Toward a post-reform agenda in education*. Routledge.

Anderson, J. D. (1988). *The education of blacks in the south, 1860–1935*. University of North Carolina Press.

Annamma, S. A. (2018). *The pedagogy of pathologization: Dis/abled girls of color in the school-prison nexus*. Routledge.

Annamma, S. A., Ferri, B. A., & Connor, D. J. (2018). Disability critical race theory: Exploring the intersectional lineage, emergence, and potential futures of DisCrit in education. *Review of Research in Education, 42*(1), 46–71.

Apple, M. W. (2004). *Ideology and curriculum*. Routledge.

Argyris, C. (1958). Creating effective research relationships in organizations. *Human Organization, 17*(1), 34–40.

Aronson, B. A., (2017) The white savior industrial complex: A cultural studies analysis of a teacher educator, savior film, and future teachers. *Journal of Critical Thought and Praxis 6*(3), 36–54.

Arum, R. (2003). *Judging school discipline: The crisis of moral authority.* Harvard University Press.

Asante, M. K. (1991). The Afrocentric idea in education. *The Journal of Negro Education, 60*(2), 170–80.

Auerbach, S. (2011). Conceptualizing leadership for authentic partnerships: A continuum to inspire practice. In S. Auerbach (Ed.), *School leadership for authentic family and community partnerships: Research perspectives for transforming practice* (pp. 29–52). Routledge.

Bahena, S., Cooc, N., Currie-Rubin, R., Kuttner, P., & Ng, M. (Eds.). (2012). *Disrupting the school-to-prison pipeline.* Harvard Education Press.

Banwo, B. (2020). *African communitarianism as black student motivation: An institutional exploration of collectivism in African-Centered education* [Unpublished doctoral dissertation]. University of Minnesota.

Banwo, B., Alston, J., & Madyun, N. (2019). Blackness and maleness: An ethnology organizational experiences framework (EOEF). In L. Bass, & H. Mackey (Eds.), *Barbara L. Jackson Scholars Network Information Age Publishing Yearbook.* Information Age Publishing, Inc.

Bass, L. (2012). When care trumps justice: The operationalization of Black feminist caring in educational leadership. *International Journal of Qualitative Studies in Education, 25*(1), 73–87.

Bell, D. (1992). *Faces at the bottom of the well: The permanence of racism.* Basic Books.

Bell, D. (2004). *Silent covenants: Brown v. Board of Education and the unfulfilled hopes for racial reform.* Oxford University Press.

Bell, Jr., D. A. (1980). Brown v. Board of Education and the interest-convergence dilemma. *Harvard Law Review, 93*(3), 518–533.

Bell, J. (1992). *Populism and elitism: Politics in the age of equality.* Regnery Publishing.

Beltman, S., Mansfield, C., & Price, A. (2011) Thriving not just surviving: A review of research on teacher resilience. *Educational Research Review, 6*(3), 185–207.

Bennett, M. (1986). A developmental approach to training intercultural sensitivity. *International Journal of Intercultural Relations, 10*(2), 179–186.

Berger, P. L., & Luckmann, T. (1967). *The social construction of reality: A treatise in the sociology of knowledge.* Anchor Books.

Berkovich, I. (2014). A socio-ecological framework of social justice leadership in education. *Journal of Educational Administration, 52*(3), 282–309.

Berlatsky, N. (2019). White parents are enabling school segregation—If it doesn't hurt their own kids. *NBC News.* https://www.nbcnews.com/think/opinion/white-parents-are-enabling-school-segregation-if-it-doesn-t-ncna978446

Bernstein Chernoff, C. R. (2016). *The crisis of caring: Compassion satisfaction and compassion fatigue among student conduct and behavior intervention professionals* (Publication No. 1789879166) [Doctoral dissertation, University of South Florida]. ProQuest Dissertations & Theses Global.

Bertrand, M., & Rodela, K. C. (2018). A framework for rethinking educational leadership in the margins: Implications for social justice leadership preparation. *Journal of Research on Leadership Education, 13*(1), 10–37. https://doi.org/10.1177/1942775117739414

Bills, A., Giles, D., & Rogers, B. (2017). Whatever it takes! Using a component theory approach with public secondary school principals "doing schooling differently." *School Leadership & Management, 37*(1–2), 188–211.

Björk, L. G., Browne-Ferrigno, T., & Kowalski, T. J. (2018). Superintendent roles as CEO and team leader. *Research in Educational Administration & Leadership, 3*(2), 179–205. https://doi.org/10.30828/real/2018.2.3

Black Lives Matter. (n.d.). *Herstory*. https://blacklivesmatter.com/herstory/

Blackmore, J. (2002). Leadership for socially just schooling: More substance and less style in high risk, low trust times? *Journal of School Leadership, 12*(2), 198–222.

Blankstein, A. M., Noguera, P., & Kelly, L. (2016). *Excellence through equity: Five principles of courageous leadership to guide achievement for every student*. ASCD.

Bliuc, A. M., Faulkner, N., Jakubowicz, A., & McGarty, C. (2018). Online networks of racial hate: A systematic review of 10 years of research on cyber-racism. *Computers in Human Behavior, 87*, 75–86.

Blumer, I., & Tatum, B. D. (1999). Creating a community of allies: How one school system attempted to create an anti-racist environment. *International Journal of Leadership in Education, 2*(3), 255–267.

Boddie, E. (2020). Why are American public schools still segregated? Interview with Ivan Natividad. *Berkeley News*. https://news.berkeley.edu/2020/03/04/why-are-american-public-schools-still-segregated/

Bogotch, I. (2002). Educational leadership and social justice: Practice into theory. *Journal of School Leadership, 12*(2), 138–156.

Bolling, G. (2016). Commitment, love, and responsibility are key. In E. R. Drame, & D. J. Irby (Eds.), *Black participatory research: Power, identity, and the struggle for justice in education* (pp. 87–103). Palgrave Macmillan.

Bonilla-Silva, E. (2001). *White supremacy and racism in the post-civil rights era*. Lynne Rienner Publishers.

Bonilla-Silva, E. (2003/2006/2018). *Racism without racists: Color-blind racism and the persistence of racial inequality in the United States*. Rowman and Littlefield.

Bonilla-Silva, E. (2012). The invisible weight of whiteness: The racial grammar of everyday life.in contemporary America. *Ethnic and Racial Studies, 35*(2), 173–194.

Bonilla-Silva, E. (2015). The structure of racism in color-blind, "post-racial" America. *American Behavioral Scientist, 58*(11), 1358–1376.

Boyatzis, R. E., & McKee, A. (2005). *Resonant leadership: Renewing yourself and connecting with others through mindfulness, hope, and compassion*. Harvard Business Review Press.

Bracho, C. A., & Hayes, C. (2020). Gay voices without intersectionality is white supremacy: Narratives of gay and lesbian teachers of color on teaching and learning. *International Journal of Qualitative Studies in Education, 33*(6), 583–592.

Bredeson, P. V., & Johansson, O. (2000). The school principal's role in teacher professional development. *Journal of In-service Education, 26*(2), 385–401.

Brewer, R. M. (2013). 21st-century capitalism, austerity, and Black economic dispossession. *Souls, 14*(3–4), 227–239.

Briscoe, F., Arriaza, G., & Henze, R. C. (2009). *The power of talk: How words change our lives*. Corwin Press.

Brock, S. E., Lazarus, J. P. J., & Jimerson, S. R. (2002). *Best practices in school crisis prevention and intervention*. National Association of School Psychologists.

Brooks, J. S. (2012). *Black school, white school: Racism and educational (mis)leadership*. Teachers College Press.

Brooks, J. S., & Arnold, N. W. (2013) *Anti-racist school leadership: Toward equity and education for America's students*. Information Age Publishing, Inc.

Brooks, J. S., Arnold, N. W., & Brooks, M. C. (2013). Educational leadership and racism: Second-generation segregation in an urban high school. *Teachers College Record, 115*(11), 1–27.

Brooks, J. S., & Jean-Marie, G. (2007). Black leadership, white leadership: Race and race relations in an urban high school. *Journal of Educational Administration, 45*(6), 756–768.

Brooks, J. S., & Miles, M. T. (2010). The social and cultural dynamics of school leadership: Classic concepts and cutting-edge possibilities. In S. D. Horsford (Ed.), *New perspectives in educational leadership: Exploring social, political, and community contexts and meaning* (pp. 7–28). Peter Lang Publishing, Inc.

Brooks, J. S., & Watson, T. N. (2018). School leadership and racism: An ecological perspective. *Urban Education 53*(9), 1–25.

Brooks, J. S., & Witherspoon Arnold, N. (Eds.). (2013). *Anti-racist school leadership: Toward equity in education for America's students*. Information Age Publishing, Inc.

Brown, E. L., Horner, C. G., Kerr, M. M., & Scanlon, C. L. (2014). United States teachers' emotional labor and professional identities. *Kedi Journal of Educational Policy, 11*(2), 205–225.

Browne-Ferrigno, T. (2011). Mandated university—district partnerships for principal preparation Professors' perspectives on required program redesign. *Journal of School Leadership, 21*(5), 735–756.

Burkam, D. T., & Lee, V. E. (2002). *Inequality at the starting gate: Social background differences in achievement as children begin school*. Economic Policy Institute. https://www.epi.org/publication/books_starting_gate/

Byrd, M. (2007). Theorizing African American women's leadership experiences: Sociocultural theoretical alternatives. *Advancing Women in Leadership Journal, 29*(1), 1–19.

Call-Cummings, M., & Martinez, S. (2017). "It wasn't racism; it was more misunderstanding": White teachers, Latino/a students, and racial battle fatigue. *Race Ethnicity and Education, 20*(4), 561–574.

Campbell, C. L. (2020). Getting at the root instead of the branch: Education, a long-ignored transitional justice project. *Law & Inequality: A Journal of Theory and Practice, 38*(2), 1–67.

Capper, C. A. (2015). The 20th-year anniversary of critical race theory in education. Implications for leading to eliminate racism. *Educational Administration Quarterly, 51*(5), 791–833.

Carter Andrews, D. J., & Gutwein, M. (2020). Middle school students' experiences with inequitable discipline practices in school: The elusive quest for cultural responsiveness. *Middle School Journal, 51*(1), 29–38.

Carver-Thomas, D. (2018). *Diversifying the teaching profession: How to recruit and retain teachers of color*. Learning Policy Institute.

Casella, R. (2006). *Selling us the fortress: The promotion of techno-security equipment for schools*. Routledge.

Castagno, A. E. (2014). *Educated in whiteness: Good intentions and diversity in schools*. University of Minnesota Press.

Changfoot, N., Andrée, P., Levkoe, C. Z., Nilson, M., & Goemans, M. (2020). Engaged scholarship in tenure and promotion: Autoethnographic insights from the fault lines of a shifting landscape. *Michigan Journal of Community Service Learning, 26*(1), 239–263.

Cherone, H. (2020, July 23). Push to keep woodlawn residents in their homes near Obama Center to include more affordable housing. *WTTW*. https://news.wttw.com/2020/07/21/push-keep-woodlawn-residents-their-homes-near-obama-center-include-more-affordable

Chesler, M., Lewis, A., & Crowfoot, J. (2005). *Challenging racism in higher education: Promoting justice*. Rowman & Littlefield Publishers, Inc.

Childress, S. M., Doyle, D. P., & Thomas, D. (2009). *Leading for equity: The pursuit of excellence in Montgomery County Public Schools*. Harvard Education Press.

Coalition to Revitalize Walter H. Dyett High School. (2015). Proposal for *Walter H. Dyett Global Leadership and Green Technology High School*. https://news.wttw.com/sites/default/files/article/file-attachments/DyettRFP_DyettGlobalAndGreenTechnologyHSProposal.pdf

Coates, R. D. (2011). *Covert racism: Theories, institutions, and experiences*. Brill.

Coates, T. (2015). *Between the world and me*. One World.

Coburn, C. E., & Penuel, W. R. (2016). Research-practice partnerships: Outcomes, dynamics, and open questions. *Educational Researcher, 45*(1), 48–54.

Cochran-Smith, M. (2000). Blind vision: Unlearning racism in teacher education. *Harvard Educational Review, 70*(2), 157–190.

Cole, M. (1996). *Cultural psychology. A once and future discipline*. Harvard University Press.

Coleman, L. B., & Reames, E. (2020). The role of the educational leadership program coordinator (PC) in university–K-12 school district partnership development. *Journal of Research on Leadership Education, 15*(4), 241–260.

Collins, J., & Hansen, M. T. (2011). *Great by choice: Uncertainty, chaos and luck-why some thrive despite them all*. Random House.

Collins, P. H. (1986). Learning from the outsider within: The sociological significance of Black feminist thought. *Social Problems, 33*(6), S14–S32. https://doi.org/10.1525/sp.1986.33.6.03a00020

Collins, P. H. (1989). The social construction of Black feminist thought. *Signs, 14*(41), 745–773.

Collins, P. H. (2000/2002). *Black feminist thought: Knowledge, consciousness, and the politics of empowerment*. Routledge.

Collins, P. H. (2015). Intersectionality's definitional dilemmas. *Annual Review of Sociology, 41*(1), 1–20.

Condron, D. (2007). Stratification and educational sorting: Explaining ascriptive inequalities in early childhood reading group placement. *Social Problems, 54*(1), 139–160.

Cooper, B. (2018). *Eloquent rage: A Black feminist discovers her superpowers*. St. Martin's Press.

Cosner, S. (2011). Supporting the initiation and early development of evidence-based grade-level collaboration in urban elementary schools: Key roles and strategies of principals and literacy coordinators. *Urban Education, 46*(4), 786–827. https://doi.org/10.1177/0042085911399932

Cox, T., & Nkomo, S. M. (1990). Invisible men and women: A status report on race as a variable in organization behavior research. *Journal of Organizational Behavior, 11*(6), 419–431.

Cranston, J., & Kusanovich, K. (2015). Learning to lead against the grain: Dramatizing the emotional toll of teacher leadership. *Issues in Teacher Education, 24*(2), 63–78.

Crenshaw, K. (1991). Mapping the margins: Intersectionality, identity politics, and violence against women of color. *Stanford Law Review, 43*(6), 1241–1299.

Crenshaw, K., Ocean, P., & Nanda, J. (2015). *Black girls matter: Pushed out, overpoliced, and underprotected* [Policy brief]. African American Policy Forum.

Cross, T. L., Pewewardy, C., & Smith, A. T. (2019). Restorative education, reconciliation, and healing: Indigenous perspectives on decolonizing leadership education. *New Directions for Student Leadership*, (163), 101–115. https://onlinelibrary.wiley.com/toc/23733357/2019/2019/163

Curry, T. (2017). *The man-not: Race, class, genre, and the dilemmas of black manhood*. Temple University Press.

Cyert, R. M., & March, J. G. (1992). *Behavioral theory of the firm*. Wiley-Blackwell Publishing.

Daly, A. J. (2009). Rigid response in an age of accountability the potential of leadership and trust. *Educational Administration Quarterly, 45*(2), 168–216. https://doi.org/10.1177/0013161x08330499

Dantley, M. E., & Tillman, L. C. (2006). Social justice and moral transformative leadership. In C. Marshall, & M. Oliva (Eds.), *Leadership for social justice: Making revolutions in education* (pp. 16–30). Pearson Education.

Darling-Hammond, L. (2007). Race, inequality and educational accountability: The irony of "No Child Left Behind." *Race Ethnicity and Education, 10*(3), 245–260.

Datnow, A., & Stringfield, S. (2000). Working together for reliable school reform. *Journal of Education for Students Placed at Risk (JESPAR), 5*(1–2), 183–204.

Davis, A. Y. (2011). *Are prisons obsolete?* Seven Stories Press.

Day, M. (2020). Teachers' unions are demanding police free schools. *Jacobin*. https://jacobinmag.com/2020/06/teachers-unions-police-schools-movement-protests

De Freitas, E., & McAuley, A. (2008). Teaching for diversity by troubling whiteness: Strategies for classrooms in isolated white communities. *Race Ethnicity and Education, 11*(4), 429–444.

DeCuir, J. T., & Dixson, A. D. (2004). "So when it comes out, they aren't that surprised that it is there": Using critical race theory as a tool of analysis of race and racism in education. *Educational Researcher, 33*(5), 26–31.

Delgado, M. (2020). *State-sanctioned violence: Advancing a social work social justice agenda*. Oxford University Press.

Delgado, R. (1989). Storytelling for oppositionists and others: A plea for narrative. *Michigan Law Review, 87*(8), 2411–2441.

Delgado, R., & Stefanic, J. (Eds.). (2000). *Critical race theory: The cutting edge* (2nd ed.). Temple University Press.

Delgado, R., & Stefancic, J. (2001/2017). *Critical race theory: An introduction*. New York University Press.

Delpit, L. (1995). *Other people's children: Cultural conflict in the classroom*. The New Press.

DeLugan, R. M., Roussos, S., & Skram, G. (2014). Linking academic and community guidelines for community-engaged scholarship. *Journal of Higher Education Outreach and Engagement, 18*(1), 155–168.

DeMatthews, D. (2018a). *Community-engaged leadership for social justice: A critical approach in urban schools*. Routledge.

DeMatthews, D. (2018b). Social justice dilemmas: Evidence on the successes and shortcomings of three principals trying to make a difference. *International Journal of Leadership in Education, 21*(5), 545–559.

DeMatthews, D., & Tarlau, R. (2019). Activist principals: Leading for social justice in Ciudad Juarez, Baltimore, and Brazil. *Teachers College Record, 121*(4), 1–36.

DeMatthews, D. E., Carey, R. L., Olivarez, A., & Moussavi Saeedi, K. (2017). Guilty as charged? Principals' perspectives on disciplinary practices and the racial discipline gap. *Educational Administration Quarterly, 53*(4), 519–555.

Demerath, P. (2009). *Producing Success: The culture of personal advancement in an American high school.* University of Chicago Press.

Diamond, J. B. (2018). Race and white supremacy in the sociology of education: Shifting the intellectual gaze. In J. Mehta, & S. Davies (Eds.), *Education in a new society: Renewing the sociology of education* (pp. 345–362). University of Chicago Press.

DiAngelo, R. (2011). White fragility. *International Journal of Critical Pedagogy, 3*(3), 54–70.

DiAngelo, R. (2012). *Developing white racial literacy.* Peter Lang Publishing Inc.

DiAngelo, R. (2018). *White fragility: Why it's so hard for white people to talk about racism.* Beacon Press.

Diem, S., & Carpenter, B. W. (2012). Social justice and leadership preparation: Developing a transformative curriculum. *Planning and Changing, 43*(1–2), 96–112.

Diem, S., Carpenter, B. W., & Lewis-Durham, T. (2019). Preparing antiracist school leaders in a school choice context. *Urban Education, 54*(5), 706–731.

Diem, S., & Welton, A. D. (2017). Disrupting spaces for education policymaking and activism. In R. Diem, & M. Berson (Eds.), *Mending walls: Historical, socio-political, economic, and geographic perspectives* (pp. 219–238). Information Age Publishing, Inc.

Diem, S., & Welton, A. D. (2021). *Anti-racist educational leadership and policy. Addressing racism in public education.* Routledge.

Dillard, C. (1995). Leading with her life: An African American feminist (re)interpretation of leadership for an urban high school principal. *Educational Administration Quarterly, 31*(4), 539–563.

Dillard, C. (2018). The school-to-deportation pipeline. *Teaching Tolerance, 60*, 40–45.

Drame, E. R., & Irby, D. J. (Eds.). (2016). *Black participatory research: Power, identity, and the struggle for justice in education.* Palgrave Macmillan.

DuBois, W. E. B. (1903) *The souls of Black folk*: A. C. McClurg & Co.

Dyer, R. (1997). *White.* Routledge.

Education Week. (2020). Map: Coronavirus and school closures. *Education Week.* https://www.edweek.org/ew/section/multimedia/map-coronavirus-and-school-closures.html

Ee, J., & Gándara, P. (2020). The impact of immigration enforcement on the nation's schools. *American Educational Research Journal, 57*(2), 840–871.

Elsen-Rooney, M. (2020, March 19). Black and Latino students admitted to NYC's specialized high schools stays flat at 11%. *New York Daily News.* https://www.nydailynews.com/new-york/education/ny-specialized-high-school-admission-20200319-2z4bhh65xrcetnfx3wwmbysqdq-story.html

Engeström, Y. (2001). Expansive learning at work: Toward an activity theoretical reconceptualization. *Journal of Education and Work, 14*(1), 133–156.

Engeström, Y. (2011). From design experiments to formative interventions. *Theory and Psychology, 21*(5), 598–628.

Epstein, D. (2011). *Measuring inequity in school funding.* Center for American Progress.

Evans, M. P. (2019). Power and authenticity in education focused community-based organizations. In S. B. Sheldon, & T. A. Turner-Vorbeck (Eds.), *The Wiley handbook of family, school, and community relationships in education* (pp. 379–397). John Wiley & Sons.

Ewing, E. L. (2015, September 21). "We shall not be moved": A hunger strike, education, and housing in Chicago. *The New Yorker.* https://www.newyorker.com/news-desk/we-shall-not-be-moved-a-hunger-strike-education-and-housing-in-chicago

Fein, A. H., Carlisle, C. S., & Isaacson, N. S. (2008). School shootings and counselor leadership: Four lessons from the field. *Professional School Counseling, 11*(4), 246–252.

Ferguson, A. A. (2000). *Bad boys: Public schools in the making of black masculinity.* University of Michigan Press.

Ferman, B. (2017). *The fight for America's schools: Grassroots organizing in education.* Harvard Education Press.

Fernández, E., & Paredes Scribner, S. M. (2018). "Venimos para que se oiga la voz": Activating community cultural wealth as parental educational leadership. *Journal of Research on Leadership Education, 13*(1), 59–78. https://doi.org/10.1177/1942775117744011

Figley, C. R. (2002). Compassion fatigue: Psychotherapists' chronic lack of self care. *Journal of Clinical Psychology, 58*(11), 1433–1441.

Fixsen, D. L., & Blase, K. A. (2009). Technical assistance in special education: Past, present, and future. *Topics in Early Childhood Special Education, 29*(1), 62–64.

Fixsen, D. L., Naoom, S. F., Blase, K. A., Friedman, R. M., & Wallace, F., (2005). *Implementation research: A synthesis of the literature.* University of South Florida, Louis de la Parte Florida Mental Health Institute, The National Implementation Research Network (FMHI Publication #231).

Flores, O. J., & Gunzenhauser, M. G. (2019). The problems with colorblind leadership revealed: A call for race-conscious leaders. *International Journal of Qualitative Studies in Education, 32*(8), 963–981.

Flores, O. J., & Kyere, E. (2021). Advancing equity-based school leadership: The importance of family–school relationships. *The Urban Review, 53*(1), 1–18.

Fluehr-Lobban, C. (2006), *Race and racism: An introduction.* AltaMira Press.

Fordham, S. (1996). *Blacked out: Dilemmas of race, identity, and success at Capital High.* University of Chicago Press.

Fore, G. A., Hess, J. L., Sorge, B., Price, M. F., Coleman, M. A., Hahn, T. W., & Hatcher, J. A. (2018). *An introduction to the Integrated Community-Engaged Learning and Ethical Reflection Framework* (I-CELER). ASEE.

Forman, T., & Lewis, A. E. (2006). Racial apathy and hurricane Katrina: The social anatomy of prejudice in the post-civil rights era. *Du Bois Review, 3*(1), 175–202.

Foster, K. M. (2010). Taking a stand: Community-engaged scholarship on the tenure track. *Journal of Community Engagement and Scholarship, 3*(2), 1–11.

Franz, N. (2011). Tips for constructing a promotion and tenure dossier that documents engaged scholarship endeavors. *Journal of Higher Education Outreach and Engagement, 15*(3), 15–29.

Fraser, N. (2008). Abnormal justice. *Critical Inquiry, 34*(3), 393–422.

Fredrickson, G. M. (2015). *Racism: A short history.* Princeton University Press.

Freire, P. (2005). *Teachers as cultural workers: Letters to those who dare teach.* Westview Press.

Fullan, M. (2003). *Change forces with a vengeance.* Routledge.

Fullan, M. (2008). *The six secrets of change: What the best leaders do to help their organizations survive and thrive.* John Wiley & Sons.

Gabel, S. L. (Ed.). (2005). *Disability studies in education: Readings in theory and method* (Vol. 3). Peter Lang Publishing, Inc.

Galloway, M. K., & Ishimaru, A. M. (2015). Radical recentering: Equity in educational leadership standards. *Educational Administration Quarterly, 51*(3), 372–408.

Gandhi, M. K. (1951). *Non-violent resistance (satyagraha).* Schocken Books.

Garcia Cano, R., & Rankin, S. (2020). Parent resistance thwarts local school desegregation efforts. *Associated Press.* https://apnews.com/article/4e818872210464f07d23fc1259a49ebf

Gardiner, M., & Enomoto, E. (2006). Urban school principals and their role as multicultural leaders. *Urban Education, 41*(6), 560–584.

Garland, D. (2001). *The culture of control: Crime and social order in contemporary society.* University of Chicago Press.

Gelmon, S., & Agre-Kippenhan, S. (2002). Promotion, tenure, and the engaged scholar: Keeping the scholarship of engagement in the review process. *AAHE Bulletin, 54*(5), 7–11. https://www.aahea.org/articles/engaged.htm

Gilmore, R. W. (2007). *Golden gulag: Prisons, surplus, crisis, and opposition in globalizing California.* University of California Press.

Ginwright, S. (2016). *Hope and healing in urban education: How urban activists and teachers are reclaiming matters of the heart.* Taylor and Francis Group.

Glassick, C. E., Huber, M. T., & Maeroff, G. I. (1997). *Scholarship assessed: Evaluation of the professoriate.* Jossey-Bass.

Goff, P. A., Jackson, M. C., Di Leone, B. A. L., Culotta, C. M., & DiTomasso, N. A. (2014). The essence of innocence: Consequences of dehumanizing Black children. *Journal of Personality and Social Psychology, 106*(4), 526–544.

Goldring, E., & Sims, P. (2005). Modeling creative and courageous school leadership through district-community-university partnerships. *Educational Policy, 19*(1), 223–249.

Goldstein, D. (2020, June 12). Do police officers make schools safer or more dangerous? *The New York Times.* https://www.nytimes.com/2020/06/12/us/schools-police-resource-officers.html

González, T., & Artiles, A. J. (2020). Wrestling with the paradoxes of equity: A cultural-historical reframing of technical assistance interventions. *Multiple Voices for Ethnically Diverse Exceptional Learners, 20*(1), 5–15.

Gonzalez, T., Love, L. D., Johnson, M. L., Picón, N., & Velázquez, J. (2017). Youth rising: Centering youth voice in the quest for equitable and inclusive schools. *Equity by Design*. Midwest & Plains Equity Assistance Center (MAP EAC). http://glec.education.iupui.edu/Images/Briefs/2017_07_20_TauciaGonzalez_YouthRising.pdf

Gooden, M. A. (2005). The role of an African American principal in an urban information technology high school. *Educational Administration Quarterly, 41*(4), 630–650. https://doi.org/10.1177/0013161X04274273

Gooden, M. A., Bell, C. M., Gonzales, R. M., & Lippa, A. P. (2011). Planning university-urban district partnerships: Implications for principal preparation programs. *Educational Planning, 20*(2), 1–13.

Gooden, M. A., & Dantley, M. (2012). Centering race in a framework for leadership preparation. *Journal of Research on Leadership Education, 7*(2), 237–253. https://doi.org/10.1177/1942775112455266

Gooden, M. A., & O'Doherty, A. (2015). Do you see what I see? Fostering aspiring leaders' racial awareness. *Urban Education, 50*(2), 225–255.

Goodman, J. (2013). Charter management organizations and the regulated environment: Is it worth the price? *Educational Researcher, 42*(2), 89–96.

Gorski, P. C. (2020). "So you think you're an anti-racist? 6 critical paradigm shifts for well-intentioned white folks." *Edchange*. http://www.edchange.org/multicultural/resources/paradigmshifts_race.html

Gorski, P. C., & Erakat, N. (2019). Racism, whiteness, and burnout in antiracism movements: How white racial justice activists elevate burnout in racial justice activists of color in the United States. *Ethnicities, 19*(5), 784–808.

Gramlich, J. (2020). *Black imprisonment in the U.S. has fallen by a third since 2006*. Pew Research Center. https://www.pewresearch.org/fact-tank/2020/05/06/black-imprisonment-rate-in-the-u-s-has-fallen-by-a-third-since-2006/

Green, T. L. (2015a). Places of inequality, places of possibility: Mapping "opportunity in geography" across urban school-communities. *The Urban Review, 47*(4), 717–741.

Green, T. L. (2015b). Leading for urban school reform and community development. *Educational Administration Quarterly, 51*(5), 679–711.

Green, T. L. (2017). Community-based equity audits: A practical approach for educational leaders to support equitable community-school improvements. *Educational Administration Quarterly, 53*(1), 3–39.

Green, T. L. (2018). School as community, community as school: Examining principal leadership for urban school reform and community development. *Education and Urban Society, 50*(2), 111–135.

Gregory, A., Skiba, R. J., & Noguera, P. A. (2010). The achievement gap and the discipline gap: Two sides of the same coin? *Educational Researcher, 39*(1), 59–68.

Gregory, A., & Weinstein, R. S. (2008). The discipline gap and African Americans: Defiance or cooperation in the high school classroom. *Journal of School Psychology, 46*(4), 455–475.

Grogan, M. (2000). Laying the groundwork for a reconception of the superintendency from feminist postmodern perspectives. *Educational Administration Quarterly, 36*(1), 117–142. https://doi.org/10.1177/0013161X00361005

Haberman, M. (2005). Teacher burnout in black and white. *The New Educator, 1*(3), 153–175. https://doi.org/10.1080/15476880590966303.

Hacker, A. (1992) *Two nations: Black and white, separate, hostile, unequal.* Scribner.

Hallinger, P., & Heck, R. H. (1998). Exploring the principal's contribution to school effectiveness: 1980–1995. *School Effectiveness and School Improvement, 9*(2), 157–191. https://doi.org/10.1080/0924345980090203

Hammer, M. (2020). *Intercultural development inventory.* https://idiinventory.com/generalinformation/

Handel, G. (2006). *Childhood socialization, social problems and social issues.* Transaction Publishers.

Harmon, A., & Burch, A. D. S. (2020, June 22). White Americans say they are waking up to racism. What will it add up to? *The New York Times.* https://www.nytimes.com/2020/06/22/us/racism-white-americans.html

Harris, D. N., Ingle, W. K., & Rutledge, S. A. (2014). How teacher evaluation methods matter for accountability: A comparative analysis of teacher effectiveness ratings by principals and teacher value-added measures. *American Educational Research Journal, 51*(1), 73–112.

Harris, J. C., Haywood, J. M., Ivery, S. M., & Shuck, J. R. (2015). Yes, I am smart!": Battling microaggressions as women of color doctoral students. In J. L. Martin (Ed.), *Racial battle fatigue: Insights from the front lines of social justice advocacy* (pp. 129–140). ABC-CLIO.

Harris-Perry, M. (2011). *Sister citizen: Shame, stereotypes, and black women in America.* Yale University Press.

Harvey, D. (2005). *A brief history of neoliberalism.* Oxford University Press.

Heifetz, R., & Linsky, M. (2017). *Leadership on the line, with a new preface: Staying alive through the dangers of change.* Harvard Business Review Press.

Heller, M. F., & Firestone, W. A. (1995) Who's in charge here? Sources of leadership for change in eight schools. *Elementary School Journal, 96*(1), 65–86.

Hernández, K. L., Muhammad, K. G., & Thompson, H. A. (2015). Introduction: Constructing the carceral state. *The Journal of American History, 102*(1), 18–24.

Herrmann, M. (2020). *Learn to lead, lead to learn: Leadership as a work in progress.* Rowman & Littlefield.

Hill, M. L. (2018). "Thank You, Black Twitter": State violence, digital counterpublics, and pedagogies of resistance. *Urban Education, 53*(2), 286–302.

Hill, T. (2017). *Combating the achievement gap: Ending failure as a default in schools*. Rowman & Littlefield.

Hinton, K. A. (2015). Should we use a capital framework to understand culture? Applying cultural capital to communities of color. *Equity & Excellence in Education, 48*(2), 299–319.

Hipp, K. A. (1996, April). *Teacher efficacy: Influence of principal leadership behavior*. Paper presented at the Annual Meeting of the American Educational Research Association. New York, NY.

Hiraldo, P. (2010). The role of critical race theory in higher education. *The Vermont Connection, 31*(1), 53–59.

Hirschfield, P. J. (2008). Preparing for prison? The criminalization of school discipline in the USA. *Theoretical Criminology, 12*(1), 79–101.

Hirschfield, P. J. (2018). Trends in school social control in the United States: Explaining patterns of decriminalization. In J. Deakin, E. Taylor, & A. Kupchik (Eds.), *The Palgrave international handbook of school discipline, surveillance, and social control* (pp. 43–64). Palgrave Macmillan.

Hite, L. M. (2004). Black and white women managers: Access to opportunity. *Human Resource Development Quarterly, 15*(2), 131–146.

Hoffman, L. P. (2009). Educational leadership and social activism: A call for action. *Journal of Educational Administration and History, 41*(4), 391–410.

Hoffman, S., Palladino, J. M., & Barnett, J. (2007). Compassion fatigue as a theoretical framework to help understand burnout among special education teachers. *Journal of Ethnographic & Qualitative Research, 2*(1), 15–22.

Holme, J. J., Diem, S., & Welton, A. (2014). Suburban school districts and demographic change: The technical, normative, and political dimensions of response. *Educational Administration Quarterly, 50*(1), 34–66.

Hong, C. P. (2021). *Minor feelings: An Asian American reckoning*. One World.

Horsford, S. (2012). This bridge called my leadership: An essay on Black women as bridge leaders in education. *International Journal of Qualitative Studies in Education. 25*, 11–22. https://doi.org/10.1080/09518398.2011.647726.

Horsford, S. (2014). When race enters the room: Improving leadership and learning through racial literacy. *Theory into Practice, 53*(2), 123–130.

Horsford, S. D. (2011). *Learning in a burning house: Educational inequality, ideology, and (dis)integration*. Teachers College Press.

Horsford, S. D. (2018). Making America's schools great now: Reclaiming democracy and activist leadership under Trump. *Journal of Educational Administration and History, 50*(1), 3–11.

Horsford, S. D., Grosland, T., & Gunn, K. M. (2011). Pedagogy of the personal and professional: Toward a framework for culturally relevant leadership. *Journal of School Leadership, 21*(4), 582–606.

Howard-Hamilton, M. F., Palmer, C., Johnson, S., & Kicklighter, M. (1998). Burnout and related factors: Differences between women and men in student affairs. *College Student Affairs Journal, 17*(2), 80–91.

Hubain, B. S., Allen, E. L., Harris, J. C., & Linder, C. (2016). Counter-stories as representations of the racialized experiences of students of color in higher education and student affairs graduate preparation programs. *International Journal of Qualitative Studies in Education, 29*(7), 946–963.

Hughes, J. N., Gleason, K. A., & Zhang, D. (2005). Relationship influences on teachers' perceptions of academic competence in academically at-risk minority and majority first grade students. *Journal of School Psychology, 43*(4), 303–320.

Humphrey, R. H. (2012). How do leaders use emotional labor? *Journal of Organizational Behavior, 33*(5), 740–744.

Irby, D. J., & Clark, S. P. (2018). Talk it (racism) out: Race talk and organizational learning. *Journal of Educational Administration, 56*(5), 504–518.

Irby, D. J., & Drame, E. R. (2016). Introduction. Black bridges, troubled waters, and the search for solid ground: The people, the problems, and educational justice. In E. R. Drame & D. J. Irby (Eds.), *Black participatory research: Power, identity, and the struggle for justice in education* (pp. 1–19). Palgrave Macmillan.

Ishimaru, A. (2013). From heroes to organizers: Principals and education organizing in urban school reform. *Educational Administration Quarterly, 49*(1), 3–51.

Ishimaru, A. M., Lott, J. L., Torres, K. E., & O'Reilly-Diaz, K. (2019). Families in the driver's seat: Catalyzing familial transformative agency for equitable collaboration. *Teachers College Record, 112*(11), 1–39.

Jackson, B. L. (1988). Education from black perspective: Implications for leadership preparation. In D. E. Griffiths, R. T. Stout, & R. B. Forsyth (Eds.), *Leaders for America's schools: The report and papers of the National Commission on Excellence in Educational Administration*. McCutchan.

Jackson, R. G., Coomer, N. M., Dagli, C., Kyser, T. S., Skelton, S. M., & Thorius, K. A. K. (2016). Reexamining workforce diversity: Authentic representations of difference. *Equity Dispatch Newsletter*. Great Lakes Equity Center.

Jackson, S. A. (2002). A study of teachers' perceptions of youth problems. *Journal of Youth Studies, 5*(3), 313–323.

Jean-Marie, G., & Mansfield, K.C. (2013). Race and racial discrimination in schools: School leaders' courageous conversations. In J. S. Brooks & N. W. Arnold, (Eds.), *Anti-racist school leadership: Toward equity in education for America's students* (pp. 19–36). Information Age Publishing, Inc.

Jean-Marie, G., Normore, A. H., & Brooks, J. S. (2009). Leadership for social justice: Preparing 21st Century school leaders for a new social order. *Journal of Research on Leadership in Education, 4*(1), 1–31.

Johnson, L. (2006). "Making her community a better place to live": Culturally responsive urban school leadership in historical context. *Leadership and Policy in Schools, 5*(1), 19–36.

Johnson, L. (2014). Culturally responsive leadership for community empowerment. *Multicultural Education Review, 6*(2), 145–170.

Jordan, C. (2007). (Ed.). *The community-engaged scholarship review, promotion & tenure package*. Community-Campus Partnerships for Health. https://www.ccphealth.org/wp-content/uploads/2017/10/CES_RPT_Package.pdf

Jordan, D., & Wilson, C. (2015). Supporting African-American student success through prophetic activism: New possibilities for public school-church partnerships. *Urban Education, 52*(1), 91–119.

Kafka, J. (2011). *The history of "zero tolerance" in American public schooling*. Palgrave Macmillan.

Kahlenberg, R. D., Potter, H., & Quick, K. (2019). School integration: How it can promote social cohesion and combat racism. *American Educator, 43*(3), 26–30.

Karpinski, C., & Lugg, C. (2006). Social justice and educational administration: Mutually exclusive? *Journal of Educational Administration, 44*(3), 278–292.

Katsiyannis, A., Gage, N. A., Rapa, L. J., & MacSuga-Gage, A. S. (2020). Exploring the disproportionate use of restraint and seclusion among students with disabilities, boys, and students of color. *Advances in Neurodevelopmental Disorders, 4*, 271–278. https://doi.org/10.1007/s41252-020-00160-z

Katz, J., & Wandersman, A. (2016). Technical assistance to enhance prevention capacity: A research synthesis of the evidence base. *Prevention Science, 17*(4), 417–428.

Keels, M., Durkee, M., & Hope, E. (2017). The psychological and academic costs of school-based racial and ethnic microaggressions. *American Educational Research Journal, 54*(6), 1316–1344.

Kelley, R. D. (2002). *Freedom dreams: The black radical imagination*. Beacon Press.

Kelly, S. (2004). Are teachers tracked? On what basis and with what consequences? *Social Psychology of Education, 7*(1), 55–72.

Kendall, F. (2013). *Understanding white privilege: Creating pathways to authentic relationships across race*. Routledge.

Kendi, I. X. (2019). *How to be an antiracist*. One World.

Khalifa, M. (2012). A re-new-ed paradigm in successful urban school leadership: Principal as community leader. *Educational Administration Quarterly, 48*(3), 424–467. https://doi.org/10.1177/0013161x11432922

Khalifa, M. (2018). *Culturally responsive school leadership*. Harvard Education Press.

Khalifa, M. A., Gooden, M. A., & Davis, J. E. (2016). Culturally responsive school leadership: A synthesis of the literature. *Review of Educational Research, 86*(4), 1272–1311.

Khalil, D., & Brown, E. (2020). Diversity dissonance as an implication of one school's relocation and reintegration initiative. *Educational Administration Quarterly, 56*(3), 499–529.

Kim, J., & Garland, J. (2019). Development cooperation and post-colonial critique: An investigation into the South Korean model. *Third World Quarterly, 40*(7), 1246–1264.

Kimball, K., & Sirontnik, K. A. (2000). The urban school principalship: Take this job and … ! *Education and Urban Society, 32*(4), 536–543.

King, Jr., Martin Luther. (1958/2010). *Stride toward freedom: The Montgomery story.* Beacon Press.

King, Jr., Martin Luther, & Washington, J. M. (1986). *A testament of hope: The essential writings of Martin Luther King, Jr.* Harper & Row.

King, T. C., & Ferguson, S. A. (2001). Charting ourselves: Leadership development with Blackprofessional women. *National Women's Studies Association Journal, 13*(2), 123–141.

Knoester, M., & Au, W. (2017). Standardized testing and school segregation: Like tinder for fire? *Race Ethnicity and Education, 20*(1), 1–14.

Koenig, A., Rodger, S., & Specht, J. (2018). Educator burnout and compassion fatigue: A pilot study. *Canadian Journal of School Psychology, 33*(4), 259–278.

Kohli, R. (2014). Unpacking internalized racism: Teachers of color striving for racially just classrooms. *Race, Ethnicity and Education, 17*(3), 367–387.

Kohli, R., Pizarro, M., & Nevárez, A. (2017). The "new racism" of K–12 schools: Centering critical research on racism. *Review of Research in Education, 41*(1), 182–202.

Koon, D. S. V. (2020). Education policy networks: The co-optation, coordination, and commodification of the school-to-prison pipeline critique. *American Educational Research Journal, 57*(1), 371–410.

Kowalski, T. J. (2005). Evolution of the school superintendent as communicator. *Communication Education, 54*(2), 101–117.

Kozleski, E. B., & Artiles, A. J. (2012). Technical assistance as inquiry: Using activity theory methods to engage equity in educational practice communities. In S. Steinberg, & G. Canella (Eds.), *Handbook on Critical Qualitative Research* (pp. 431–445). Peter Lang Publishing, Inc.

Kozleski, E. B., & Artiles, A. J. (2015). Mediating systemic change in educational systems through sociocultural methods. In P. Smeyers, D. Bridges, M. Griffiths, & N. Burbules (Eds.), *International handbook of interpretation in educational research methods* (pp. 805–822). Springer.

Kronick, R. F., Lester, J. N., & Luter, D. G. (2013). Conclusion to higher education's role in public school reform and community engagement. *Peabody Journal of Education, 88*(5), 657–664.

Kumashiro, K. K. (2002). Against repetition: Addressing resistance to anti-oppressive change in the practices of learning, teaching, supervising, and researching. *Harvard Educational Review, 72*(1), 67–93.

Kurt, T., Duyar, I., & Çalik, T. (2011). Are we legitimate yet? A closer look at the casual relationship mechanisms among principal leadership, teacher self-efficacy, and collective efficacy. *Journal of Management Development, 31*(1), 71–86.

Kyser, T. S., Coomer, N. M., Moore, T., Cosby, G., Jackson, R. G., & Skelton, S. M. (2015). Parents/caregivers as authentic partners in education. *Equity Dispatch* Newsletter. Great Lakes Equity Center.

Kyser, T. S., Skelton, S. M., Warren, C. L., & Whiteman, R. S. (2016). *Policy equity analysis toolkit*. Great Lake Equity Assistance Center. https://greatlakesequity.org/resource/policy-equity-analysis-toolkit-0

Lac, V. T., & Cumings Mansfield, K. (2018). What do students have to do with educational leadership? Making a case for centering student voice. *Journal of Research on Leadership Education, 13*(1), 38–58.

Ladson-Billings, G. (1994a). *The dreamkeepers: Successful teachers of African American children*. John Wiley & Sons, Inc.

Ladson-Billings, G. (1994b). What we can learn from multicultural education research. *Educational Leadership, 51*(8), 22–26.

Ladson-Billings, G. (1995). Toward a theory of culturally relevant pedagogy. *American Educational Research Journal, 32*(3), 465–491.

Ladson-Billings, G. (2006). From the achievement gap to the education debt: Understanding achievement in U.S. schools. *Educational Researcher, 35*(7), 3–12.

Ladson-Billings, G. (2014). Culturally relevant pedagogy 2.0: a.k.a. the remix. *Harvard Educational Review, 84*(1), 74–84.

LaFave, S. (2020, May 4). How school closures for COVID-19 amplify inequality. *The Hub*. https://hub.jhu.edu/2020/05/04/school-closures-inequality/

Lakota People's Law Project (n.d.). *DAPL and environmental justice*. https://lakotalaw.org/resources/dapl-environmental-justice

Larson, C. L., & Murtadha, K. (2002). Leadership for social justice. In J. Murphy (Ed.), *The educational leadership challenge: Redefining leadership for the 21st Century* (pp. 134–161), University of Chicago Press.

Lassiter, C. (2018). *Everyday courage for school leaders*. Corwin.

Laura, C. T. (2014). *Being bad: My baby brother and the school-to-prison Pipeline*. Teachers College Press.

LeChasseur, K. (2014). Critical race theory and the meaning of "community" in district partnerships. *Equity & Excellence in Education, 47*(3), 305–320.

Lee, J., & Wong, K. K. (2004). The impact of accountability on racial and socioeconomic equity: Considering both school resources and achievement outcomes. *American Educational Research Journal, 41*(4), 797–832. https://doi.org/10.3102/00028312041004797

Leithwood, K. (2012). *The Ontario leadership framework 2012*. Institute for Education Leadership. http://iel.Immix.ca/storage/6/1345688978/Final_Research_Report_-_EN.pdf.

Leonard, J., Walker, E. N., Bloom, V. R., & Joseph, N. M. (2020). Mathematics literacy, identity resilience, and opportunity sixty years since "Brown v. Board": Counternarratives of a five-generation family. *Journal of Urban Mathematics Education, 13*, 12–37.

Leonardo, Z. (2004). The color of supremacy: Beyond the discourse of "white privilege." *Educational Philosophy and Theory, 36*(2), 137–152.

Leonardo, Z. (2009). *Race, whiteness, and education*. Routledge.

Leonardo, Z. (2013). The story of schooling: Critical race theory and the educational racial contract. *Discourse: Studies in the Cultural Politics of Education, 34*(4), 599–610.

Leonardo, Z., & Porter, R. K. (2010). Pedagogy of fear: Toward a Fanonian theory of "safety" in race dialogue. *Race Ethnicity and Education, 13*(2), 139–157.

Levi-Strauss, C. (1966). *The savage mind.* The University of Chicago Press.

Lewis, A. E. (2003). *Race in the schoolyard: Negotiating the color line in classrooms and communities.* Rutgers University Press.

Lewis, A. E., & Diamond, J. B. (2015). *Despite the best intentions: How racial inequality thrives in good schools.* Oxford University Press.

Lewis, A. E., & Manno, M. J. (2011). The best education for some: Race and schooling in the United States today. In M-K Jung, J. C. Vargas, & E. Bonilla-Silva (Eds.), *State of white supremacy: Racism, governance, and the United States* (pp. 93–109). Stanford University Press.

Lewis, D. (2019). *Bobbie Raymond—A whirlwind for social change.* The Oak Park Regional Housing Center. https://oprhc.org/2019/05/in-memoriam-of-bobbie-raymond/

Lewis, K. (2016). Social justice leadership and inclusion: A genealogy. *Journal of Educational Administration and History, 48*(4), 324–341.

Lightfoot, S. L. (2004). *The essential conversation: What parents and teachers can learn from each other.* Ballantine Books.

Linton, R. (1936). *The study of man: An introduction.* D. Appleton-Century.

Linton, S. (1998). *Claiming disability: Knowledge and identity.* New York University Press.

Liou, D. D., & Liang, J. G. (2020). Toward a theory of sympathetic leadership: Asian American school administrators' expectations for justice and excellence. *Educational Administration Quarterly.* https://doi.org/10.1177%2F0013161X20941915

Liou, D. D., Leigh, P. R., Rotheram-Fuller, E., & Deits Cutler, K. (2019). The influence of teachers' colorblind expectations on the political, normative, and technical dimensions of educational reform. *International Journal of Educational Reform, 28*(1), 122–148.

Lipman, P. (2011). *The new political economy of urban education: Neoliberalism, race, and the right to the city.* Routledge.

Lipman, P. (2015). School closings: The nexus of white supremacy, state abandonment, and accumulation by dispossession. In B. Picower, & E. Mayorga (Eds.), *What's race got to do with it? How current school reform policy maintains racial and economic inequality* (pp. 59–79). Peter Lang Publishing, Inc.

Lipsitz, G. (1998). *The possessive investment in whiteness: How white people profit from identity politics.* Temple University Press.

Litwack, L. F. (1998). *Trouble in mind: Black southerners in the age of Jim Crow.* Knopf.

Liu, G. (2007–08). Improving Title I funding equity across state, districts, and schools. *Iowa Law Review, 93*(3), 973–1013.

Loder-Jackson, T. (2011). Bridging the legacy of activism across generations: Life stories of African American educators in post-civil rights Birmingham. *The Urban Review*, *43*(2), 151–174.

Lomotey, K. (1993). African-American principals: Bureaucrat/administrators and ethno-humanists. *Urban Education*, *27*(4), 395–412.

Lomotey, K., & Lowery, K. (2015). Urban schools, Black principals, and Black students: Culturally responsive education and the ethno-humanist role identity. In M. Khalifa, N. W. Arnold, A. F. Osanloo, & C. M. Grant (Eds.), *Handbook of urban educational leadership* (pp. 118–134). Rowman & Littlefield Publishers.

Long, D. (2012). The foundations of student affairs: A guide to the profession. In L. J. Hinchliffe, & M. A. Wong (Eds.), *Environments for student growth and development: Librarians and student affairs in collaboration* (pp. 1–39). Association of College & Research Libraries.

López, G. R. (2003). The (racially neutral) politics of education. A critical race theory perspective. *Educational Administration Quarterly*, *39*(1), 68–94.

Losen, D. J., & Gillespie, J. (2012). *Opportunities suspended: The disparate impact of disciplinary exclusion from school*. UCLA Civil Rights Project/Proyecto Derechos Civiles.

Love, B. (2019). *We want to do more than survive: Abolitionist teaching and the pursuit of educational freedom*. Beacon Press.

Lynch, R. J. (2017). *Breaking the silence: A phenomenological exploration of secondary traumatic stress in US College student affairs professionals* [Doctoral dissertation, Old Dominion University]. Old Dominion University Digital Commons: https://digitalcommons.odu.edu/efl_etds/43.

Macey, E. M., Thorius, K. A. K., & Skelton, S. M. (2012). Engaging school communities in critical reflection on policy. *Equity by Design*. https://greatlakesequity.org/resource/engaging-school-communities-critical-reflection-policy

Magee, M. P. (2019). *A little opposition is a good thing and other lessons from the science of advocacy*. The 50-State Campaign for Achievement.

Mansfield, C. F., Beltman, S., Price, A., & McConney, A. (2012). "Don't sweat the small stuff": Understanding teacher resilience at the chalkface. *Teaching and Teacher Education*, *28*(3), 357–367.

March, J. G. (1991). Exploration and exploitation in organizational learning. *Organization Science*, *2*(1), 71–87.

Marks, H. M., & Printy, S. M. (2003). Principal leadership and school performance: An integration of transformational and instructional leadership. *Educational Administration Quarterly*, *39*(3), 370–397.

Marshall, C., & Anderson, A. L. (Eds.) (2008). *Activist educators: Breaking past limits*. Routledge.

Marshall, C., & Olivia, M. (2006). *Leadership for social justice: Making revolutions in education*. Allyn & Bacon.

Marshall, C., & Oliva, M. (2007). *Leadership for social justice: Making revolutions in education*. 2nd edn. Pearson.

Martinez, E., & Garcia, G. (1997). *What is neoliberalism?* https://corpwatch.org/article/what-neoliberalism

Martinez Hoy, Z. R., & Gilbert, K., (2011). A narrative inquiry into the experiences of higher education service providers working with undocumented Latino young adults. Unpublished paper.

Martinez Hoy, Z. R., & Nguyen, D. H. K. (2019). Higher education professionals navigating anti-immigration policy for undocumented students. *Educational Policy*. https://doi.org/10.1177/0895904819857823.

Mawhinney, L. (2016). Be catty and piss on your work: A cautionary tale of researching while black. In E. R. Drame, & D. J. Irby (Eds.), *Black participatory research: Power, identity, and the struggle for justice in education* (pp. 105–121). Palgrave Macmillan.

Mawhinney, L., Irby, D. J., & Roberts, E. S. (2016). Passed along: Black women reflect on the long-term effects of social promotion and retention in schools. *International Journal of Educational Reform*, *25*(2), 154–69.

May, C., & Finch, T. (2009). Implementing, embedding, and integrating practices: An outline of normalization process theory. *Sociology*, *43*(3), 535–554.

Mazrui, A. A., & Levine, T. K. (1986). *The Africans: A reader*. Praeger Publishers.

McCardle, T. (2020). A critical historical examination of tracking as a method for maintaining racial segregation. *Educational Considerations*, *45*(2), 1–14.

McConn, M. (2019). A university and local school partnership: Utilizing tension as a catalyst for growth. *Studying Teacher Education*, *15*(2), 235–253.

McInerney, M., & Hamilton, J. (2007). Elementary and middle schools technical assistance center: An approach to support the effective implementation of scientifically based practices in special education. *Exceptional Children*, *73*(2), 242–255.

McIntosh, P. (1988). *White privilege and male privilege: A personal account of coming to see correspondences through work in women's studies* (Working paper/Wellesley College, Center for Research on Women, no. 189). Wellesley College, Center for Research on Women. http://citeseerx.ist.psu.edu/viewdoc/download?doi=10.1.1.732.4979&rep=rep1&type=pdf

McKenzie, K. B., Christman, D. E., Hernandez, F., Fierro, E., Capper, C. A., Dantley, M., … Scheurich, J. J. (2008). From the field: A proposal for educating leaders for social justice. *Educational Administration Quarterly*, *44*(1), 111–138. https://doi.org/10.1177/0013161X07309470

McKenzie, K. B., & Scheurich, J. J. (2004). Equity traps: A useful construct for preparing principals to lead schools that are successful with racially diverse students. *Educational Administration Quarterly*, *40*(5), 601–632. https://doi.org/10.1177/0013161X04268839

McMahon, B. (2007). Educational administrators' conceptions of whiteness, anti-racism and social justice. *Journal of Educational Administration, 45*(6), 684–696.

Mead, G. H. (1934). *Mind, self, and society from the standpoint of a social behaviorist.* University of Chicago Press.

Mediratta, K., & Fructher, N. (2001). *Mapping the field of organizing for school improvement: A report on education organizing in Baltimore, Chicago, Los Angeles the Mississippi Delta, New York City, Philadelphia, San Francisco, and Washington DC.* New York University, Institute for Education and Social Policy, with California Tomorrow, Designs for Change, and Southern Echo. https://files.eric.ed.gov/fulltext/ED471052.pdf

Mediratta, K., Shah, S., & McAlister, S. (2009). *Community organizing for stronger schools: Strategies and successes.* Harvard Education Press.

Mehta, J. (2020). Equity work: Too much talk, too little action. *Next Generation Learning Challenges.* https://www.nextgenlearning.org/articles/equity-work-too-much-talk-too-little-action

Meier, D. (2002). *The power of their ideas.* Beacon Press.

Meier, K. J., Stewart, J., & England, R. E. (1989). *Race, class, and education: The politics of second-generation discrimination.* University of Wisconsin Press.

Meiners, E. R. (2007). *Right to be hostile: Schools, prisons, and the making of public enemies.* Routledge.

Merchant, B., & Garza, E. (2015). The Urban School Leaders Collaborative: Twelve years of promoting leadership for social justice. *Journal of Research on Leadership Education, 10*(1), 39–62. https://doi.org/10.1177/1942775115569576

Merriam, S. B., Caffarella, R. S., & Baumgartner L. M. (2007). *Learning in adulthood: A comprehensive guide.* John Wiley & Sons, Inc.

Mezirow, J. (1991). *Transformative dimensions of adult learning.* Jossey-Bass.

Metzl, J. M., & Roberts, D. E. (2014). Structural competency meets structural racism: Race, politics, and the structure of medical knowledge. *AMA Journal of Ethics, 16*(9), 674–690.

Michael, A., & Conger, M. C. (2009). Becoming an anti-racist white ally: How a white affinity group can help. *Perspectives on Urban Education, 6*(1), 56–60.

Mickelson, R. A. (2001). Subverting Swann: First- and second-generation segregation in the Charlotte-Mecklenburg Schools. *American Educational Research Journal, 38*(2), 215–25.

Midwest and Plains Equity Assistance Center. (2017). *Equity context analysis process (ECAP).* Author.

Midwest and Plains Equity Assistance Center. (2019). *Leading equity-focused initiatives partnership academy.* Author.

Mills, C. W. (2014). *The racial contract.* Cornell University Press.

Mintrop, H., & Sunderman, G. L. (2009). Predictable failure of federal sanctions-driven accountability for school improvement—and why we may retain it anyway. *Educational Researcher, 38*(5), 353–364. https://doi.org/10.3102/0013189x09339055

Mintrop, H., & Trujillo, T. (2007). The practical relevance of accountability systems for school improvement: A descriptive analysis of California schools. *Educational Evaluation and Policy Analysis, 29*(4), 319–352. https://doi.org/10.3102/0162373707309219

Mitchinson, A., & Morris, R. (2014). *Learning about learning agility* (white paper). Center for Creative Leadership.

Monteiro-Ferreira, A. (2014). *The demise of the inhuman: Afrocentricity, modernism, and postmodernism.* SUNY Press.

Moore, M., & Alonso, A. (2017) *Creating public value: School superintendents as strategic managers of public schools.* President and Fellows of Harvard College.

Morris, M. (2016). *Pushout: The criminalization of black girls in schools.* The New Press.

Morris, M. (2019). *Sing a rhythm, dance a blues: Education for the liberation of black and brown girls.* The New Press.

Mosley, M. (2010). "That really hit me hard": Moving beyond passive anti-racism to engage with critical race literacy pedagogy. *Race, Ethnicity and Education, 13*(4), 449–471.

Murtadha, K., & Watts, D. M. (2005). Linking the struggle for education and social justice: Historical perspectives of African American leadership in schools. *Educational Administration Quarterly, 41*(4), 591–608.

Nadal, K. L., Davidoff, K. C., Allicock, N., Serpe, C. R., & Erazo, T. (2017). Perceptions of police, racial profiling, and psychological outcomes: A mixed methodological study. *Journal of Social Issues, 73*(4), 808–830.

Nance, J. (2015). Students, police, and the school-to-prison pipeline. *Washington University Law Review 93*(4), 919–987.

National Center for Education Statistics. (2020). *Racial/ethnic enrollment in public schools.* https://nces.ed.gov/programs/coe/indicator_cge.asp

Nayak, A. (2007). Critical whiteness studies. *Sociology Compass, 1*(2), 737–755.

Ngounou, G., & Gutierrez, N. (2017). Learning to lead for racial equity. *Phi Delta Kappan 99*(3), 37–41.

Nguyen, B. M. D., Noguera, P., Adkins, N., & Teranishi, R. T. (2019). Ethnic discipline gap: Unseen dimensions of racial disproportionality in school discipline. *American Educational Research Journal, 56*(5), 1973–2003.

Nguyen, D. H. K., & Ward, L. W. (2019). Innocent until proven guilty: A critical interrogation of the legal aspects of job fit in higher education. In B. J. Reece, V. T. Tran, E. N. DeVore, & G. Porcaro (Eds.), *Debunking the myth of job fit in higher education and student affairs.* Stylus Publishing, LLC.

Noguera, P. A. (2003). The trouble with Black boys: The role and influence of environmental and cultural factors on the academic performance of African American males. *Urban Education, 38*(4), 431–459.

Nolan, K. (2011). *Police in the hallways: Discipline in an urban high school.* University of Minnesota Press.

Nyerere, J. K. (1964). *UJAMAA: Essays on socialism.* Oxford University Press.

O'Connor, C. (2020). Education research and the disruption of racialized distortions: Establishing a wide-angle view. *Educational Researcher, 20*(10), 1–12.

O'Connor, C., Hill, L. D., & Robinson, S. R. (2009). Who's at risk in school and what's race got to do with it? *Review of Research in Education, 33*(1), 1–33.

O'Neil, J. (1992). On tracking and individual differences: A conversation with Jeannie Oakes. *Educational Leadership, 50*(2), 18–21.

Oakes, J. (1985/2005). *Keeping track: How schools structure inequality.* Yale University Press.

Oakes, J., Rogers, J., & Lipton, M. (2006). *Learning power: Organizing for education and justice.* Teachers College Press.

Office, G. A. (2009). *Seclusion and restraints: Selected cases of death and abuse at public and private schools and treatment centers.* Author. https://www.gao.gov/assets/gao-09-719t.pdf

Ogawa, R. T., & Bossert, S. T. (1995). Leadership as an organizational quality. *Educational Administration Quarterly, 31*(2), 224–243.

Ohito, E. O. (2016). Making the emperor's new clothes visible in anti-racist teacher education: Enacting a pedagogy of discomfort with white preservice teachers. *Equity & Excellence in Education, 49*(4), 454–467.

Okonofua, J. A., Walton, G. M., & Eberhardt, J. L. (2016). A vicious cycle: A social-psychological account of extreme racial disparities in school discipline. *Perspectives on Psychological Science, 11*(3), 381–398.

Oluo, I. (2018). *So you want to talk about race?* Seal Press.

Orfield, G., Kucsera, J., & Siegel-Hawley, G. (2012). *E pluribus… separation? Deepening double segregation for more students.* UCLA Civil Rights Project/Proyecto Derechos Civiles.

Osofsky, J. D., Putnam, F. W., & Lederman, J. C. S. (2008). How to maintain emotional health when working with trauma. *Juvenile and Family Court Journal, 59*(4), 91–102.

Padilla, A. M. (1994). Ethnic minority scholars, research, and mentoring: Current and future issues. *Educational Researcher, 23*(4), 24–27.

Parker, L., & Lynn, M. (2002). What's race got to do with it?: Critical race theory's conflicts with and connections to qualitative research methodology and epistemology. *Qualitative Inquiry, 8*(1), 7–22.

Parker, M., & Henfield, M. S. (2012). Exploring school counselors' perceptions of vicarious trauma: A qualitative study. *Professional Counselor, 2*(2), 134–142.

Patton, L. D., & Haynes, C. (2020). Dear white people: Reimagining whiteness in the struggle for racial equity. *Change: The Magazine of Higher Learning, 52*(2), 41–45.

Patton, M. Q. (2002). Two decades of developments in qualitative inquiry: A personal, experiential perspective. *Qualitative Social Work, 1*(3), 261–283.

Payne, C. M. (2008). *So much reform, so little change: The persistence of failure in urban schools.* Harvard Education Press.

Pearlman, L. A., & Saakvitne, K. W. (1995). *Trauma and the therapist: Countertransference and vicarious traumatization in psychotherapy with incest survivors*. W. W. Norton & Company.

Peguero, A. A. (2019). Introduction to the special issue on significant of race/ethnicity in bullying. *International Journal of Bullying Prevention, 1*, 159–160: https://doi.org/10.1007/s42380-019-00032-8

Penuel, W. R., & Gallagher, D. J. (2017). *Creating research-practice partnerships in education*. Harvard Education Press.

Peterson, M. (2019). *The revolutionary practices of black feminisms*. Smithsonian National Museum of African American History and Culture.https://nmaahc.si.edu/explore/stories/collection/revolutionary-practice-black-feminism

Phelps Moultrie, J., Magee, P. A., & Paredes Scribner, S. M. (2017). Talk about a racial eclipse: Narratives of institutional evasion in an urban school–university partnership. *Journal of Cases in Educational Leadership, 20*(1), 6–21.

Piert, J. (2015). *Alchemy of the soul: An African-centered education*. Peter Lang Publishing, Inc.

Pizarro, M., & Kohli, R. (2018). "I stopped sleeping": Teachers of color and the impact of racial battle fatigue. *Urban Education*. https://doi.org/10.1177/0042085918805788.

Postman, N., & Weingartner, C. (1971). *The soft revolution: A student handbook for turning schools around*. Delacorte Press.

Pour-Khorshid, F. (2018). Cultivating sacred spaces: A racial affinity group approach to support critical educators of color. *Teaching Education, 29*(4), 318–329.

Prison Policy Initiative. (n.d.). *Prison gerrymandering project: The problem*. https://www.prisonersofthecensus.org/impact.html

Quaye, S. J., Karikari, S. N., Rashad Allen, C., Kwamogi Okello, W., & Demere Carter, K. (2019). Strategies for practicing self-care from racial battle fatigue. *Journal Committed to Social Change on Race and Ethnicity, 5*(2), 95–131.

Quijano, A. (2000). Coloniality of power and Eurocentrism in Latin America. *International Sociology, 15*(2), 215–232.

Raby, R. (2004). "There's no racism at my school, it's just joking around": Ramifications for anti-racist education. *Race Ethnicity and Education, 7*(4), 367–383.

Radd, S. I., Generett, G. G., Gooden, M. A., & Theoharis, G. (2021). *Five practices for equity-focused school leadership*. ASCD.

Radd, S. I., & Grosland, T. J. (2018). Desegregation policy as social justice leadership? The case for critical consciousness and racial literacy. *Educational Policy, 32*(3), 395–422. https://doi.org/10.1177/0895904816637686

Radd, S. I., & Grosland, T. J. (2019). Desirablizing whiteness: A discursive practice in social justice leadership that entrenches white supremacy. *Urban Education, 54*(5), 656–676. https://doi.org/10.1177/0042085918783824

Radd, S. I., Grosland, T. J., & Steepleton, A. G. (2020). Desegregation policy as cultural routine: A critical examination of the Minnesota Desegregation Rule, *Journal of Education Policy, 35*(6), 765–784. https://doi.org/10.1080/02680939.2019.1609092

Raimondi, T. P. (2019). Compassion fatigue in higher education: Lesson from other helping fields. *Change: The Magazine of Higher Learning, 51*(3), 52–58.

Rapp, D. (2002). Social justice and the importance of rebellious imaginations. *Journal of School Leadership, 12*(3), 226–245.

Ray, V. (2019). A theory of racialized organizations. *American Sociological Review, 84*(1), 26–53.

Research, H. (2014). *Recruiting and retaining diverse personnel*. Author.

Rickford, R. (2016). Black Lives Matter: Toward a modern practice of mass struggle. *New Labor Forum, 25*(1), 34–42.

Riehl, C. J. (2000). The principal's role in creating inclusive schools for diverse students: A review of normative, empirical, and critical literature on the practice of educational administration. *Review of Educational Research, 70*(1), 55–81.

Robinson, C. J. (2000). *Black Marxism: The making of the Black radical tradition*. The University of North Carolina Press.

Robinson, L. R. (2010). *Processes and strategies school leaders are using to move their multicultural schools toward culturally responsive education* (Doctoral dissertation). ProQuest Dissertations and Theses. (UMI No. 3402432)

Rodela, K. C., & Bertrand, M. (2018). Rethinking educational leadership in the margins: Youth, parent, and community leadership for equity and social justice. *Journal of Research on Leadership Education, 13*(1), 3–9.

Roithmayr, D. (2014). *Reproducing racism: How everyday choices lock in white advantage*. New York University Press.

Rosiek, J. (2019). School segregation: A realist's view. *Phi Delta Kappan, 100*(5), 8–13.

Rudd, T. (2014). *Racial disproportionality in school discipline: Implicit bias is heavily implicate* [Issue brief]. Kirwan Institute for the Study of Race and Ethnicity.

Rury, J. L. (1999). Race, space, and the politics of Chicago's Public Schools: Benjamin Willis and the tragedy of urban education. *History of Education Quarterly, 39*(2), 117–142. https://doi.org/10.2307/370035

Ryan, J. (2010). Promoting social justice in schools: Principals' political strategies. *International Journal of Leadership in Education, 13*(4), 357–376. https://doi.org/10.1080/13603124.2010.503281

Sabo, B. (2006). Compassion fatigue and nursing work: can we accurately capture the consequences of caring work? *International Journal of Nursing Practice, 12*(3), 136–142.

Saldaña, J. (2013). *The coding manual for qualitative researchers,* 2nd edn. SAGE.

Saldaña, J. (2015). *The coding manual for qualitative researchers*. 3rd edn. SAGE.

Saltmarsh, J., Giles Jr, D. E., O'Meara, K., Sandmann, L., Ward, E., & Buglione, S. M. (2009). Community engagement and institutional culture in higher education: An investigation of faculty reward policies at engaged campuses. In B. E. Moely, S. H. Billig, & B. A. Holland (Eds.), *Advances in service-learning research. Creating our identities in service-learning and community engagement* (pp. 3–29). Information Age Publishing, Inc.

Sanders, M., & Harvey, A. (2002). Beyond the school walls: A case study of principal leadership for school-community collaboration. *Teachers College Record, 104*(7), 1345–1368.

Santoro, D. A. (2018). *Demoralized: Why teachers leave the profession they love and how they can stay*. Harvard Education Press.

Saull, R. (2010). Hegemony and the global political economy. In R. A. Denemark (Ed.), *The International Studies Encyclopedia*. Wiley–Blackwell.

Schalock, M. D., Fredericks, B., Dalke, B. A., & Alberto, P. A. (1994). The house that TRACES built: A conceptual model of service delivery systems and implications for change. *The Journal of Special Education, 28*(2), 203–223.

School Diversity Advisory Group. (2019). *Making the grade II: New programs for better schools*. Author.

Schiele, J. H. (1994). Afrocentricity: Implications for higher education. *Journal of Black Studies*, 150–69.

Schutz, A. (2006). Home is a prison in the global city: The tragic failure of school-based community engagement strategies. *Review of Educational Research, 76*(4), 691–743.

Senge, P. M. (1990). *The fifth discipline: The art & practice of the learning organization*. Doubleday.

Senge, P. M., & Sterman, J. D. (1992). Systems thinking and organizational learning: Acting locally and thinking globally in the organization of the future. *European Journal of Operational Research, 59*(1), 137–150.

Shapiro, E. (2019a, March 26). Segregation has been the story of New York City's schools for 50 years. *The New York Times*. https://www.nytimes.com/2019/03/26/nyregion/school-segregation-new-york.html

Shapiro, E. (2019b, November 15). Why white parents were at the front of the line for the school tour. *The New York Times*. https://www.nytimes.com/2019/11/15/nyregion/beacon-high-school-admissions-nyc.html

Shapiro, E. (2020, June 11). A school admissions process that caused segregation fell apart in weeks. *The New York Times*. https://www.nytimes.com/2020/06/11/nyregion/coronavirus-nyc-schools-admissions.html

Shedd, C. (2015). *Unequal city: Race, schools, and perceptions of injustice*. Russell Sage Foundation.

Shirley, D. (1997). *Community organizing for urban school reform*. The University of Texas Press.

Silverman, M. M., & Glick, R. L. (2010). Crisis and crisis intervention on college campuses. In J. Kay & V. Schwartz (Eds.), *Mental health care in the college community* (pp. 157–78). Wiley-Blackwell.

Singleton, G. E. (2014). *Courageous conversations about race: A field guide for achieving equity in schools*. Corwin Press.

Singleton, G. E., & Linton, C. (2005). *Facilitators' guide to courageous conversations about race: A field guide for achieving equity in schools*. Corwin Press.

Skiba, R. J. (2014). The failure of zero tolerance. *Reclaiming Children and Youth, 22*(4), 27–33.

Skiba, R. J., Horner, R. H., Chung, C. G., Rausch, M. K., May, S. L., & Tobin, T. (2011). Race is not neutral: A national investigation of African American and Latino disproportionality in school discipline. *School Psychology Review, 40*(1), 85–107.

Skiba, R. J., & Peterson, R. L. (2000). School discipline at a crossroads: From zero tolerance to early response. *Exceptional Children, 66*(3), 335–346.

Skrla, L., McKenzie, K. B., & Scheurich, J. J. (Eds.). (2009). *Using equity audits to create equitable and excellent schools*. Corwin Press.

Skrla, L., Scheurich, J. J., Garcia, J., & Nolly, G. (2004). Equity audits: A practical leadership tool for developing equitable and excellent schools. *Educational Administration Quarterly, 40*(1), 133–161.

Smith, P. A. (2016). Does racism exist in the hiring and promotion of K-12 school administrators? *Urban Education Research & Policy Annuals, 4*(1), 122–136.

Smith, W. A. (2008). Higher education: Racial battle fatigue. *Encyclopedia of Race, Ethnicity, and Society, 1*, 616–618.

Smith, W. A. (2014). *Racial battle fatigue in higher education: Exposing the myth of post-racial America*. Rowman & Littlefield.

Smith, W. A., Allen, W. R., & Danley, L. L. (2007). "Assume the position ... you fit the description" psychosocial experiences and racial battle fatigue among African American male college students. *American Behavioral Scientist, 51*(4), 551–578.

Sojoyner, D. M. (2013). Black radicals make for bad citizens: Undoing the myth of the school to prison pipeline. *Berkeley Review of Education, 4*(2), 241–263.

Solorzano, D. G., & Bernal, D. D. (2001). Examining transformational resistance through a critical race and LatCrit theory framework: Chicana and Chicano students in an urban context. *Urban Education, 36*(3), 308–42.

Solorzano, D. G., & Yosso, T. J. (2001). From racial stereotyping and deficit discourse toward a critical race theory in teacher education. *Multicultural Education, 9*(1), 2–8.

Solorzano, D. G., & Yosso, T. J. (2002). Critical race methodology: Counter-storytelling as ananalytical framework for education research. *Qualitative Inquiry, 8*(1), 23–44.

Southern Poverty Law Center & The Center for Civil Rights Remedies. (2019). *The striking outlier: The persistent, painful, and problematic practice of corporal punishment in schools*. Authors. https://www.splcenter.org/sites/default/files/com_corporal_punishment_final_web.pdf

Spring, J. (2017). *American education*. Routledge.

Stanford Center for Education Policy Analysis. (2020). *Achievement disparities search*. https://cepa.stanford.edu/search/node/achievement%20disparities

Stanford Center for Education Policy Analysis. (2020). *Racial and ethnic achievement gaps*. https://cepa.stanford.edu/educational-opportunity-monitoring-project/achievement-gaps/race/

Stanley, D., & Venzant Chambers, T. T. (2018). Tracking myself: African American high school students talk about the effects of curricular differentiation. *International Journal of Educational Policy & Leadership, 13*(1), 1–16.

Starck, J. G., Riddle, T., Sinclair, S., & Warikoo, N. (2020). Teachers are people too: Examining the racial bias of teachers compared to other American adults. *Educational Researcher, 49*(4), 273–284.

Steele, C. M. (1997). A threat in the air: How stereotypes shape intellectual identity and performance. *American Psychologist, 52*(6), 613–629.

Steele, D. M., & Cohn-Vargas, B. (2013). *Identity safe classrooms, grades K-5: Places to belong and learn.* Corwin Press.

Stephens, D., & Boldt, D. (2004). School/university partnerships: Rhetoric, reality, and intimacy. *Phi Delta Kappan, 85*(9), 703–707.

Stevenson, H. (2014). *Promoting racial literacy in schools: Differences that make a difference.* Teachers College Press.

Stevenson, Z., & Shetley, P. (2015). School district and university leadership development collaborations: How do three partnerships line up with best practices? *Journal of Education for Students Placed at Risk (JESPAR), 20*(1–2), 169–181.

STOP School Violence Act of 2018. 34 USC 10551 (2020) https://uscode.house.gov/view.xhtml?req=(title:34%20section:10551%20edition:prelim

Stovall, D. (2006). Forging community in race and class: Critical race theory and the quest for social justice in education. *Race Ethnicity and Education, 9*(3), 243–259.

Stovall, D. (2013). 14 souls, 19 days and 1600 dreams: Engaging critical race praxis while living on the "edge" of race. *Discourse: Studies in the Cultural Politics of Education, 34*(4), 562–579.

Stovall, D. O. (2016). *Born out of struggle: Critical race theory, school creation, and the politics of interruption.* SUNY Press.

Stoves, D. (2014). *Compelled to act: The negotiation of compassion fatigue among student affairs professionals* (Publication No. 3620005) [Doctoral dissertation, Texas A&M-Corpus Christi]. ProQuest Dissertations and Theses Global.

Strauss, V. (2015, September 6). Why hunger strikers are not stopping their action over a Chicago high school. *Washington Post.* https://www.washingtonpost.com/news/answer-sheet/wp/2015/09/06/why-hunger-strikers-are-not-stopping-their-action-over-a-chicago-high-school/

Stroh, D. P. (2015). *Systems thinking for social change: A practical guide to solving complex problems, avoiding unintended consequences, and achieving lasting results.* Chelsea Green Publishing.

Sue, D. W. (2010). *Microaggressions in everyday life: Race, gender, and sexual orientation.* John Wiley & Sons, Inc.

Sue, D. W. (2015). *Race talk and the conspiracy of silence: Understanding and facilitating difficult dialogues on race.* John Wiley & Sons, Inc.

Sugrue, T. J. (2014). *The origins of the urban crisis: Race and inequality in postwar Detroit updated edition.* Princeton University Press.

Sullivan, A. L., & Proctor, S. L. (2016). The shield or the sword?: Revisiting the debate on racial disproportionality in special education and implications for school psychologists. *School Psychology Forum: Research in Practice, 10*(3), 278–288.

Superville, D. R. (2020, September 23). Principals need help building anti-racist schools. *Education Week.* https://www.edweek.org/leadership/principals-need-help-building-anti-racist-schools/2020/09?cmp=SOC-SHR-FB

Swanson, J., & Welton, A. (2019). When good intentions only go so far: White principals leading discussions about race. *Urban Education, 54*(5), 732–759.

Swasey, B. (2020, June 28). Trump retweets video of apparent supporter saying "white power". *National Public Radio.* https://www.npr.org/sections/live-updates-protests-for-racial-justice/2020/06/28/884392576/trump-retweets-video-of-apparent-supporter-saying-white-power

Takaki, R. (1993). *A different mirror: A history of multicultural America.* Little, Brown and Company Publishers Inc.

Tan, P., & Thorius, K. K. (2019). Toward equity in mathematics education for students with dis/abilities: A case study of professional learning. *American Educational Research Journal, 56*(3), 995–1032.

Tanner, M. N., & Welton, A. D. (2021). Using anti-racism to challenge whiteness in educational leadership. In C. A. Mullen (Ed.), *Handbook of social justice interventions in education.* Springer. https://doi.org/10.1007/978-3-030-29553-0_123-1

Tasler, N. (2017). Stop using the excuse "Organizational change is hard." *Harvard Business Review.* https://hbr.org/2017/07/stop-using-the-excuse-organizational-change-is-hard

Tate, IV, W. F. (1997). Critical race theory and education: History, theory and implications. *Review of Research in Education, 22*, 195–247.

Tate, IV, W. F. (2008). "Geography of opportunity": Poverty, place, and educational outcomes. *Educational Researcher, 37*(7), 397–411. https://doi.org/10.3102/0013189X08326409

Tatum, B. D. (1994). Teaching white students about racism: The search for white allies and the restoration of hope. *Teachers College Record, 95*(4), 462–76.

Tatum, B. D. (2003). *Why are all the black kids sitting together in the cafeteria? And other conversations about race.* Basic Books.

Theoharis, G. (2009). *The school leaders our children deserve: Seven keys to equity, social justice, and school reform.* Teachers College Press.

Theoharis, G., & Haddix, M. (2013). White principals and race-conscious leadership. In J. S. Brooks, & N. W. Arnold (Eds.), *Antiracist school leadership: Toward equity in education for America's students* (pp. 1–18). Information Age Publishing, Inc.

Thorius, K. A. K. (2016). Stimulating tensions in special education teachers' figured world: An approach toward inclusive education. *International Journal of Inclusive Education, 20*(12), 1326–1343. https://doi.org/10.1080/13603116.2016.1168877

Thorius, K. A. K. (2019). Facilitating en/counters with special education's cloak of benevolence in professional learning to eliminate racial disproportionality in special education. *International Journal of Qualitative Studies in Education, 32*(3), 323–340.

Thorkildsen, R., & Scott Stein, M. R. (1996). Fundamental characteristics of successful university school partnerships. *The School Community Journal, 6*(2), 79–92.

Todd-Breland, E. (2018). *A political education: Black politics and education reform in Chicago since the 1960s.* The University of North Carolina Press.

Trohanis, P. L. (1982). Technical assistance and the improvement of services to exceptional children. *Theory into Practice, 21*(2), 119–128.

Tuck, E. (2009). Suspending damage: A letter to communities. *Harvard Educational Review, 79*(3), 409–427.

Turner, E. O., & Beneke, A. J. (2020). "Softening" school resource officers: The extension of police presence in schools in an era of Black Lives Matter, school shootings, and rising inequality. *Race Ethnicity and Education, 23*(2), 221–240.

Turner, E. O., & Spain, A. K. (2020). The multiple meanings of (in) equity: Remaking school district tracking policy in an era of budget cuts and accountability. *Urban Education, 55*(5), 783–812.

Tyson, K. (2011). *Integration interrupted: Tracking, black students, & acting white after Brown.* Oxford University Press.

Ullucci, K. (2011). Learning to see: The development of race and class consciousness in white teachers. *Race Ethnicity and Education, 14*(4), 561–577.

United States Department of Education. (2016). *Key data highlights on equity and opportunity gaps in our nation's public schools.* Rep., Off. Civil Rights, US Dep. Educ., Washington, DC. https://www2.ed.gov/about/offices/list/ocr/docs/2013-14-first-look.pdf.

United States Department of Education. (2019). *National teacher and principal survey (NTPS).* National Center for Education Statistics.

United Teachers of Los Angeles. (2020). Imagine police-free schools with the supports students deserve. United Teachers of Los Angeles [website]. https://www.utla.net/news/imagine-police-free-schools-supports-students-deserve

Valencia, R. (2010). *Dismantling contemporary deficit thinking: Educational thought and practice.* Taylor & Francis Group.

Valencia, R. (2015). *Students of color and the achievement gap: Systemic challenges, systemic transformations.* Taylor & Francis Group.

Valenzuela, A. (1999). *Subtractive schooling: U.S.-Mexican youth and the politics of caring.* State University of New York Press.

Vaught, S. E., & Castagno, A. E. (2008) "I don't think I'm a racist": Critical race theory, teacher attitudes, and structural racism. *Race Ethnicity and Education, 11*(2), 95–113.

Vavrus, F., & Cole, K. M. (2002). "I didn't do nothin": The discursive construction of school suspension. *The Urban Review, 34*(2), 87–111.

Venzant Chambers, T. T., & Spikes, D. D. (2016). "Tracking [is] for Black people": A structural critique of deficit perspectives of achievement disparities. *Educational Foundations, 29*(1–4), 29–53.

Vinovskis, M. A. (1999). *The road to Charlottesville: The 1989 Education Summit.* National Education Goals Panel.

Vygotsky, L. (1978). *Mind in society. The development of higher psychological processes.* Harvard University Press.

Wagner, P., & Kopf, D. (2015). The racial geography of mass incarceration. *Prison Policy Initiative.* https://www.prisonpolicy.org/racialgeography/report.html

Wahlstrom, K. L., & Louis, K. S. (2008). How teachers experience principal leadership: Theroles of professional community, trust, efficacy, and shared responsibility. *Educational Administration Quarterly, 44*(4), 458–495.

Waitoller, F. R., & Thorius, K. A. K. (2016). Cross-pollinating culturally sustaining pedagogy and universal design for learning: Toward an inclusive pedagogy that accounts for dis/ability. *Harvard Educational Review, 86*(3), 366–89.

Walsh, M. E., & Backe, S. (2013). School–university partnerships: Reflections and opportunities. *Peabody Journal of Education, 88*(5), 594–607.

Ward, G. K. (2012). *The black child-savers: Racial democracy and juvenile justice.* University of Chicago Press.

Warren, M. R. (1998). Community building and political power: A community organizing approach to democratic renewal. *American Behavioral Scientist, 42*(1), 78–92.

Warren, M. R. (2005). Communities and schools: A new view of urban education reform. *Harvard Educational Review, 75*(2), 133–173. https://doi.org/10.17763/haer.75.2.m718151032167438

Warren, M. R., & Mapp, K. L. (2011). *A match on dry grass: Community organizing as a catalyst for school reform.* Oxford University Press.

Warren, M. R., Park, S. O., & Tieken, M. C. (2016). The formation of community-engaged scholars: A collaborative approach to doctoral training in education research. *Harvard Educational Review, 86*(2), 233–260.

Watkins, W. H. (2001). *The white architects of black education: Ideology and power in America, 1865–1954.* Teachers College Press.

Watson, N., & Fullan, M. (1992). Beyond school district-university partnerships. In M. Fullan & A. Hargreaves (Eds.), *Teacher development and educational change* (pp. 213–242). Routledge.

Weathers, E. S., & Sosina, V. E., (2019). *Separate remains unequal: Contemporary segregation and racial disparities in school district revenue.* CEPA Working Paper No. 19-02. Stanford Center for Education Policy Analysis.

Weinstein, R. S. (2002). *Reaching higher: The power of expectations in schooling.* Harvard University Press.

Weiss, C. H., & Cambone, J. (1994). Principals, shared decision making, and school reform. *Educational Evaluation and Policy Analysis, 16*(3), 287–301.

Welner, K., & Oakes, J. (2005). Mandates still matter: Examining a key policy tool for promoting successful equity-minded reform. In J. Petrovich & A. S. Wells (Eds.), *Bringing equity back: Research for a new era in American educational policy* (pp. 77–102). Teachers College Press.

Welsh, R. O., & Little, S. (2018). The school discipline dilemma: A comprehensive review of disparities and alternative approaches. *Review of Educational Research, 88*(5), 752–794.

Welton, A. (2020). The whitening of anti-racist education. *Voices & Viewpoints.* Online: University of Illinois. https://occrl.illinois.edu/our-products/voices-and-viewpoints-detail/current-topics/2020/06/25/the-whitening-of-anti-racism-in-education

Welton, A., Diem, S., & Carpenter, B. W. (2019). Introduction to the special issue: Negotiating the politics of antiracist leadership: The challenges of leading under the predominance of whiteness. *Urban Education, 54*(5), 627–630.

Welton, A. D. (2013). Even more racially isolated than before: Problematizing the "vision for diversity" in a racially mixed high school. *Teachers College Record, 115*(11), 1–42.

Welton, A. D., Diem, S., & Holme, J. J. (2015). Color conscious, cultural blindness: Suburban school districts and demographic change. *Education and Urban Society, 47*(6), 695–722. https://doi.org/10.1177/0013124513510734

Welton, A. D., & Freelon, R. (2018). Community organizing as educational leadership: Lessons from Chicago on the politics of racial justice. *Journal of Research on Leadership Education, 13*(1), 79–104.

Welton, A. D., & Freelon, R. (2019). A critical examination of the educational leadership standards: A community organizing perspective., In A. B. Danzig & W. R. Black (Eds.), *Who controls the preparation of education administrators?* (pp. 187–218). Information Age Publishing, Inc.

Welton, A. D., Owens, D. R., & Zamani-Gallaher, E. M. (2018). Anti-racist change: A conceptual framework for educational institutions to take systemic action. *Teachers College Record, 120*(14), 1–22.

West, C. (2017). *Race matters, 25th anniversary: With a new introduction.* Beacon Press.

Western, B. (2006). *Punishment and inequality in America.* Russell Sage.

Wilderson, III, F. B. (2018). "We're trying to destroy the world": Anti-blackness and police violence after Ferguson. In M. Grzinic & A. Stojnic (Eds.), *Shifting corporealities in contemporary performance: Danger, immobility and politics* (pp. 45–60). Palgrave Macmillan.

Wilson, C. M. (2014). Starting the bandwagon: A historiography of African American mothers' leadership during voluntary school desegregation, 1954–1971. *Advancing Women in Leadership Journal, 34,* 38–47.

Wilson, C., & Johnson, L. (2015). Black educational activism for community empowerment: International leadership perspectives. *International Journal of Multicultural Education, 17*(1), 102–120.

Wilson, M. A. F., Yull, D. G., & Massey, S. G. (2020). Race and the politics of educational exclusion: Explaining the persistence of disproportionate disciplinary practices in an urban school district. *Race, Ethnicity, and Education, 23*(1), 134–157.

Wing, D. W. (2015). *Race talk and the conspiracy of silence: Understanding and facilitating difficult dialogues on race*. Wiley.

Winn, M. T., & Behizadeh, N. (2011). The right to be literate: Literacy, education, and the school-to-prison pipeline. *Review of Research in Education, 35*(1), 147–173.

Witziers, B., Bosker, R. J., & Krüger, M. L. (2003). Educational leadership and student achievement: The elusive search for an association. *Educational Administration Quarterly, 39*(3), 398–425.

Wood, E., Hong, Y., Price, M. F., Stanton-Nichols, K., Hatcher, J. A., Craig, D. M., … Palmer, K. L. (2016). *Public scholarship at Indiana University-Purdue University Indianapolis*. IUPUI Center for Service and Learning; IUPUI Office of Academic Affairs. https://scholarworks.iupui.edu/bitstream/handle/1805/9713/PublicScholarship_V6.5.31%5b1%5d.pdf?sequence=5&isAllowed=y

Woodson, C. G. (1933). *The miseducation of the negro*. The Associated Publisher.

Yancy, G. (2016). *Black bodies, white gazes: The continuing significance of race in America*. Rowman & Littlefield Publishers.

Yonezawa, S., Wells, A. S., & Serna, I. (2002). Choosing tracks: "Freedom of choice" in detracking schools. *American Educational Research Journal, 39*(1), 37–67. https://doi.org/10.3102/00028312039001037

Yoon, I. H. (2012). The paradoxical nature of whiteness-at-work in the daily life of schools and teacher communities. *Race Ethnicity and Education, 15*(5), 587–613. https://doi.org/10.1080/13613324.2011.624506

Yosso, T. J. (2005). Whose culture has capital? A critical race theory discussion of community cultural wealth. *Race Ethnicity and Education, 8*(1), 69–91. https://doi.org/10.1080/1361332052000341006

Young, M. D. (1999). Multifocal educational policy research: Toward a method for enhancing traditional educational policy studies. *American Educational Research Journal, 36*(4), 677–714. https://doi.org/10.3102/00028312036004677

Young, M. D. (2019. July). *Developing advocacy leaders*. BELMAS Convention Keynote. Leicestershire, United Kingdom.

Young, M. D., Anderson, E., & Miles Nash, A. (2017). Preparing school leaders: Standards-based curriculum in the United States. *Leadership and Policy in Schools, 16*(2), 228–271.

Young, M. D., & Laible, J. (2000). White racism, antiracism, and school leadership preparation. *Journal of School Leadership, 10*(5), 374–415.

Zirkel, S., & Pollack, T. M. (2016). A critical case analysis of public discourse about race, merit, and worth. *American Educational Research Journal, 53*(6), 1522–1555. https://doi.org/10.3102/0002831216676568

Index

abolitionist mode 190
absolvist mode 187
accountability 39, 43, 46, 47, 49, 66, 111, 115, 217
activism
    anti-racist modes of 188–90
    inactivism and 191
    neutral modes of 188
    racist modes of 186–8
activist leadership 121–4
    community needs 129
    in CPS 124–5
    engaging 131–2
    forming partnerships 129–30
    immigration rights 125–6
    mutualistic service 130–1
    permeability 127–8
advocacy leadership 109–12, 118–20
    accountability 115
    capacities for 116–17
    capacity building 113
    cultivation 117–18
    instructional programs 114–15
    organizational development 113–14
    setting directions 112
advocate mode 189–90
African-centered school leaders 93–5
    culture 103
    ethno-cultural responsiveness 96–9
    marginalized space 97–9
    organizational inquiry 94, 95, 100–4
    pedagogical approach 104
    purpose and design 103
    structure 103
Afrocentricity 95
Alchemist mode 187
ally mode 189
Alonso, A. 65, 66
Anderson, B. 96, 100
Anderson, G. L. 110, 117–18
antagonist mode 186–7
anti-Blackness 2, 18, 50, 166

anticipation 216
anti-racism 182, 185, 191
    activism 188–90
    defining 3–4
    as identity 218
    racism and 185–91
anti-racist leaders 55–7
    community focus 64–7
    intellectual and multidisciplinary approach 62–3
    mindsets, dispositions, and behaviors 57–9
    personal characteristics and attributes 59–62
    principles 56
    TA for 213–18
apathetic mode 188
Apple, M. W. 93, 94
architectural mode 186
Artiles, A. J. 211
Auerbach, S. 139
authentic partnerships 139

Bell, D. 162–3, 170
Berger, P. L. 93, 94
Bills, A. 102
Black, Indigenous, and People of Color (BIPOC) 159–60, 196, 197
    actions 163–5
    compassion fatigue 161
    Critical Race Theory 162–3
    organizational culture 166–7
    racial battle fatigue 161–2
    secondary traumatic stress 161
    TA for 217
Black Lives Matter movement 2, 47, 84, 166
Black women 169–70
    CRT and 170–1
    mammification and policing 177–9
    suppression 177
Black youth 48, 169

Boddie, E. 208
bricolage 115
Brown v. Board of Education of Topeka 207–8

capacity building 113
Castagno, A. E. 18
Center for Creative Leadership (Mitchinson & Morris) 60–1
Chicago Public Schools (CPS) 121, 124–5. *See also* activist leadership
Chicago Teachers Union (CTU) 49
Civil Rights movement 122, 123, 208
civil rights organizations 47–8
classroom
    behavior 36–9, 82
    race and school discipline 85
    tracking 21
Coalition to Revitalize Walter H. Dyett High School 139–40
Coates, T. 71
Cole, K. M. 86
Collins, P. H. 176
colorblindness 78, 164
colorblind racism 33, 34
community
    and anti-racist leaders 64–7
    Black 101, 126, 127
    care 127, 217
    of color 48–9, 91, 127, 129, 131–4, 184
    imagined 96–8, 100
    meeting space and playground 126–7
    needs 129
community-based leadership 134, 135, 137
community-based organizations (CBOs) 48, 140–1
compassion fatigue 161
counter-narratives 77
counter-storytelling 11, 170, 171
Covid-19 pandemic 1, 3, 17, 87
crime control discourses 43–4
critical consciousness 118, 136, 140, 160–3, 184
Critical Race Theory (CRT) 11, 162–3
    and Black Feminism 170–1
critical reflection 112, 117–18
Culturally Responsive Leadership Framework 58–9
culturally responsive school leadership (CRSL) 97–8, 109, 111, 112, 115

Culturally Responsive School Leadership (Khalifa) 64
cultural taxation 163

Dantley, M. 204
Davis, A. Y. 98
decision-making 29, 40, 66, 78, 91, 115, 136–7, 213, 214
DeCuir, J. T. 162
DeLugan, R. M. 155
detracking 20–1, 27–8
Developmental Model of Intercultural Sensitivity 201
Diamond, J. 33–4
Diem, S. 29
difference competence 202–4
Disciplined Courage 60
district administration 24–6
Dixson, A. D. 162
double-stimulation 212

economic recession 42–3
education
    higher 153, 159–62
    neoliberal education policy 46–7
    public 21, 141, 209, 211
    technical assistance in 210–11
E3 Group 28
Empathetic Courage 60
Equity Assistance Centers (EACs) 207, 209–11, 218. *See also* technical assistance (TA)
equity, diversity, and inclusion (EDI) 166
ethno-cultural responsiveness 96–9
(de)Europification 101
Everyday Courage for School Leaders (Lassiter) 59–60
expansive learning 212

forming partnerships 129–30
Fullan, M. 153

Gifted and Talented (G&T) programs 20
Ginwright, S. 39
Gooden, M. A. 98, 204
Gorski, P. 58
Gutierrez, N. 67

Hallinger, P. 112
Hamilton, J. 210
Handel, G. 93, 94

hard revolution 189
Heck, R. H. 112
Heifetz, R. 75
Hinton, K. A. 148, 149, 154
Hiraldo, P. 162
homogeneity 202–4
Homogenous Whole phenomenon 194–6
  anti-racism 199
  community lacks 198–9
  difference competence 202–4
  differences and racial neutrality 197
  individual leaders 201–2
  "make the case" and relevance 204–5
  marginalization experience 199–200
  pressure to conform 197–8
  self-replicating cycle 195–6
  white population 196–7
Horsford, S. 63

imagined community 97, 98, 100
Immigration and Customs Enforcement (ICE) 41, 125, 126, 129
immigration rights 125–6
instructional programs 114–15
Intellectual Courage 59
Intercultural Development Inventory 201

Kendi, I. X. 57, 59, 218
Kenwood Oakland Community Organization (KOCO) 140–2
Khalifa, M. 64, 97–8, 109
Kohli, R. 35, 162
Kozleski, E. B. 211
K-12 schooling 19

Ladson-Billings, G. 162
Laible, J. 90
Lassiter, C. 59–60
Laura, C. 38
leadership. *See also* activist leadership; advocacy leadership
  community-based organizations 140–1
  lived experiences 135–7
  local knowledge 138–40
  public systems 141–3
  racial equity 73, 74
  resistant capital 137–8
  school 17–19
  social justice 122, 123, 129

leadership preparation programs 56–9, 63–7, 90–1, 119, 135, 143–4. *See also* anti-racist leaders
learning agility assessment instrument (LAAI) 60
learning agility behavior 60–1
Learning to Lead for Racial Equity (Ngounou and Gutierrez) 67
Leithwood, K. 113
Leonardo, Z. 84
Levine, T. K. 96
Linsky, M. 75
Little, S. 34
local knowledge 138–40, 143, 147
Local School Council (LSC) 136–7
Lomotey, K. 99
Love, B. L. 62
Luckmann, T. 93, 94

McInerney, M. 210
McIntosh, P. 165
McMahon, B. 85
March, J. G. 94
marginalized space 97–9
Mazrui, A. A. 96
Mehta, J. 57
Meiners, E. R. 51
Mezirow, J. 118
Midwest and Plains Equity Assistance Center (MAP Center) 209, 216
Mills, C. W. 82
Moore, M. 65, 66
Moral Courage 59
multiculturalism 104–5
multiple perspectives 63, 116–18
mutualistic service 130–1

neoliberalism 46–7
Nevarez, A. 35
New York City Public Schools (NYCPS) 20
Ngounou, G. 67
No Child Left Behind Act (NCLB) 46
NYC Leadership Academy 58
Nyerere, J. K. 104

Oakes, J. 19
Oak Park and River Forest High School (OPRFHS) 23–4, *24*
Obama, B. 45–6, 142
  Community Benefits Agreement Coalition 142–3

O'Connor, C. 40
OLF 111, 113
Oluo, I. 67
one best systems 117
organizational development 113–14
organizational inquiry 94, 95, 100–4
Owens, D. R. 66–7

Padilla, A. M. 163
Palomino Elementary School 86–90
paradigm shifts 58
parent engagement 136–7
Park, S. O. 155
Pearlman, L. A. 163
pedagogical approach 97, 104, 114
permeability 127–8
Pizarro, M. 35, 162
Point Four Program 210
police-free schools 48, 49
policy appropriation 117
Positive Behavioral Intervention Supports (PBIS) 45–6
poverty 38, 43, 45, 47, 204, 208, 210
predominantly white school district (PWSD) 193–5, 197–202, 204–5. *See also* Homogenous Whole phenomenon
Prison Industrial Complex (PIC) 44–5
Professional Standards for Educational Leaders (PSEL) 4
public education 21, 141, 209, 211

race 26, 70–5, 183, 184, 187, 218
  consciousness 4, 50, 83, 87
  and criminality 90–1
  and discipline 83–6
  social constructionism and 94
  talk 201–2
race-neutrality 7, 12, 33–9, 43–4, 78, 82, 83, 87, 145, 146
racial
  battle fatigue 161–2
  capitalism 41–2, 47, 50, 51
  difference 197
  equity audits 76
  equity leadership 73, 74
  justice 2, 3, 22, 29–30, 33, 47, 70, 72, 74, 133–5, 137, 215, 216
  neutrality 197
  trauma 72, 163, 164

racial inequity 7, 8, 13, 22, 36, 39, 40, 51, 75–6, 208, 214
  collective and reflective dialogue 77–9
  counter-narratives 77
  numerical data 76–7
  root causes 76
  school leaders 79
racism 18, 35, 42, 71–6, 78, 191, 208–9. *See also* anti-racism
  activism 186–8
  Black women 171–2, 176
  colorblind 33, 34
  covert 184–5
  CRT and Black Feminism 170–1
  defining 183–5
  mammification and policing 177–9
  school and 75–6
  structural 32, 62, 159
  suppression 177
  systemic 1–3, 17, 22, 60, 61, 76, 77, 79, 166, 200, 213, 216
  white 18, 19, 22, 29, 70–4, 185, 217
resilience 61, 82, 159, 163
resistant capital 137–8
Roussos, S. 155

Saakvitne, K. W. 163
school
  in Arizona 83
  discipline 34–6, 45–6, 83–6, 91
  discourses and policies 44
  leadership 17–19
  police-free 48, 49
  race and discipline 75–6, 84–5
  safety 45, 46, 82, 87
  suburban 23–4, *24*
schooling 18, 20, 35, 102, 135, 136, 216
school–prison nexus 41–2, 50–1
  Black youth activists 48
  civil rights organizations 47–8
  community-based groups 48
  crime control discourses 43–4
  neoliberal education policy 46–7
  Prison Industrial Complex 44–5
  race-neutral 43–4
  recession, poverty, and the shrinking state 42–3
  white, middle-class and upper-middle-class families 47
  zero-tolerance policies and police in schools 44, 48–9

School Resource Officer (SRO) programs 44
school segregation 208
secondary traumatic stress 161
seeing the system 113–14, 117
Shetley, P. 146
shrinking tax base 43
silver bullets 117
Skram, G. 155
social constructionism 93, 94
social justice leadership 122, 123, 129
societal level 83–4
soft revolution 189
Stanley, D. 21
status quo versions 215–16
Stevenson, Z. 146
strategic thinking 114–15
Strategic Triangle Framework 65–6
student
    Black 19, 20, 49, 50, 83, 85, 87, 90, 104, 169, 172, 190
    of color 18, 22, 25, 29, 30, 35, 37, 39, 41, 44, 46, 47, 49, 50, 69, 78, 83, 187
    marginalized space 97–9
    performance 8, 23, 79, 116
    population 23–5, 78, 109, 110, 149
    race and school discipline 85–6
    racial peers 193, 194
    success 25, 86
Student Code of Conduct 36
Supportive School Discipline Initiative 45
Swann v. Charlotte-Mecklenberg Board of Education 208
systemic racism 1–3, 17, 22, 60, 61, 76, 77, 79, 166, 200, 213, 216

teachers
    and administrators 37–9
    ladder of consequences 36–9
    and teachers unions 48–9
technical assistance (TA) 207, 209
    approaches 210–11
    for BIPOC 217
    equity-expansive 211–13
    MAP Center 209
    origins of 210–11
    partnerships for persistence 218
    professional development 214
    status quo versions 215–16

This Bridge Called My Leadership: An Essay on Black Women as Bridge Leaders in Education (Horsford) 63
Thorius, K. A. K. 212
Tieken, M. C. 155
tracking 19, 21, 47, 49, 50, 78
Transformational Teaching and Learning 25–6

university–district partnerships 145–55
    experiences 148–9
    theory 148
US Departments of Education and Justice 45

Valenzuela, A. 38
Vavrus, F. 86
Venzant Chambers, T. T. 21
violence 2, 17–18, 29, 42, 181, 183, 191, 196
vulnerability 71–2, 172

Warren, M. R. 155
Watkins, W. H. 93
Watson, N. 153
Welsh, R. O. 34
Welton, A. D. 29, 66–7, 213, 216
white
    population 196–7
    privilege 47, 66, 70, 87, 217
    racism 18, 19, 22, 29, 185, 217
    saviorism 187
    supremacy 18, 21–3, 33–4, 42, 46, 70, 73, 74, 77, 83, 90, 91, 94, 95, 101, 122, 196, 200, 208
white leaders 70–4
    politics of 74–5
whiteness 18, 19, 21–3, 30, 70, 74, 77, 86, 90, 196, 198–201
Wilson, M. A. F. 51
Woodson, C. G. 35

Yonezawa, S. 20, 21
Yosso, T. J. 138, 148
Young, M. D. 90, 118

Zamani-Gallaher, E. M. 66–7
zero-tolerance policies 44, 48–9, 83, 86, 90

www.ingramcontent.com/pod-product-compliance
Lightning Source LLC
Chambersburg PA
CBHW062123300426
44115CB00012BA/1793